W9-CBE-405

JUMBLE®

Unscramble these four Jumbles,
one letter to each square, to
form four ordinary words.

SNABI

THIRM

SINOUF

UPDELD

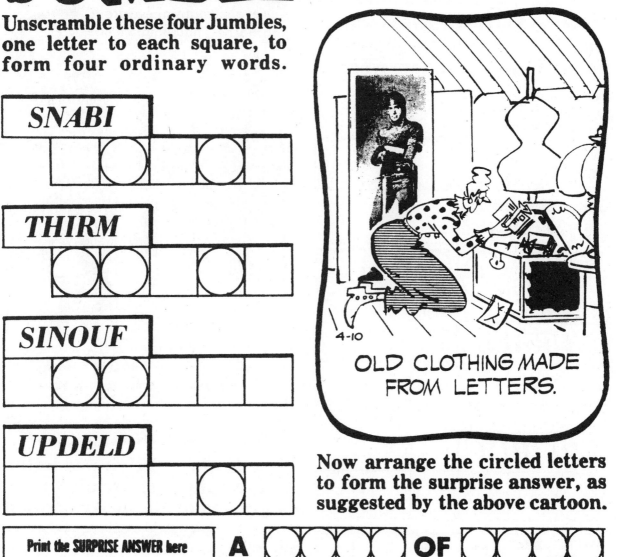

4-10

OLD CLOTHING MADE
FROM LETTERS.

Now arrange the circled letters
to form the surprise answer, as
suggested by the above cartoon.

Print the SURPRISE ANSWER here

A ⬡⬡⬡⬡⬡ OF ⬡⬡⬡⬡

JUMBLE®

Unscramble these four Jumbles, one letter to each square, to form four ordinary words.

TRIGE

DUTIA

KURBEE

HOARIM

Cures rheumatism, eyestrain, toothache, housemaid's knee . . .

WHAT THE MEDICINE MAN HAD TROUBLE SELLING.

Now arrange the circled letters to form the surprise answer, as suggested by the above cartoon.

Print the SURPRISE ANSWER here

A ⚪⚪⚪⚪ ON THE ⚪⚪⚪⚪⚪⚪

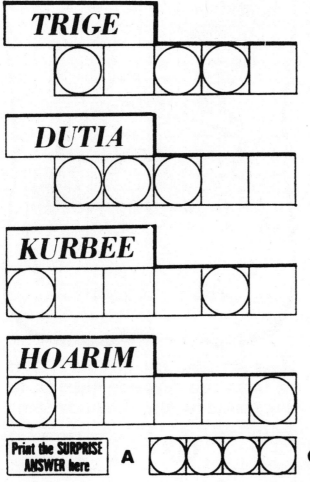

JUMBLE®

A BIG BOOK FOR BIG FANS

by Henri Arnold, Bob Lee,
and Mike Argirion

TRIUMPH
BOOKS
CHICAGO

This book is available at special discounts
for your group or organization.

For further information, contact:

Triumph Books
601 South LaSalle Street
Suite 500
Chicago, Illinois 60605
(312) 939-3330
(312) 663-3557 FAX

ISBN 1-57243-314-0

Printed in the USA

"My favorite pastime is doing Jumbles®.
I anxiously await for each Jumble® book
to come out so I can try my best in
solving all of them"

**BERNIE REDER
CINCINNATI, OH**

"Being retired, my wife Lucy and I
look forward to lunch out most days. Of
course, our Jumble® book always goes
with us and is part of our enjoyment
and conversation. Thanks for the fun!"

**CLARENCE STRAND
ROCHESTER, MI**

CONTENTS

Classic

JUMBLE

"We have enjoyed
doing Jumbles® for
several years and
look forward to
each book that
comes out."

**MYRTLE & GORDON BEALS
FORESTVILLE, CT**

JUMBLE®

Unscramble these four Jumbles, one letter to each square, to form four ordinary words.

TACUE

SAYID

REWEPT

SCUMEL

WHAT HAPPENED TO THE BAKED GOODS?

Now arrange the circled letters to form the surprise answer, as suggested by the above cartoon.

Print the ANSWER here

THEY WERE "◯◯◯◯-◯◯◯◯◯◯"

JUMBLE®

Unscramble these four Jumbles, one letter to each square, to form four ordinary words.

WAULF

ORFYT

FORTIP

THIMER

Print the SURPRISE ANSWER here

Oh, honey!

$100

WHAT COLD CASH OFTEN MAKES PEOPLE DO.

Now arrange the circled letters to form the surprise answer, as suggested by the above cartoon.

JUMBLE®

Unscramble these four Jumbles, one letter to each square, to form four ordinary words.

ODARR

NEKIF

TAISER

CORRET

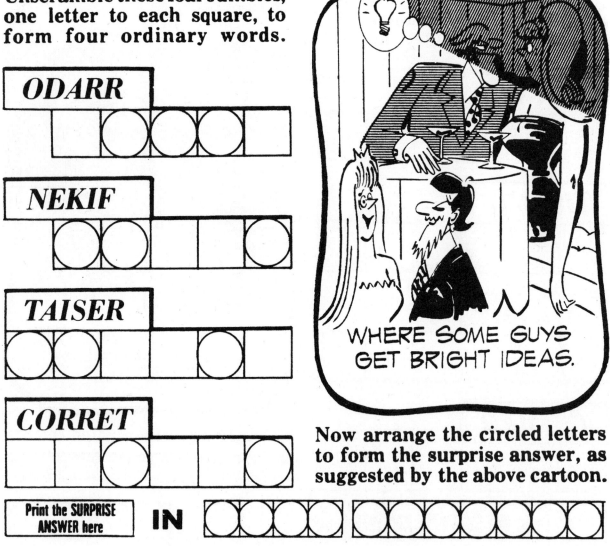

WHERE SOME GUYS GET BRIGHT IDEAS.

Now arrange the circled letters to form the surprise answer, as suggested by the above cartoon.

Print the SURPRISE ANSWER here   IN

JUMBLE®

Unscramble these four Jumbles,
one letter to each square, to
form four ordinary words.

NACEP

CREMY

BUTSOE

KENVIO

Now arrange the circled letters
to form the surprise answer, as
suggested by the above cartoon.

Print the SURPRISE ANSWER here   A

JUMBLE®

Unscramble these four Jumbles,
one letter to each square, to
form four ordinary words.

DUTOO

THOLC

ADUMAR

ENCLAG

Print the **SURPRISE ANSWER** here

A NOTE OF HARMONY
IN MOST HOUSEHOLDS

Now arrange the circled letters
to form the surprise answer, as
suggested by the above cartoon.

" ◯◯◯◯◯◯ "

JUMBLE®

Unscramble these four Jumbles, one letter to each square, to form four ordinary words.

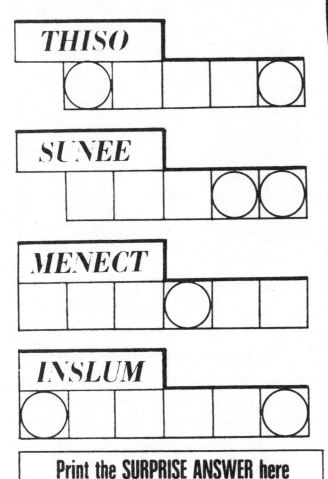

THISO

SUNEE

MENECT

INSLUM

Print the SURPRISE ANSWER here

How far you going?

THIS TELLS YOU WHAT THE FARE IS.

Now arrange the circled letters to form the surprise answer, as suggested by the above cartoon.

JUMBLE®

Unscramble these four Jumbles,
one letter to each square, to
form four ordinary words.

BAEBY

NARCK

TAUNER

YELMIT

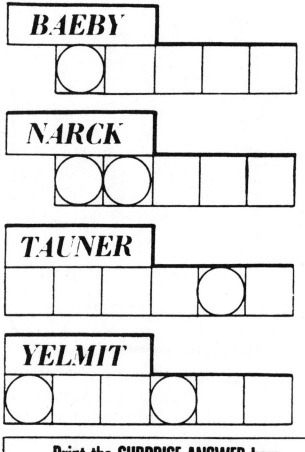

BIGMOUTHED AT
THE SUMMIT!

Now arrange the circled letters
to form the surprise answer, as
suggested by the above cartoon.

Print the SURPRISE ANSWER here

A

JUMBLE®

Unscramble these four Jumbles, one letter to each square, to form four ordinary words.

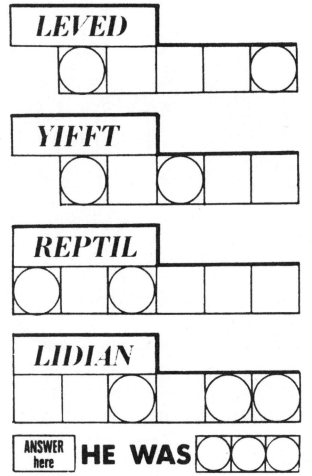

LEVED

YIFFT

REPTIL

LIDIAN

You check out perfect

WHY THE RESULTS OF HIS PHYSICAL WERE MUSIC TO HIS EARS.

Now arrange the circled letters to form the surprise answer, as suggested by the above cartoon.

ANSWER here   HE WAS ⬡⬡⬡ AS A ⬡⬡⬡⬡⬡⬡⬡

JUMBLE®

Unscramble these four Jumbles, one letter to each square, to form four ordinary words.

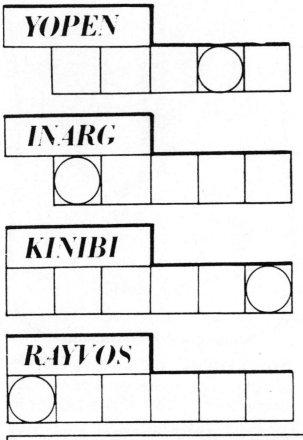

YOPEN

INARG

KINIBI

RAYVOS

Great to be free . . .

You got a suspended sentence last time

25¢

ONCE IS OK, BUT A REPEAT MEANS PRISON.

Now arrange the circled letters to form the surprise answer, as suggested by the above cartoon.

Print the SURPRISE ANSWER here

JUMBLE®

Unscramble these four Jumbles,
one letter to each square, to
form four ordinary words.

YUMOS

PYLAP

NEEWAK

UMLUTT

Aha, madam—you weren't quick enough!

WHAT THE STUPID SHOPLIFTER WAS.

Now arrange the circled letters
to form the surprise answer, as
suggested by the above cartoon.

Print the
ANSWER here

ON THE

JUMBLE ®

Unscramble these four Jumbles,
one letter to each square, to
form four ordinary words.

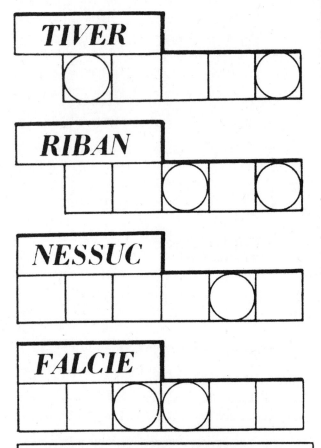

TIVER

RIBAN

NESSUC

FALCIE

Print the SURPRISE ANSWER here

THE CARTOONIST
DREW THIS IN ORDER
TO HIDE WHAT
HE WAS DOING.

Now arrange the circled letters
to form the surprise answer, as
suggested by the above cartoon.

A

JUMBLE®

Unscramble these four Jumbles, one letter to each square, to form four ordinary words.

TECOT

DESET

INLOPP

ROVACT

WHAT THE SCARED TREE WAS.

Now arrange the circled letters to form the surprise answer, as suggested by the above cartoon.

Print the SURPRISE ANSWER here

◯◯◯◯◯◯◯ TO THE ◯◯◯◯

JUMBLE®

Unscramble these four Jumbles,
one letter to each square, to
form four ordinary words.

BISSA

NAYRE

CORVEL

UNPOCE

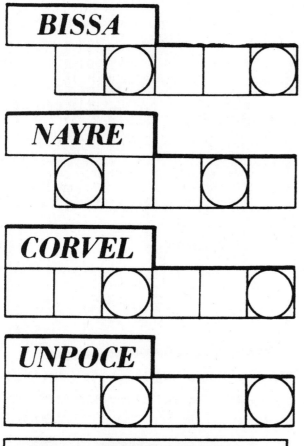

OPENINGS PROVIDED
FOR STEREO SOUND.

Now arrange the circled letters
to form the surprise answer, as
suggested by the above cartoon.

Print the SURPRISE ANSWER here

JUMBLE®

Unscramble these four Jumbles,
one letter to each square, to
form four ordinary words.

FERIG

WETET

SAKMAD

PINELP

HOW WOMEN
ARE AFTER
SHOPPING SPREES.

Now arrange the circled letters
to form the surprise answer, as
suggested by the above cartoon.

Print the SURPRISE
ANSWER here

◯◯◯◯◯ —AND ◯◯◯◯◯◯

JUMBLE®

Unscramble these four Jumbles, one letter to each square, to form four ordinary words.

PHOWO

NORST

BLABED

WURCEF

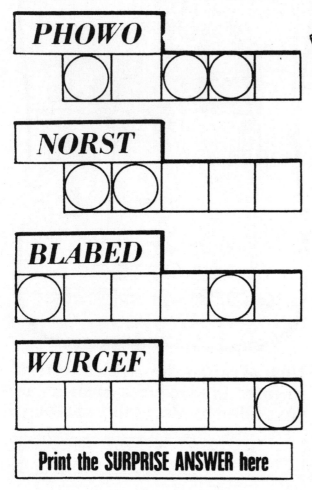

Print the SURPRISE ANSWER here

WHAT THE TRAFFIC COP TURNED DOCTOR WARNED HIS PATIENT TO DO.

Now arrange the circled letters to form the surprise answer, as suggested by the above cartoon.

JUMBLE®

Unscramble these four Jumbles, one letter to each square, to form four ordinary words.

TAFOO

MIRGY

INGARD

CHELEK

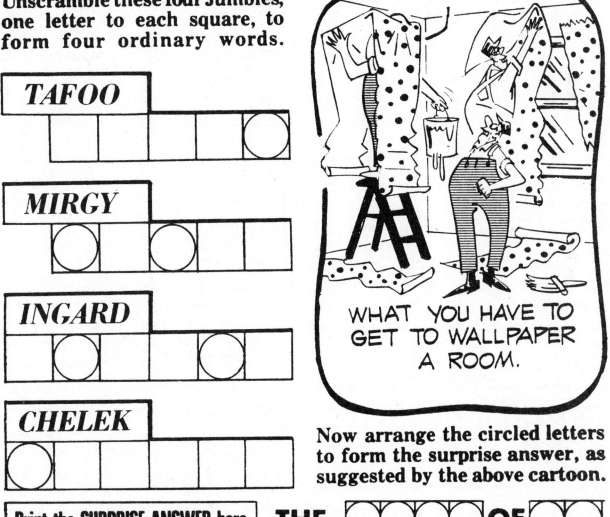

Refill, please

WHAT YOU HAVE TO GET TO WALLPAPER A ROOM.

Now arrange the circled letters to form the surprise answer, as suggested by the above cartoon.

Print the SURPRISE ANSWER here

THE ☐☐☐☐☐ OF ☐☐

JUMBLE®

Unscramble these four Jumbles,
one letter to each square, to
form four ordinary words.

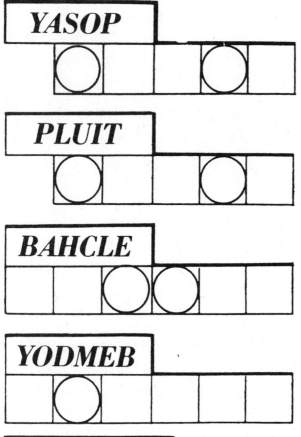

YASOP

PLUIT

BAHCLE

YODMEB

WHAT ONE WOMAN'S
PAST OFTEN IS.

Now arrange the circled letters
to form the surprise answer, as
suggested by the above cartoon.

Print the SURPRISE ANSWER here   **ANOTHER'S**

JUMBLE®

Unscramble these four Jumbles,
one letter to each square, to
form four ordinary words.

KROOB

LAGOW

TIENNY

DEMPIN

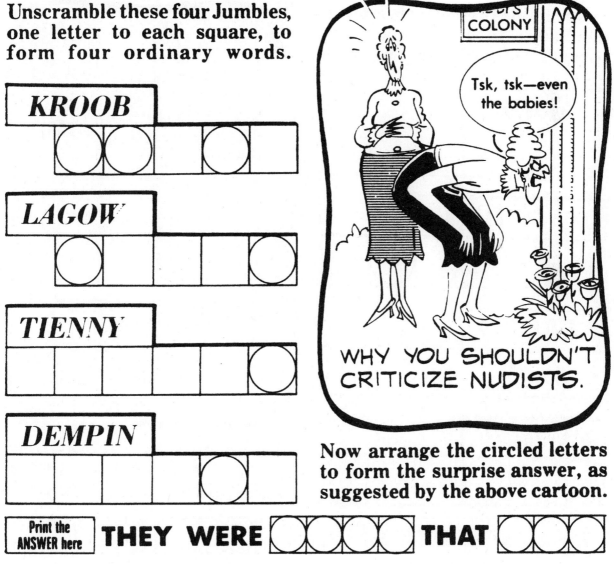

Tsk, tsk—even
the babies!

COLONY

WHY YOU SHOULDN'T
CRITICIZE NUDISTS.

Now arrange the circled letters
to form the surprise answer, as
suggested by the above cartoon.

Print the
ANSWER here   THEY WERE ◯◯◯◯◯ THAT ◯◯◯

JUMBLE®

Unscramble these four Jumbles, one letter to each square, to form four ordinary words.

IXOCT

SNURP

CEEDDO

ENOMAY

WHAT TO AVOID IF YOU MARRIED YOUR WIFE FOR HER LOOKS.

Now arrange the circled letters to form the surprise answer, as suggested by the above cartoon.

Print the SURPRISE ANSWER here

JUMBLE®

Unscramble these four Jumbles, one letter to each square, to form four ordinary words.

PHAMC

DUJEG

BRUMPE

DAGAPO

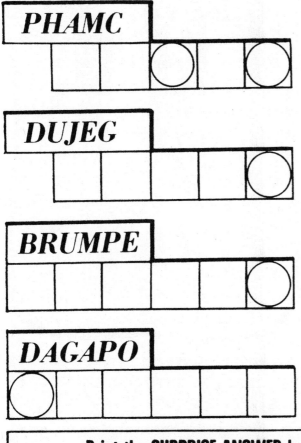

"Groovy, man!"

WHAT THE HIP GROCER SAID HIS "BAG" WAS.

Now arrange the circled letters to form the surprise answer, as suggested by the above cartoon.

Print the SURPRISE ANSWER here

JUMBLE®

Unscramble these four Jumbles, one letter to each square, to form four ordinary words.

Uh oh! What did you do this time?

ONIGG

EVVAL

YORPOL

HOMFAT

YOUR WIFE MIGHT DO THIS WHEN YOU GIVE.

Now arrange the circled letters to form the surprise answer, as suggested by the above cartoon.

Print the SURPRISE ANSWER here

JUMBLE®

Unscramble these four Jumbles,
one letter to each square, to
form four ordinary words.

RINBY

LAWRC

MILGRY

TRAFYC

Of course, dear

WHAT SOME WOMEN
DO IF AT FIRST
THEY DON'T SUCCEED.

Now arrange the circled letters
to form the surprise answer, as
suggested by the above cartoon.

Print the SURPRISE
ANSWER here

◯◯◯, ◯◯◯ ◯◯◯◯◯

JUMBLE®

Unscramble these four Jumbles,
one letter to each square, to
form four ordinary words.

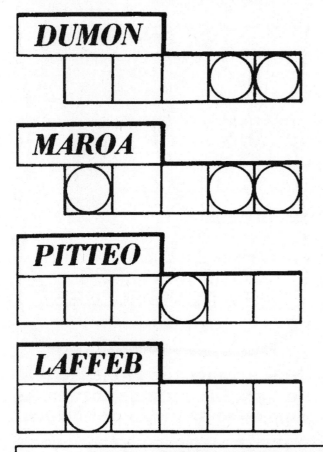

DUMON

MAROA

PITTEO

LAFFEB

WHAT ADAM WASN'T.

Now arrange the circled letters
to form the surprise answer, as
suggested by the above cartoon.

Print the SURPRISE ANSWER here

JUMBLE®

Unscramble these four Jumbles,
one letter to each square, to
form four ordinary words.

DIADE

VREEV

SCEPHY

PLAICH

Print the SURPRISE
ANSWER here

TO

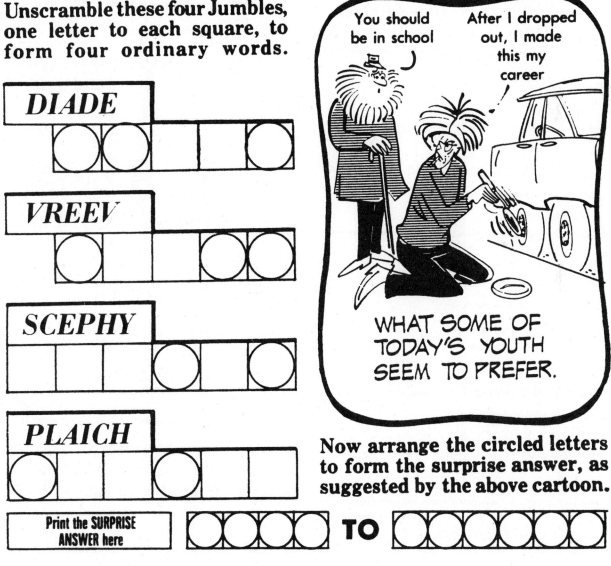

You should be in school

After I dropped out, I made this my career

WHAT SOME OF TODAY'S YOUTH SEEM TO PREFER.

Now arrange the circled letters
to form the surprise answer, as
suggested by the above cartoon.

JUMBLE®

Unscramble these four Jumbles, one letter to each square, to form four ordinary words.

IVGLI

ARSYC

HIRTED

ATTARR

ESIDENT

Back to work!

A DRESS SHOULD BE THIS WHEN IT'S ATTRACTIVE.

Now arrange the circled letters to form the surprise answer, as suggested by the above cartoon.

Print the SURPRISE ANSWER here

JUMBLE®

Unscramble these four Jumbles,
one letter to each square, to
form four ordinary words.

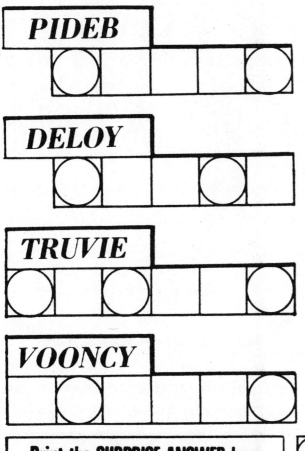

PIDEB

DELOY

TRUVIE

VOONCY

Print the SURPRISE ANSWER here

THIS LEAVES
NO ONE OUT!

Now arrange the circled letters
to form the surprise answer, as
suggested by the above cartoon.

JUMBLE®

Unscramble these four Jumbles, one letter to each square, to form four ordinary words.

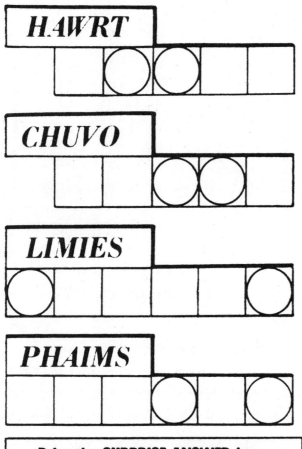

HAWRT

CHUVO

LIMIES

PHAIMS

Print the SURPRISE ANSWER here

Am I late, dear?

THE ONLY THING SOME WOMEN EVER DO ON TIME.

Now arrange the circled letters to form the surprise answer, as suggested by the above cartoon.

JUMBLE®

Unscramble these four Jumbles,
one letter to each square, to
form four ordinary words.

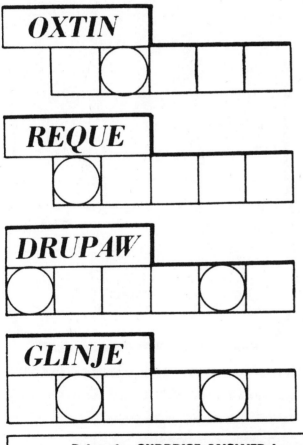

OXTIN

REQUE

DRUPAW

GLINJE

A MORE LASTING
FINISH FOR A CAR
THAN LACQUER.

Now arrange the circled letters
to form the surprise answer, as
suggested by the above cartoon.

Print the SURPRISE ANSWER here

JUMBLE®

Unscramble these four Jumbles, one letter to each square, to form four ordinary words.

SENWY

DUGAR

ROTHEX

PERTAT

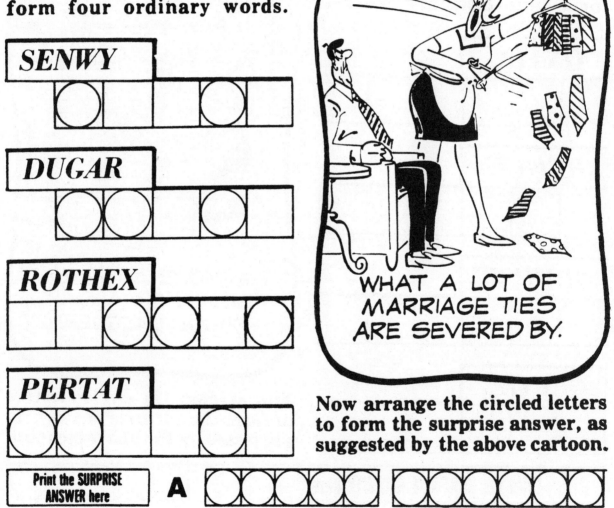

WHAT A LOT OF MARRIAGE TIES ARE SEVERED BY.

Now arrange the circled letters to form the surprise answer, as suggested by the above cartoon.

Print the SURPRISE ANSWER here

A

JUMBLE®

Unscramble these four Jumbles,
one letter to each square, to
form four ordinary words.

AWNTY

EXVIN

LARMIN

THIGEY

Gone! All gone!

But (chuckle) WE'RE not!

GROWING OLD ISN'T
SO BAD IF YOU
CONSIDER THIS.

Now arrange the circled letters
to form the surprise answer, as
suggested by the above cartoon.

Print the SURPRISE
ANSWER here

THE

JUMBLE®

Unscramble these four Jumbles,
one letter to each square, to
form four ordinary words.

MAITY

RECSS

PREDIM

UNSADE

Whew! Just
made it!

More dough
next month

WHAT BOTH LANDLORDS
AND TENANTS OFTEN
TRY TO DO.

Now arrange the circled letters
to form the surprise answer, as
suggested by the above cartoon.

Print the SURPRISE ANSWER here

THE

JUMBLE®

Unscramble these four Jumbles, one letter to each square, to form four ordinary words.

BOZIM

KRYJE

EBONGY

HYDING

WHAT THOSE WHO DRINK TO FORGET ALWAYS SEEM TO REMEMBER.

Now arrange the circled letters to form the surprise answer, as suggested by the above cartoon.

Print the SURPRISE ANSWER here   TO

35

JUMBLE®

Unscramble these four Jumbles,
one letter to each square, to
form four ordinary words.

DYPUG

LUSKK

POURRA

VELENE

WHAT A MAN
WHOSE HAND IS
QUICKER THAN THE
EYE MIGHT GET.

Now arrange the circled letters
to form the surprise answer, as
suggested by the above cartoon.

Print the SURPRISE ANSWER here

JUMBLE®

Unscramble these four Jumbles,
one letter to each square, to
form four ordinary words.

POKAK

RIQUE

SARATY

LAISOR

WHAT YOU CAN
EXPECT A DOZEN
ROSEBUDS TO
COME TO.

Now arrange the circled letters
to form the surprise answer, as
suggested by the above cartoon.

Print the SURPRISE ANSWER here

JUMBLE®

Unscramble these four Jumbles, one letter to each square, to form four ordinary words.

ILFOO

GEBOF

NISSIT

PROWED

It looks like my new system will work

You might try LOOKING for work!

THE EASIEST WAY TO MAKE ENDS MEET.

Now arrange the circled letters to form the surprise answer, as suggested by the above cartoon.

Print the SURPRISE ANSWER here

YOUR ☐☐☐ !

JUMBLE®

Unscramble these four Jumbles,
one letter to each square, to
form four ordinary words.

UNTOK

SMUCA

MANOSH

LAUBBE

A LIGHT KIND
OF BOOK.

Now arrange the circled letters
to form the surprise answer, as
suggested by the above cartoon.

Print the SURPRISE ANSWER here A

JUMBLE®

Unscramble these four Jumbles, one letter to each square, to form four ordinary words.

LAIGY

BLAYM

YARAFF

FLUGEN

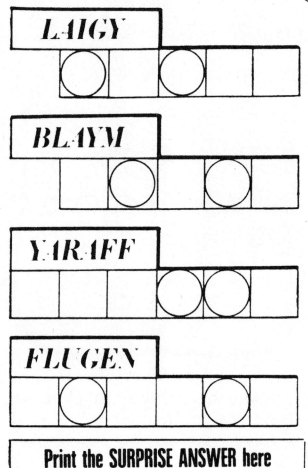

WHAT GETTING UP IN THE MORNING CAN BE.

Now arrange the circled letters to form the surprise answer, as suggested by the above cartoon.

Print the SURPRISE ANSWER here

◯◯◯◯◯◯◯◯◯!

JUMBLE®

Unscramble these four Jumbles, one letter to each square, to form four ordinary words.

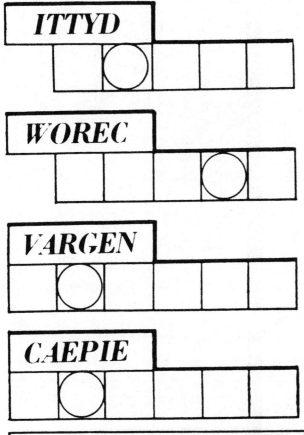

ITTYD

WOREC

VARGEN

CAEPIE

Come and get it!

READY TO EAT!

Now arrange the circled letters to form the surprise answer, as suggested by the above cartoon.

Print the SURPRISE ANSWER here

JUMBLE®

Unscramble these four Jumbles,
one letter to each square, to
form four ordinary words.

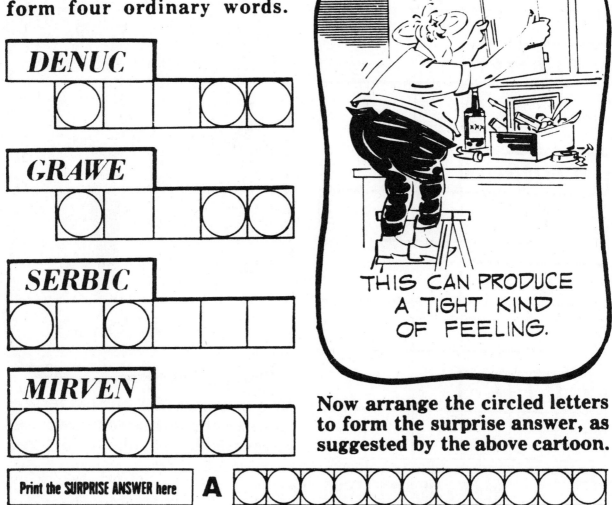

THIS CAN PRODUCE
A TIGHT KIND
OF FEELING.

DENUC

GRAWE

SERBIC

MIRVEN

Now arrange the circled letters
to form the surprise answer, as
suggested by the above cartoon.

Print the SURPRISE ANSWER here

A

JUMBLE®

Unscramble these four Jumbles, one letter to each square, to form four ordinary words.

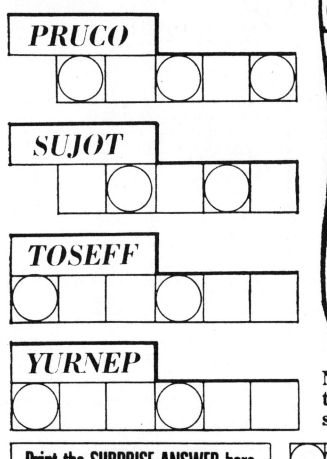

PRUCO

SUJOT

TOSEFF

YURNEP

WHAT LADLES DO.

Now arrange the circled letters to form the surprise answer, as suggested by the above cartoon.

Print the SURPRISE ANSWER here

JUMBLE®

Unscramble these four Jumbles,
one letter to each square, to
form four ordinary words.

GARBE

ELLAD

MIGNIT

BILDOY

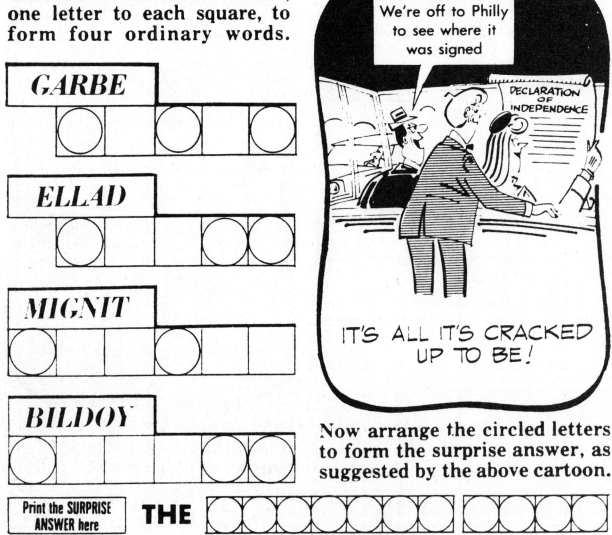

We're off to Philly
to see where it
was signed

DECLARATION
OF
INDEPENDENCE

IT'S ALL IT'S CRACKED
UP TO BE!

Now arrange the circled letters
to form the surprise answer, as
suggested by the above cartoon.

Print the SURPRISE
ANSWER here   **THE**

JUMBLE®

Unscramble these four Jumbles,
one letter to each square, to
form four ordinary words.

INBAC

UDGIE

BELJUM

HUMILE

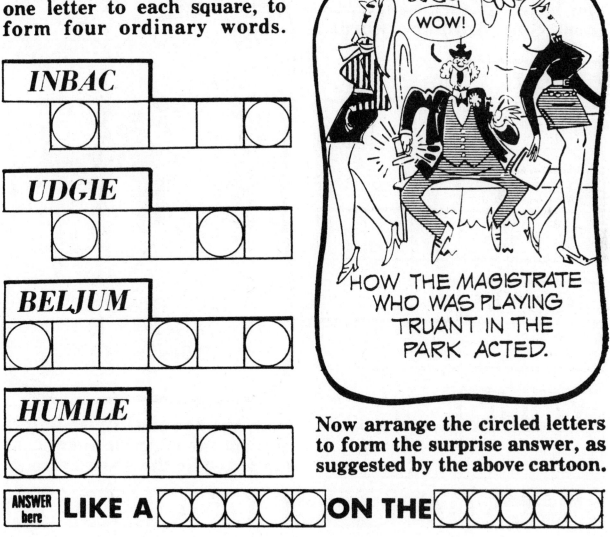

WOW!

HOW THE MAGISTRATE
WHO WAS PLAYING
TRUANT IN THE
PARK ACTED.

Now arrange the circled letters
to form the surprise answer, as
suggested by the above cartoon.

ANSWER here LIKE A ⬡⬡⬡⬡⬡ ON THE ⬡⬡⬡⬡⬡

JUMBLE®

Unscramble these four Jumbles,
one letter to each square, to
form four ordinary words.

SALIE

RETEX

MUGNIP

NACTAV

FURS

NOW!! ONLY $25,000

There's another
sale we'll skip

ONE THING YOU
CAN SAY FOR
BEING POOR.

Now arrange the circled letters
to form the surprise answer, as
suggested by the above cartoon.

Print the SURPRISE
ANSWER here   IT'S

JUMBLE®

Unscramble these four Jumbles, one letter to each square, to form four ordinary words.

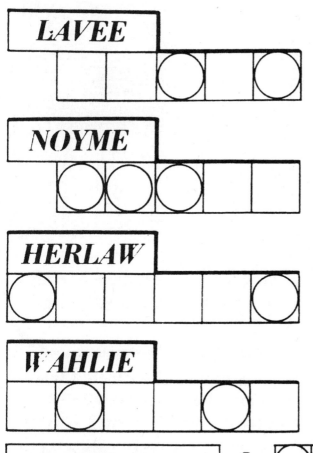

LAVEE

NOYME

HERLAW

WAHLIE

It looks better now

WHAT THE RAKE WAS TURNED INTO AFTER HE GOT MARRIED.

Now arrange the circled letters to form the surprise answer, as suggested by the above cartoon.

 Print the SURPRISE ANSWER here

A

JUMBLE®

Unscramble these four Jumbles,
one letter to each square, to
form four ordinary words.

PEWID

TRAFE

HOMIDS

YARNLE

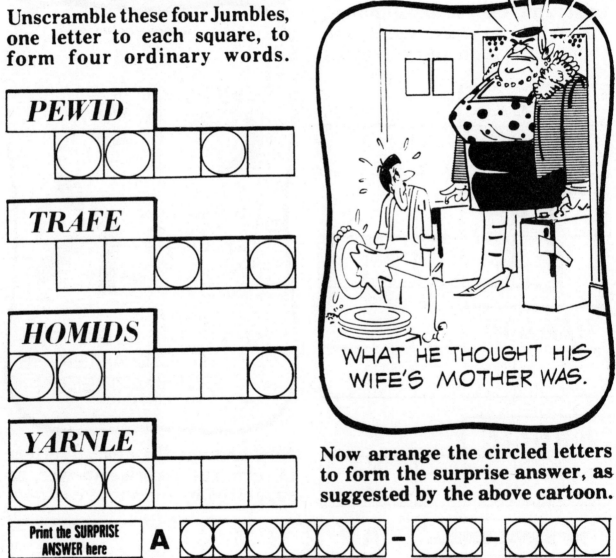

WHAT HE THOUGHT HIS
WIFE'S MOTHER WAS.

Now arrange the circled letters
to form the surprise answer, as
suggested by the above cartoon.

Print the SURPRISE
ANSWER here

A ◯◯◯◯◯◯◯ - ◯◯ - ◯◯◯

JUMBLE®

Unscramble these four Jumbles, one letter to each square, to form four ordinary words.

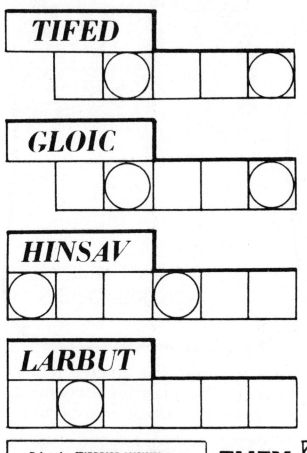

TIFED

GLOIC

HINSAV

LARBUT

CRASH!!

That does it!

BROKEN HOMES

HOW MODERN HOUSE-WIVES SOMETIMES GET RID OF UNSATIS-FACTORY DISHWASHERS.

Now arrange the circled letters to form the surprise answer, as suggested by the above cartoon.

Print the SURPRISE ANSWER here

THEY 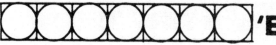 'EM

JUMBLE®

Unscramble these four Jumbles, one letter to each square, to form four ordinary words.

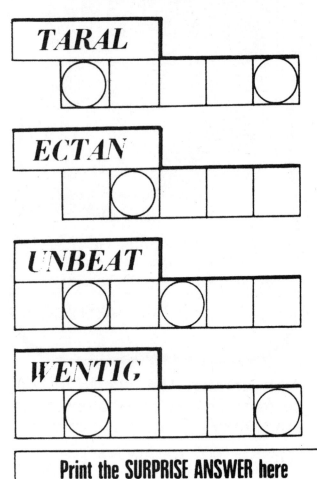

TARAL

ECTAN

UNBEAT

WENTIG

Print the SURPRISE ANSWER here

Will it be a boy or a girl?

YOU DON'T KNOW IF YOU'RE THIS!

Now arrange the circled letters to form the surprise answer, as suggested by the above cartoon.

JUMBLE®

Unscramble these four Jumbles, one letter to each square, to form four ordinary words.

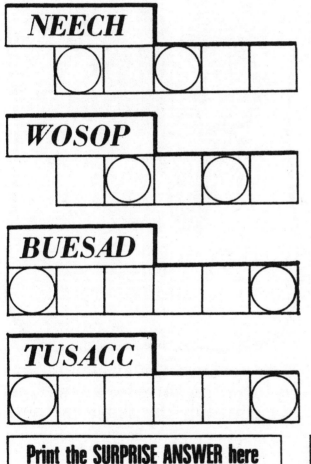

NEECH

WOSOP

BUESAD

TUSACC

Print the SURPRISE ANSWER here

From the finest geese

PAY NOW AND $AVE

JUST MARRIED

THE BEST THING TO USE FOR FEATHERING YOUR NEST.

Now arrange the circled letters to form the surprise answer, as suggested by the above cartoon.

JUMBLE®

Unscramble these four Jumbles, one letter to each square, to form four ordinary words.

VELOC

REESA

CLAGEY

RAVEEB

HOW THE REDUCING BUSINESS IS CARRIED ON.

Now arrange the circled letters to form the surprise answer, as suggested by the above cartoon.

Print the SURPRISE ANSWER here

ON A

JUMBLE®

Unscramble these four Jumbles, one letter to each square, to form four ordinary words.

BATOU

SECAE

WYLLOH

CLARNE

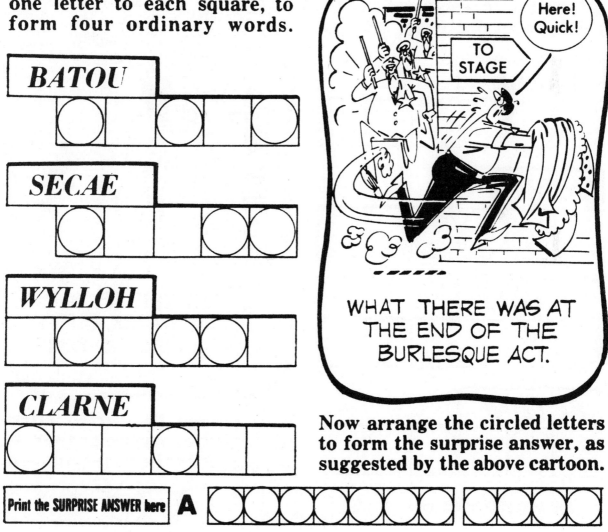

Here! Quick!

TO STAGE

WHAT THERE WAS AT THE END OF THE BURLESQUE ACT.

Now arrange the circled letters to form the surprise answer, as suggested by the above cartoon.

Print the SURPRISE ANSWER here A

JUMBLE®

Unscramble these four Jumbles,
one letter to each square, to
form four ordinary words.

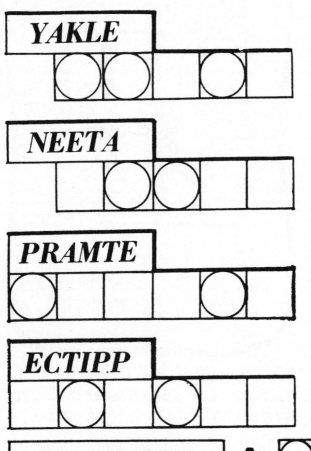

YAKLE

NEETA

PRAMTE

ECTIPP

Where were
you last
night?

UP TO THE NECK IN
HOT WATER BUT
CONTINUES TO SING.

Now arrange the circled letters
to form the surprise answer, as
suggested by the above cartoon.

Print the SURPRISE ANSWER here

A

JUMBLE®

Unscramble these four Jumbles,
one letter to each square, to
form four ordinary words.

NIFET

MYNEE

TRONIA

UMCAUV

WHEN YOU WANT TO
SLEEP THIS WAY,
BETTER PUT YOUR WATCH
UNDER YOUR PILLOW.

Now arrange the circled letters
to form the surprise answer, as
suggested by the above cartoon.

Print the SURPRISE ANSWER here

"◯◯◯◯◯ ◯◯◯◯◯"

JUMBLE®

Unscramble these four Jumbles, one letter to each square, to form four ordinary words.

DEEGH

COSUR

DELMAT

SELUNS

WHAT POLITICIANS WHO PROMISE PIE IN THE SKY OFTEN DO.

Now arrange the circled letters to form the surprise answer, as suggested by the above cartoon.

Print the SURPRISE ANSWER here

YOUR

JUMBLE®

Unscramble these four Jumbles, one letter to each square, to form four ordinary words.

DYSAN

WADAR

BOSULE

FROGLE

Print the SURPRISE ANSWER here

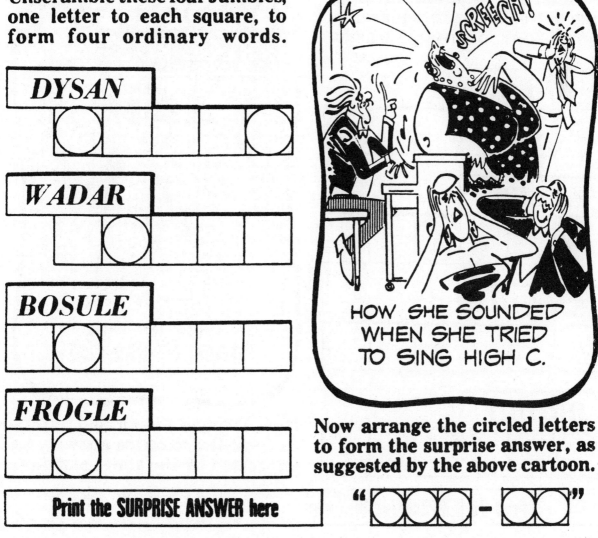

SCREECH!

HOW SHE SOUNDED
WHEN SHE TRIED
TO SING HIGH C.

Now arrange the circled letters to form the surprise answer, as suggested by the above cartoon.

" ◯◯◯ – ◯◯ "

JUMBLE®

Unscramble these four Jumbles, one letter to each square, to form four ordinary words.

BIBAR

GELEY

KNABIG

DROBIF

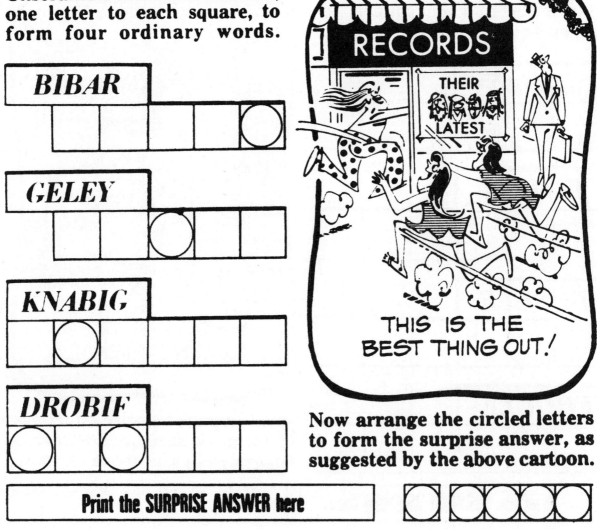

RECORDS

THEIR LATEST

THIS IS THE BEST THING OUT!

Now arrange the circled letters to form the surprise answer, as suggested by the above cartoon.

Print the SURPRISE ANSWER here

JUMBLE®

Unscramble these four Jumbles, one letter to each square, to form four ordinary words.

DACKE

YORRS

DECORF

ENCAME

BECAUSE OF THIS SOME MOVIE STARS ARE "COOL."

Now arrange the circled letters to form the surprise answer, as suggested by the above cartoon.

Print the SURPRISE ANSWER here

JUMBLE®

Unscramble these four Jumbles,
one letter to each square, to
form four ordinary words.

HIGEW

SYTTA

DIBEHN

NUCKOL

Hatching another
culinary masterpiece?

WHY MOST THINGS
DON'T HAVE TO BE
THOUGHT OUT IN
MODERN KITCHENS.

Now arrange the circled letters
to form the surprise answer, as
suggested by the above cartoon.

Print the SURPRISE
ANSWER here

THEY'RE

JUMBLE®

Unscramble these four Jumbles,
one letter to each square, to
form four ordinary words.

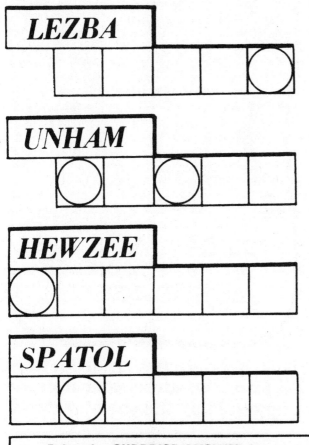

LEZBA

UNHAM

HEWZEE

SPATOL

Print the SURPRISE ANSWER here

Parts of Speech

WHAT THE INATTENTIVE
STUDENT SAID WHEN
THE TEACHER ASKED HIM
TO NAME TWO PRONOUNS.

Now arrange the circled letters
to form the surprise answer, as
suggested by the above cartoon.

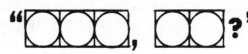

"◯◯◯, ◯◯?"

JUMBLE®

Unscramble these four Jumbles,
one letter to each square, to
form four ordinary words.

CEENI

PROWE

DANNEC

YISMAL

Durn
revenooer!!

YOU CAN MAKE THIS
BUT YOU'LL NEVER
LIVE TO SEE IT!

Now arrange the circled letters
to form the surprise answer, as
suggested by the above cartoon.

Print the SURPRISE ANSWER here

JUMBLE®

Unscramble these four Jumbles, one letter to each square, to form four ordinary words.

AGDEA

BIBER

VISPLE

PIMOCY

MEN LOOK HARDER AT GIRLS WHO LOOK THIS WAY.

Now arrange the circled letters to form the surprise answer, as suggested by the above cartoon.

" ◯◯◯◯◯◯ "

Print the SURPRISE ANSWER here

JUMBLE.®

Unscramble these four Jumbles,
one letter to each square, to
form four ordinary words.

YORFE

VENAK

YAXLAG

ENBOAM

WHAT A TAXPAYER
HOPES FOR.

Now arrange the circled letters
to form the surprise answer, as
suggested by the above cartoon.

Print the SURPRISE
ANSWER here

A ☐☐☐☐☐ IN THE ☐☐☐☐

JUMBLE®

Unscramble these four Jumbles,
one letter to each square, to
form four ordinary words.

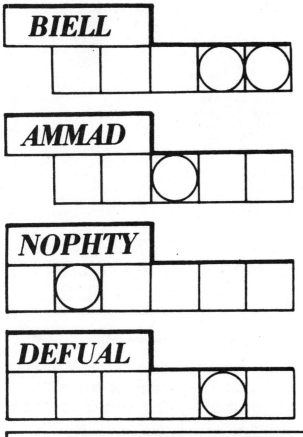

BIELL

AMMAD

NOPHTY

DEFUAL

I'll be late
for school if
I come back

SERVES TO HOLD
IMPORTANT THINGS UP.

Now arrange the circled letters
to form the surprise answer, as
suggested by the above cartoon.

Print the SURPRISE ANSWER here

A

JUMBLE®

Unscramble these four Jumbles,
one letter to each square, to
form four ordinary words.

CROFE

RICLY

INGRYP

HINEAL

WHAT THE PRUDE SAID
MINISKIRTS COULDN'T
BE WORN FOR.

Now arrange the circled letters
to form the surprise answer, as
suggested by the above cartoon.

Print the SURPRISE ANSWER here

JUMBLE®

Unscramble these four Jumbles,
one letter to each square, to
form four ordinary words.

RILLT

VAHEY

VIMOTE

GORUBE

Print the SURPRISE ANSWER here

HOW THE MISER HELD
ON TO HIS DOUGH.

Now arrange the circled letters
to form the surprise answer, as
suggested by the above cartoon.

JUMBLE®

Unscramble these four Jumbles, one letter to each square, to form four ordinary words.

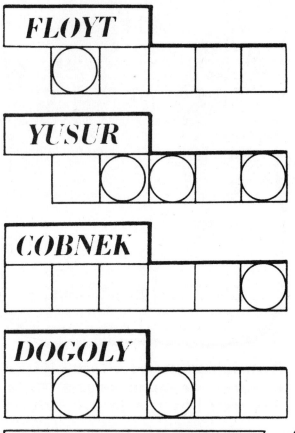

FLOYT

YUSUR

COBNEK

DOGOLY

HOW HE SLEPT WHEN HE SNORED.

Now arrange the circled letters to form the surprise answer, as suggested by the above cartoon.

Print the SURPRISE ANSWER here

"⬭⬭⬭⬭⬭-⬭⬭"

JUMBLE®

Unscramble these four Jumbles,
one letter to each square, to
form four ordinary words.

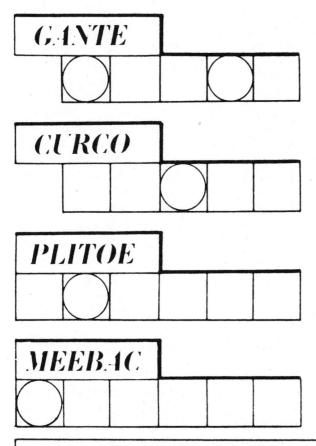

GANTE

CURCO

PLITOE

MEEBAC

Eggs will be ready in a second

AN AUTHOR TO READ AT THE BREAKFAST TABLE.

Now arrange the circled letters
to form the surprise answer, as
suggested by the above cartoon.

Print the SURPRISE ANSWER here

JUMBLE®

Unscramble these four Jumbles, one letter to each square, to form four ordinary words.

NOARP

TIFAN

SEEBID

MEESID

Print the SURPRISE ANSWER here

SOMETIMES CONNECTED WITH A STATE OF UNREST.

Now arrange the circled letters to form the surprise answer, as suggested by the above cartoon.

JUMBLE®

Unscramble these four Jumbles,
one letter to each square, to
form four ordinary words.

NUBEG

GIHLT

HALVIS

SHURTH

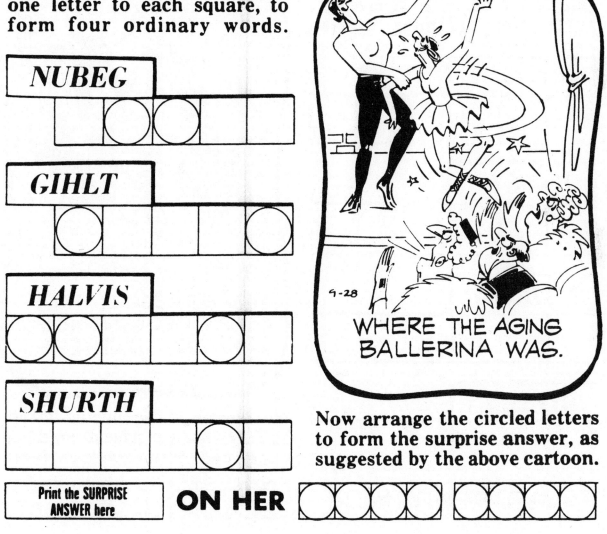

9-28

WHERE THE AGING
BALLERINA WAS.

Now arrange the circled letters
to form the surprise answer, as
suggested by the above cartoon.

Print the SURPRISE
ANSWER here

ON HER

JUMBLE®

Unscramble these four Jumbles,
one letter to each square, to
form four ordinary words.

VITOD

ESTUG

KABREY

MORLAN

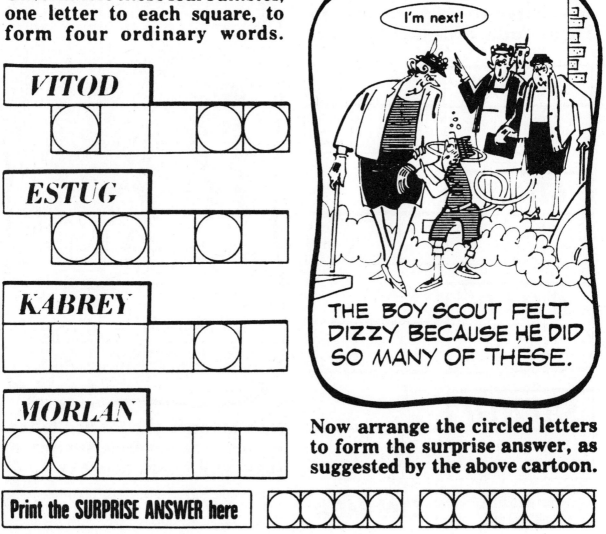

I'm next!

THE BOY SCOUT FELT
DIZZY BECAUSE HE DID
SO MANY OF THESE.

Now arrange the circled letters
to form the surprise answer, as
suggested by the above cartoon.

Print the SURPRISE ANSWER here

JUMBLE®

Unscramble these four Jumbles, one letter to each square, to form four ordinary words.

DEYNE

HUGAL

CORHUG

FATLEY

WHAT THE DOCTOR SAID TO THE PATIENT WHO WAS ALWAYS COMPLAINING OF SINUS.

Now arrange the circled letters to form the surprise answer, as suggested by the above cartoon.

Print the SURPRISE ANSWER here   IT'S ⬡⬡⬡ IN YOUR ⬡⬡⬡⬡

JUMBLE®

Unscramble these four Jumbles, one letter to each square, to form four ordinary words.

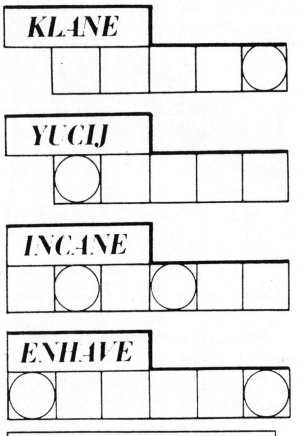

KLANE

YUCIJ

INCANE

ENHAVE

Print the SURPRISE ANSWER here

...WITH THE LIGHT BROWN HAIR...

ANTI-SEPTIC

HOW THE HEALTH OFFICIAL GREETED HIS WIFE.

Now arrange the circled letters to form the surprise answer, as suggested by the above cartoon.

"◯◯, ◯◯◯◯!"

JUMBLE®

Unscramble these four Jumbles, one letter to each square, to form four ordinary words.

DUNET

FICEH

SETTAL

VARMEL

WHAT THEY SAID WHEN THEY WERE LOCKED OUT OF THE MARKET.

Now arrange the circled letters to form the surprise answer, as suggested by the above cartoon.

Print the SURPRISE ANSWER here " ◯◯◯◯◯◯◯◯ ◯◯ "

JUMBLE®

Unscramble these four Jumbles, one letter to each square, to form four ordinary words.

MOTEC

DAFEM

CEPTIK

VOGNER

Print the SURPRISE ANSWER here

THIS MIGHT SEPARATE TWO QUARRELING THIEVES.

Now arrange the circled letters to form the surprise answer, as suggested by the above cartoon.

JUMBLE®

Unscramble these four Jumbles,
one letter to each square, to
form four ordinary words.

OXMIA

WYDON

ZAHDAR

ENGOIP

WHAT EVENTUALLY
HAPPENED TO THE GUY
WHO STAYED UP ALL
NIGHT WONDERING
WHERE THE SUN WENT
TO WHEN IT SET.

Now arrange the circled letters
to form the surprise answer, as
suggested by the above cartoon.

Print the SURPRISE
ANSWER here

IT ☐☐☐☐☐☐☐ ON ☐☐☐

JUMBLE.®

Unscramble these four Jumbles,
one letter to each square, to
form four ordinary words.

HORAB

UNYTT

PLARIL

ROQUIL

HOW THE DENTIST AND
HIS MANICURIST
WIFE FOUGHT.

Now arrange the circled letters
to form the surprise answer, as
suggested by the above cartoon.

Print the SURPRISE ANSWER here

&

JUMBLE®

Unscramble these four Jumbles, one letter to each square, to form four ordinary words.

GINCI

SEEBO

WIMDLE

LUITED

WHAT THE GREASE MONKEY GOT AFTER WORKING HOURS.

Now arrange the circled letters to form the surprise answer, as suggested by the above cartoon.

Print the SURPRISE ANSWER here

"⬭⬭⬭⬭⬭⬭"

JUMBLE®

Unscramble these four Jumbles,
one letter to each square, to
form four ordinary words.

LANUN

TAFUL

ABBOMO

GINMOH

Print the SURPRISE ANSWER here

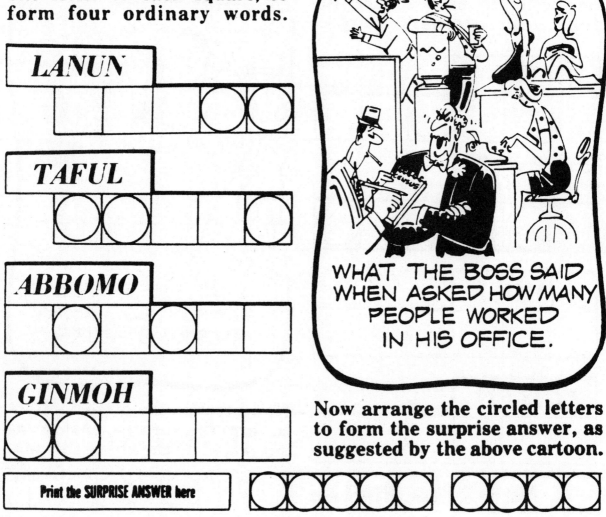

WHAT THE BOSS SAID
WHEN ASKED HOW MANY
PEOPLE WORKED
IN HIS OFFICE.

Now arrange the circled letters
to form the surprise answer, as
suggested by the above cartoon.

JUMBLE®

Unscramble these four Jumbles, one letter to each square, to form four ordinary words.

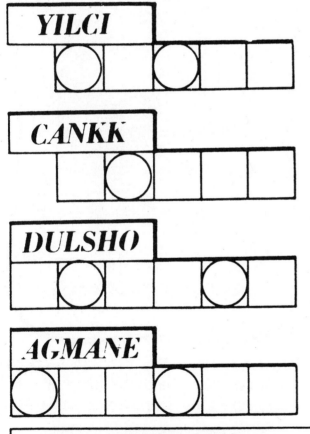

YILCI

CANKK

DULSHO

AGMANE

Print the SURPRISE ANSWER here

All alone in that big house?

WHAT THE MANICURIST WANTED TO DO.

Now arrange the circled letters to form the surprise answer, as suggested by the above cartoon.

JUMBLE®

Unscramble these four Jumbles,
one letter to each square, to
form four ordinary words.

DOPKE

VAIST

KLUNIE

CISNEC

HOME COOKING

WHAT HE THOUGHT THE
RESTAURANT WAS.

Now arrange the circled letters
to form the surprise answer, as
suggested by the above cartoon.

Print the SURPRISE ANSWER here

JUMBLE®

Unscramble these four Jumbles,
one letter to each square, to
form four ordinary words.

NUWDE

VORAB

PHONIS

VANDIE

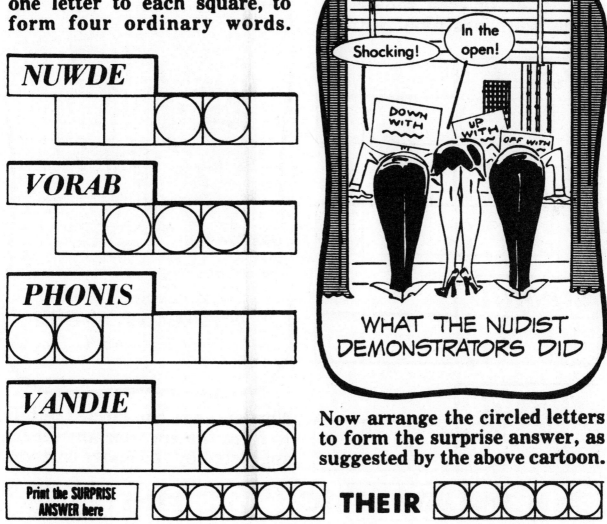

Shocking!

In the
open!

DOWN WITH

UP WITH

OFF WITH

WHAT THE NUDIST
DEMONSTRATORS DID

Now arrange the circled letters
to form the surprise answer, as
suggested by the above cartoon.

Print the SURPRISE
ANSWER here

THEIR

JUMBLE®

Unscramble these four Jumbles,
one letter to each square, to
form four ordinary words.

POATI

YARRA

COSHOL

THRENE

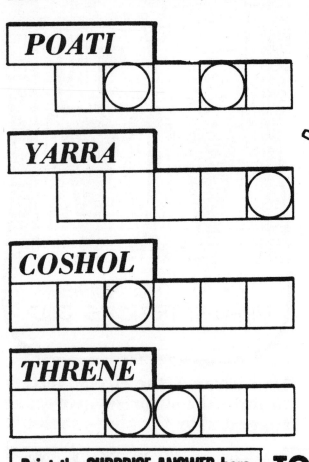

WHY HE TOOK
A HAMMER TO BED
WITH HIM.

Now arrange the circled letters
to form the surprise answer, as
suggested by the above cartoon.

Print the SURPRISE ANSWER here   TO ⬡⬡⬡ THE ⬡⬡⬡

JUMBLE®

Unscramble these four Jumbles,
one letter to each square, to
form four ordinary words.

POCUE

KERPI

FONTIY

RELPHE

EAR
DOCTOR

Come in

HOW TO STOP
THAT RINGING
IN YOUR EARS.

Now arrange the circled letters
to form the surprise answer, as
suggested by the above cartoon.

Print the SURPRISE
ANSWER here

⟨ ⟩⟨ ⟩⟨ ⟩⟨ ⟩ ⟨ ⟩⟨ ⟩ **THE** ⟨ ⟩⟨ ⟩⟨ ⟩⟨ ⟩⟨ ⟩

JUMBLE®

Unscramble these four Jumbles, one letter to each square, to form four ordinary words.

ATQUO

YITED

YALTIX

HYSERR

... And another thing, I'm sick and tired of ...

WHAT SHE KNEW HOW TO DO.

Now arrange the circled letters to form the surprise answer, as suggested by the above cartoon.

Print the SURPRISE ANSWER here

" ⬭⬭⬭⬭ ⬭⬭ ⬭⬭⬭ "

JUMBLE®

Unscramble these four Jumbles,
one letter to each square, to
form four ordinary words.

VOFAR

UGLIE

DECLUD

SEXOUD

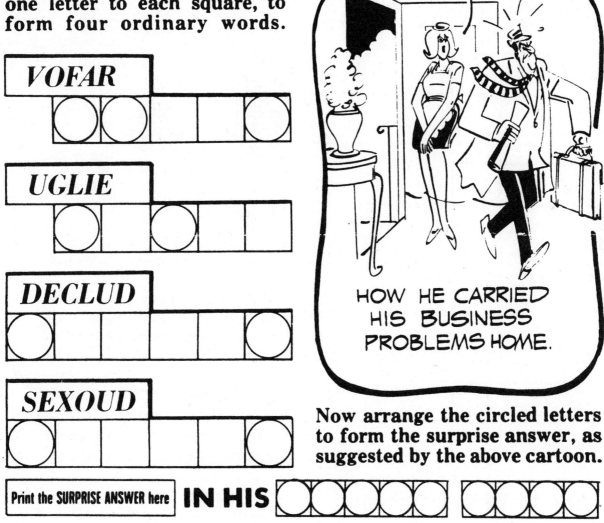

Have a nice day, dear?

HOW HE CARRIED
HIS BUSINESS
PROBLEMS HOME.

Now arrange the circled letters
to form the surprise answer, as
suggested by the above cartoon.

Print the SURPRISE ANSWER here IN HIS ⬭⬭⬭⬭⬭ ⬭⬭⬭⬭

JUMBLE®

Unscramble these four Jumbles,
one letter to each square, to
form four ordinary words.

NAMEG

DIPAL

PREEMA

CAJALK

WHERE THE USHER PUT
AN OVERATTENTIVE
THEATERGOER.

Now arrange the circled letters
to form the surprise answer, as
suggested by the above cartoon.

Print the SURPRISE ANSWER here

HIS

JUMBLE®

Unscramble these four Jumbles,
one letter to each square, to
form four ordinary words.

PYMUB

AFTEC

SAUNAE

CALAPA

Print the SURPRISE ANSWER here

THE CAVEMAN'S
FAVORITE SANDWICH.

3 DECKER!

Now arrange the circled letters
to form the surprise answer, as
suggested by the above cartoon.

JUMBLE®

Unscramble these four Jumbles, one letter to each square, to form four ordinary words.

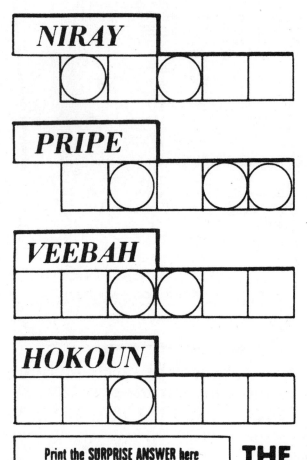

NIRAY

PRIPE

VEEBAH

HOKOUN

He'll be taking over

WHAT THE RICH WIGMAKER'S SON WAS.

Now arrange the circled letters to form the surprise answer, as suggested by the above cartoon.

Print the SURPRISE ANSWER here

THE

JUMBLE®

Unscramble these four Jumbles, one letter to each square, to form four ordinary words.

ZYIZD

HAABS

DEDUIG

NAANAB

WHAT THE LUNCH WAGON OWNER NAMED HIS DAUGHTER.

Now arrange the circled letters to form the surprise answer, as suggested by the above cartoon.

Print the SURPRISE ANSWER here

JUMBLE®

Unscramble these four Jumbles,
one letter to each square, to
form four ordinary words.

LUNCE

TYTUP

FRODIL

BEJARB

WHAT SHE WAS WHEN
HE COMPLAINED
ABOUT HER OVER-
COOKED BISCUITS.

Now arrange the circled letters
to form the surprise answer, as
suggested by the above cartoon.

Print the SURPRISE ANSWER here "⬡⬡⬡⬡⬡⬡ ⬡⬡"

JUMBLE®

Unscramble these four Jumbles, one letter to each square, to form four ordinary words.

PUTER

KIMPS

RUVESS

EIVIDD

Humph! ANY-THING goes!

THERE'S A FEMALE IN THE MIDDLE OF THIS TYPE OF SOCIETY.

Now arrange the circled letters to form the surprise answer, as suggested by the above cartoon.

Print the SURPRISE ANSWER here "◯◯◯ - ◯◯◯◯◯ - ◯◯◯".

JUMBLE®

Unscramble these four Jumbles,
one letter to each square, to
form four ordinary words.

REDOO

RALNS

PUMACS

FOYFAP

There was this traveling
salesman, see . . .

THE WOOL SALESMAN'S
STOCK-IN-TRADE.

Now arrange the circled letters
to form the surprise answer, as
suggested by the above cartoon.

Print the SURPRISE ANSWER here

JUMBLE®

Unscramble these four Jumbles, one letter to each square, to form four ordinary words.

ARICH

HAWTE

ROCEAT

FEENAD

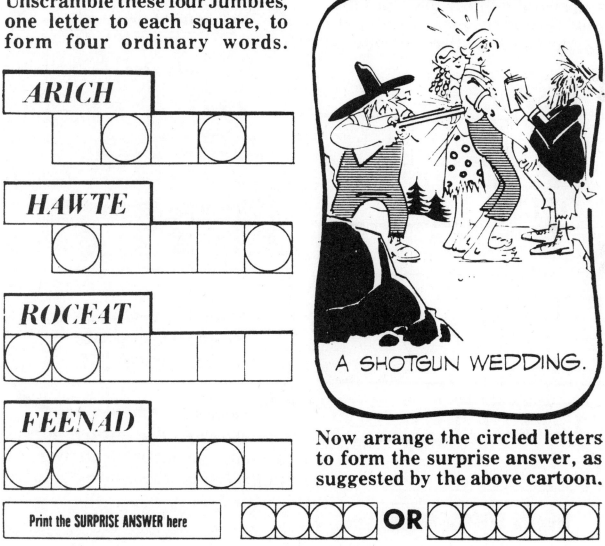

A SHOTGUN WEDDING.

Now arrange the circled letters to form the surprise answer, as suggested by the above cartoon.

Print the SURPRISE ANSWER here

☐☐☐☐☐ OR ☐☐☐☐☐

JUMBLE®

Unscramble these four Jumbles, one letter to each square, to form four ordinary words.

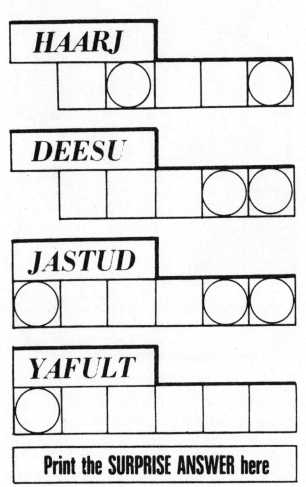

HAARJ

DEESU

JASTUD

YAFULT

Print the SURPRISE ANSWER here

This'll keep the weight off

WHAT LOW-CALORIE SHAMPOOS ARE GOOD FOR.

Now arrange the circled letters to form the surprise answer, as suggested by the above cartoon.

JUMBLE®

Unscramble these four Jumbles, one letter to each square, to form four ordinary words.

CAGIM

KIHCT

WHOANY

DELGEP

Almost didn't make it

HOW SANTA ARRIVED.

Now arrange the circled letters to form the surprise answer, as suggested by the above cartoon.

Print the SURPRISE ANSWER here

IN THE " ◯◯◯◯◯ " OF ◯◯◯◯◯

JUMBLE®

Unscramble these four Jumbles,
one letter to each square, to
form four ordinary words.

GLOIN

MARDA

YARDOP

LAWASY

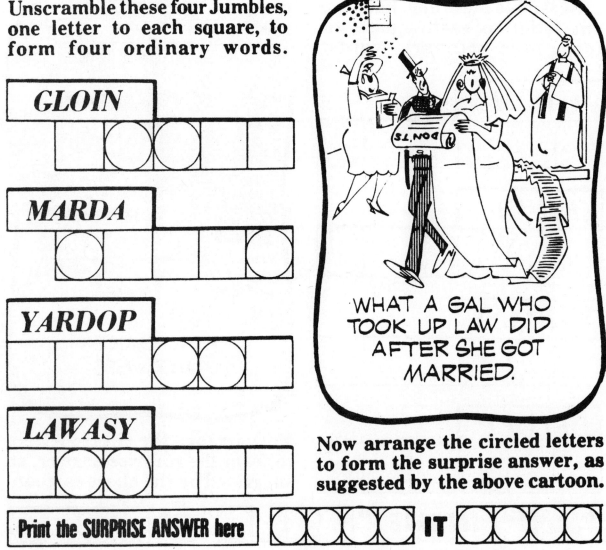

WHAT A GAL WHO
TOOK UP LAW DID
AFTER SHE GOT
MARRIED.

Now arrange the circled letters
to form the surprise answer, as
suggested by the above cartoon.

Print the SURPRISE ANSWER here

⬡⬡⬡⬡⬡ IT ⬡⬡⬡⬡

JUMBLE®

Unscramble these four Jumbles,
one letter to each square, to
form four ordinary words.

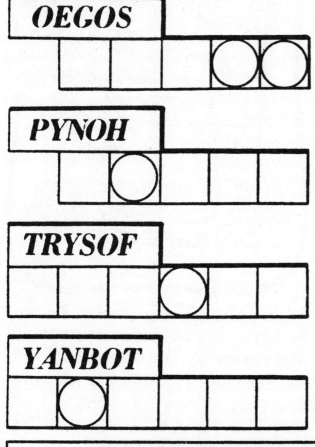

OEGOS

PYNOH

TRYSOF

YANBOT

Print the SURPRISE ANSWER here

I'm right!

DRUGS

No, I'm right!

ODD IF THEY'RE BOTH RIGHT!

Now arrange the circled letters
to form the surprise answer, as
suggested by the above cartoon.

JUMBLE®

Unscramble these four Jumbles,
one letter to each square, to
form four ordinary words.

DONUP

POURC

LAUMSY

SHOPIN

Second helping, anyone?

THIS IS NEITHER VERY GOOD NOR VERY BAD—SO, REPEAT IT!

Now arrange the circled letters
to form the surprise answer, as
suggested by the above cartoon.

Print the SURPRISE ANSWER here

Daily JUMBO JUMBLE

"Words cannot
express the
pleasure and
satisfaction I
derive from the
Jumble® books;
they have given
me many hours
of joy."

FRIEDA SHNIPER
KIAMESHA LAKE, NY

JUMBLE®

Unscramble these four Jumbles, one letter to each square, to form four ordinary words.

TOOPH

LIDAY

BELTOT

DRIFOL

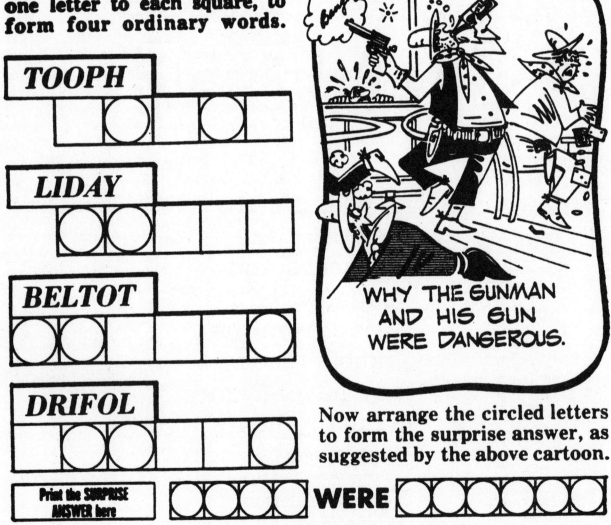

WHY THE GUNMAN AND HIS GUN WERE DANGEROUS.

Now arrange the circled letters to form the surprise answer, as suggested by the above cartoon.

Print the SURPRISE ANSWER here

⬡⬡⬡⬡ **WERE** ⬡⬡⬡⬡⬡⬡

JUMBLE®

Unscramble these four Jumbles, one letter to each square, to form four ordinary words.

DOEPT

NEALK

BROIMD

EPALUG

Print the SURPRISE ANSWER here

Happy birthday!

That was yesterday— and you've overslept

LATE IN BED AND DELAYED.

Now arrange the circled letters to form the surprise answer, as suggested by the above cartoon.

" ☐☐-☐☐☐☐☐-☐ "

JUMBLE®

Unscramble these four Jumbles,
one letter to each square, to
form four ordinary words.

HARCI

APITO

SUFOAM

GAMNEA

MATERNITY

Thanks
Thanks

TWICE A MOTHER.

Now arrange the circled letters
to form the surprise answer, as
suggested by the above cartoon.

Print the SURPRISE ANSWER here

JUMBLE®

Unscramble these four Jumbles, one letter to each square, to form four ordinary words.

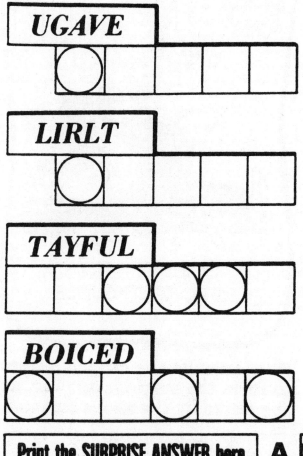

UGAVE

LIRLT

TAYFUL

BOICED

It's about time!

THIS WOULD INDICATE THAT SOMEONE HAS JUST STOPPED SMOKING.

Now arrange the circled letters to form the surprise answer, as suggested by the above cartoon.

Print the SURPRISE ANSWER here A

JUMBLE®

Unscramble these four Jumbles,
one letter to each square, to
form four ordinary words.

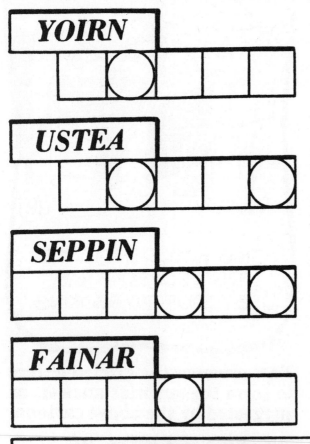

YOIRN

USTEA

SEPPIN

FAINAR

GOES OFF TO
REPORT TROUBLE.

Now arrange the circled letters
to form the surprise answer, as
suggested by the above cartoon.

Print the SURPRISE ANSWER here

JUMBLE®

Unscramble these four Jumbles, one letter to each square, to form four ordinary words.

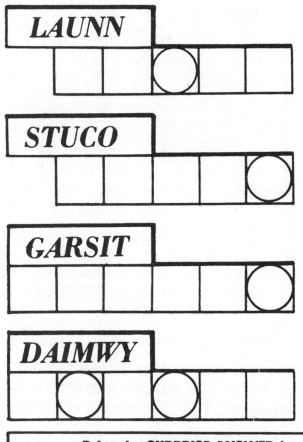

LAUNN

STUCO

GARSIT

DAIMWY

Print the SURPRISE ANSWER here

Oh, sir!!!

IT'S MORE USUAL TO HAVE ONLY HALF OF THIS.

Now arrange the circled letters to form the surprise answer, as suggested by the above cartoon.

JUMBLE®

Unscramble these four Jumbles,
one letter to each square, to
form four ordinary words.

DRUIL

PAWMS

VALERM

HIPLAC

INQUIRIES

COMPLETELY TIED UP IN
POSTAL REGULATIONS!

Now arrange the circled letters
to form the surprise answer, as
suggested by the above cartoon.

Print the SURPRISE ANSWER here

JUMBLE®

Unscramble these four Jumbles,
one letter to each square, to
form four ordinary words.

FECOR

ROBAR

WARMOR

GEPLED

Print the SURPRISE ANSWER here

MIGHT BE MAD
ABOUT THE ENGINE.

Now arrange the circled letters
to form the surprise answer, as
suggested by the above cartoon.

"◯◯◯◯"

JUMBLE®

Unscramble these four Jumbles,
one letter to each square, to
form four ordinary words.

COUNE

UFORR

POAFFY

FEECAD

Print the SURPRISE ANSWER here

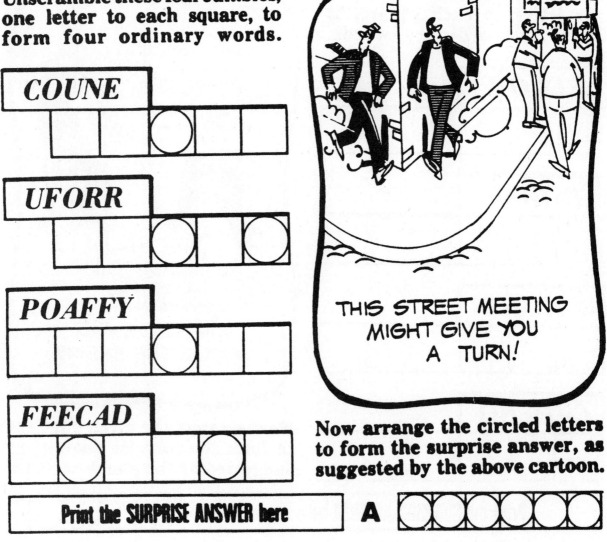

THIS STREET MEETING
MIGHT GIVE YOU
A TURN!

Now arrange the circled letters
to form the surprise answer, as
suggested by the above cartoon.

A ⭕⭕⭕⭕⭕⭕⭕

JUMBLE®

Unscramble these four Jumbles,
one letter to each square, to
form four ordinary words.

INNEL

STAIV

TEPROY

VOXCEN

Print the SURPRISE ANSWER here

Your
pay

GREASE!

YOUR FINANCIAL
PROBLEMS MELT AWAY
WHEN YOU'RE THIS!

Now arrange the circled letters
to form the surprise answer, as
suggested by the above cartoon.

JUMBLE®

Unscramble these four Jumbles,
one letter to each square, to
form four ordinary words.

DAAHE

WOSON

YIRCKT

GELIGG

HOW GOOD MODELS
ARE BUILT.

WOW!

Now arrange the circled letters
to form the surprise answer, as
suggested by the above cartoon.

Print the SURPRISE ANSWER here

JUMBLE®

Unscramble these four Jumbles, one letter to each square, to form four ordinary words.

TUINY

HERIK

SOYSIF

FLATUR

Show him who's the boss!

Yes, Mother

PROVIDES MARRIAGE GUIDANCE.

Now arrange the circled letters to form the surprise answer, as suggested by the above cartoon.

Print the SURPRISE ANSWER here

JUMBLE®

Unscramble these four Jumbles,
one letter to each square, to
form four ordinary words.

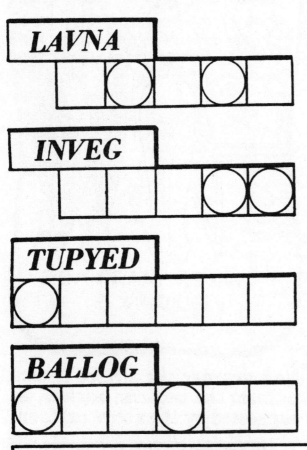

LAVNA

INVEG

TUPYED

BALLOG

SOMETIMES GOES
AROUND TO
PROVIDE COMFORT.

Now arrange the circled letters
to form the surprise answer, as
suggested by the above cartoon.

Print the SURPRISE ANSWER here

A

JUMBLE®

Unscramble these four Jumbles, one letter to each square, to form four ordinary words.

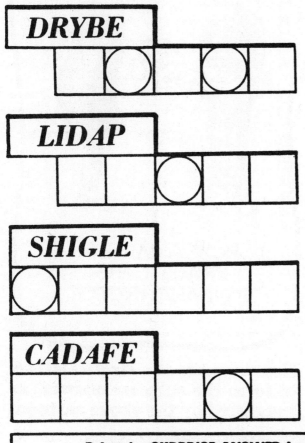

DRYBE

LIDAP

SHIGLE

CADAFE

JOE'S TATTOO PARLOR

WHAT THE TATTOO ARTIST TURNED GUNMAN DREW ON HIS VICTIMS.

Now arrange the circled letters to form the surprise answer, as suggested by the above cartoon.

Print the SURPRISE ANSWER here

JUMBLE®

Unscramble these four Jumbles,
one letter to each square, to
form four ordinary words.

GALUH

NYLOP

HILERS

TUNFAL

Print the SURPRISE ANSWER here

Thanks for the penny

HOW A MISER
PRACTICES
PHILANTHROPY.

Now arrange the circled letters
to form the surprise answer, as
suggested by the above cartoon.

JUMBLE®

Unscramble these four Jumbles, one letter to each square, to form four ordinary words.

TADAP

NALTS

LUPCOE

YARROS

BEAUTY PARLO

HOW TO GET GOOD LOOKS.

Now arrange the circled letters to form the surprise answer, as suggested by the above cartoon.

Print the SURPRISE ANSWER here

JUMBLE®

Unscramble these four Jumbles, one letter to each square, to form four ordinary words.

ATAGE

EFING

YONDOB

MOCNOM

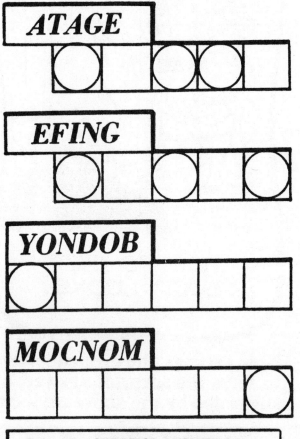

She's new

No telephone calls . . .
No loud records . . .

APERS

HE WON'T STAND
FOR ANYTHING!

Now arrange the circled letters to form the surprise answer, as suggested by the above cartoon.

Print the SURPRISE ANSWER here

JUMBLE®

Unscramble these four Jumbles,
one letter to each square, to
form four ordinary words.

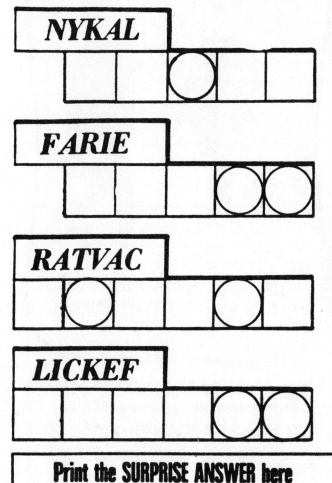

NYKAL

FARIE

RATVAC

LICKEF

PAYMASTER

YOU HAVE TO BE IT
WITH THE FIRST LETTER
BEFORE YOU CAN BE IT
WITHOUT THE FIRST.

Now arrange the circled letters
to form the surprise answer, as
suggested by the above cartoon.

Print the SURPRISE ANSWER here

◯ - ◯◯◯◯◯◯

JUMBLE.®

Unscramble these four Jumbles, one letter to each square, to form four ordinary words.

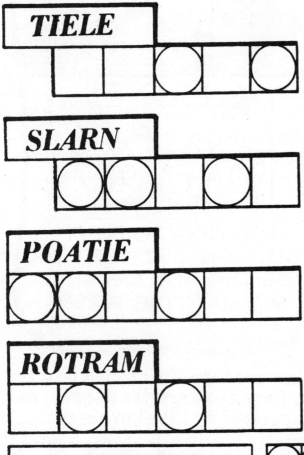

TIELE

SLARN

POATIE

ROTRAM

Print the SURPRISE ANSWER here

Is this the place for the opening?

GALLERY

THEATER PERFORMANCES NOT OPEN TO THE PUBLIC.

Now arrange the circled letters to form the surprise answer, as suggested by the above cartoon.

JUMBLE®

Unscramble these four Jumbles,
one letter to each square, to
form four ordinary words.

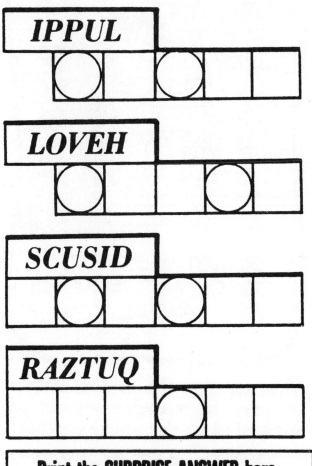

IPPUL

LOVEH

SCUSID

RAZTUQ

Print the SURPRISE ANSWER here

He charges
too much

THIS WOULD DESCRIBE A
HIGH-SPIRITED CHISELER.

Now arrange the circled letters
to form the surprise answer, as
suggested by the above cartoon.

JUMBLE®

Unscramble these four Jumbles, one letter to each square, to form four ordinary words.

MEFAD

VONEY

CLOTUC

LUPPIT

Who's next, Lucrezia?

Him!

SOMETIMES CARRIES POISON AND SOUNDS AWFUL.

Now arrange the circled letters to form the surprise answer, as suggested by the above cartoon.

Print the SURPRISE ANSWER here

"  "

JUMBLE®

Unscramble these four Jumbles, one letter to each square, to form four ordinary words.

TAIRE

LUVEA

REEWKS

HABLEC

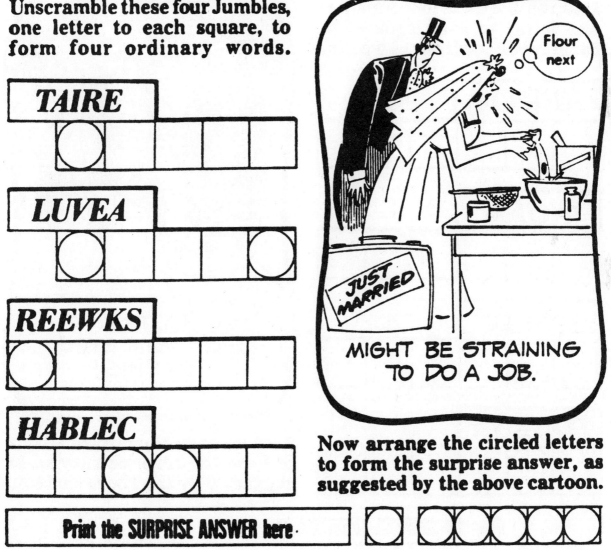

Flour next

JUST MARRIED

MIGHT BE STRAINING TO DO A JOB.

Now arrange the circled letters to form the surprise answer, as suggested by the above cartoon.

Print the SURPRISE ANSWER here

JUMBLE®

Unscramble these four Jumbles,
one letter to each square, to
form four ordinary words.

KEWOA

INORM

TINCLE

TOBENN

YOU JUST CAN'T
SHUT YOUR EYES
TO THIS!

Now arrange the circled letters
to form the surprise answer, as
suggested by the above cartoon.

Print the SURPRISE ANSWER here

JUMBLE®

Unscramble these four Jumbles, one letter to each square, to form four ordinary words.

LIVIG

KNAWE

HERTHS

WEARLY

THIS VIEW MAY HELP YOU GET A JOB.

Now arrange the circled letters to form the surprise answer, as suggested by the above cartoon.

Print the SURPRISE ANSWER here

AN ◯◯◯◯◯◯◯◯◯◯◯

JUMBLE®

Unscramble these four Jumbles,
one letter to each square, to
form four ordinary words.

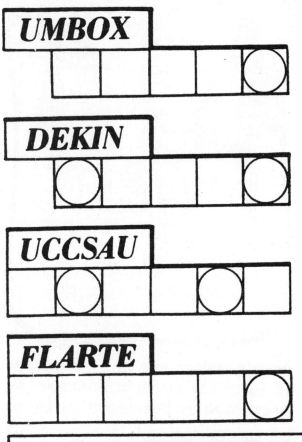

UMBOX

DEKIN

UCCSAU

FLARTE

Print the SURPRISE ANSWER here

You can see it in the dark

THIS MIGHT BE
COMPOSED OF
MUD AND AIR.

Now arrange the circled letters
to form the surprise answer, as
suggested by the above cartoon.

JUMBLE®

Unscramble these four Jumbles,
one letter to each square, to
form four ordinary words.

YASID

RECEL

OURSEA

DRUTSY

Print the SURPRISE ANSWER here

Here are
your notes

THEY INSURE THE
CORRECT DELIVERY
OF SPEECHES.

Now arrange the circled letters
to form the surprise answer, as
suggested by the above cartoon.

JUMBLE®

Unscramble these four Jumbles,
one letter to each square, to
form four ordinary words.

GUBEN

ORVAS

SHRAIG

TORFIP

Print the SURPRISE ANSWER here

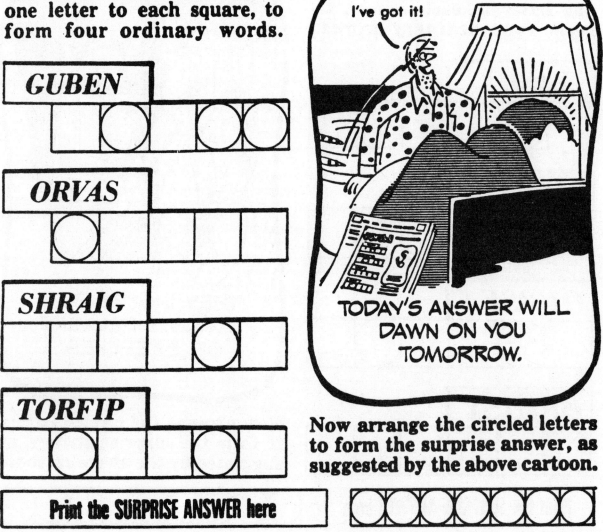

I've got it!

TODAY'S ANSWER WILL
DAWN ON YOU
TOMORROW.

Now arrange the circled letters
to form the surprise answer, as
suggested by the above cartoon.

JUMBLE.

Unscramble these four Jumbles, one letter to each square, to form four ordinary words.

STULY

ENFEC

ORSOUP

LISGRY

Sick friend

I'll be here

Just as I thought!

FROM A RUSE, YOU CAN MAKE CERTAIN OF THIS.

Now arrange the circled letters to form the surprise answer, as suggested by the above cartoon.

Print the SURPRISE ANSWER here

JUMBLE®

Unscramble these four Jumbles,
one letter to each square, to
form four ordinary words.

BROEP

DRATY

LADLAB

BONGIB

TOBACCONIS

P.D.

WHAT HE WAS WAS
APPARENT.

Now arrange the circled letters
to form the surprise answer, as
suggested by the above cartoon.

Print the SURPRISE ANSWER here

JUMBLE®

Unscramble these four Jumbles,
one letter to each square, to
form four ordinary words.

MUPIO

NOJEY

TRALEY

DRIZAL

Huh?

ONCE AROUSED
YOU MAY LOSE IT!

Now arrange the circled letters
to form the surprise answer, as
suggested by the above cartoon.

Print the SURPRISE ANSWER here

JUMBLE®

Unscramble these four Jumbles,
one letter to each square, to
form four ordinary words.

COPHE

PRAAT

BATEEK

ORFALL

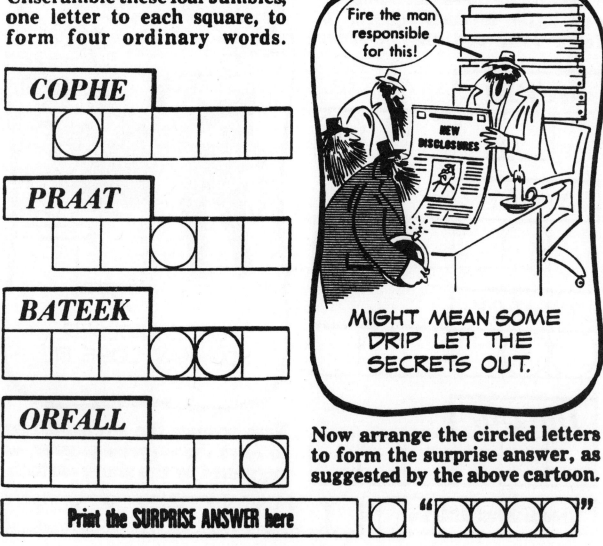

Fire the man responsible for this!

NEW DISCLOSURES

MIGHT MEAN SOME
DRIP LET THE
SECRETS OUT.

Now arrange the circled letters
to form the surprise answer, as
suggested by the above cartoon.

Print the SURPRISE ANSWER here

"〇〇〇〇"

JUMBLE®

Unscramble these four Jumbles,
one letter to each square, to
form four ordinary words.

SUMIC

PETIR

NAWDDE

ENIAMA

WHAT YOU'D EXPECT
FROM A LITTLE DEVIL

Now arrange the circled letters
to form the surprise answer, as
suggested by the above cartoon.

Print the SURPRISE ANSWER here

"◯◯◯ – ◯◯◯◯◯◯◯"

JUMBLE®

Unscramble these four Jumbles,
one letter to each square, to
form four ordinary words.

EVVER

OTTOH

CEIVED

RABENN

Jury is back

TRY AND GIVE THIS
TO A PRISONER.

Now arrange the circled letters
to form the surprise answer, as
suggested by the above cartoon.

Print the SURPRISE ANSWER here

JUMBLE®

Unscramble these four Jumbles, one letter to each square, to form four ordinary words.

RODOP

LUTEX

WEABER

UMLOVE

THIS IS OWING TO BEING LATE.

Now arrange the circled letters to form the surprise answer, as suggested by the above cartoon.

Print the SURPRISE ANSWER here

JUMBLE®

Unscramble these four Jumbles, one letter to each square, to form four ordinary words.

WENYL

NABOR

LENPOL

UNTAUM

COUNSELOR

Happens all the time

MAKE NOTHING OF IT!

Now arrange the circled letters to form the surprise answer, as suggested by the above cartoon.

Print the SURPRISE ANSWER here

JUMBLE.®

Unscramble these four Jumbles, one letter to each square, to form four ordinary words.

NOONI

LITAP

DETHOB

HYCTOU

Print the **SURPRISE ANSWER** here

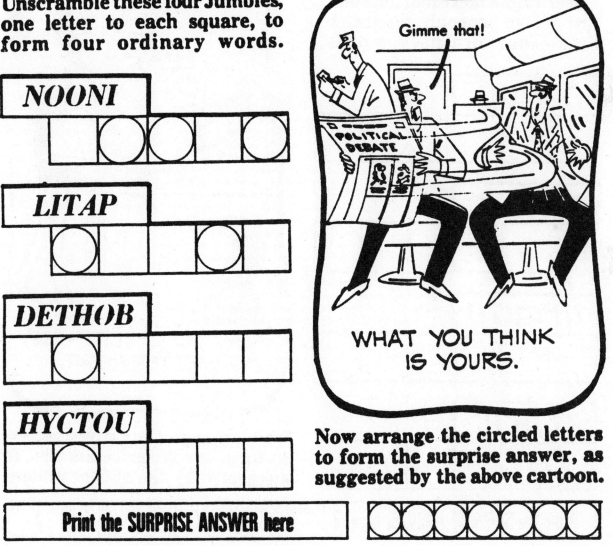

Gimme that!

POLITICAL DEBATE

WHAT YOU THINK IS YOURS.

Now arrange the circled letters to form the surprise answer, as suggested by the above cartoon.

JUMBLE®

Unscramble these four Jumbles, one letter to each square, to form four ordinary words.

YANDD

WETTE

HERBTO

TURIAL

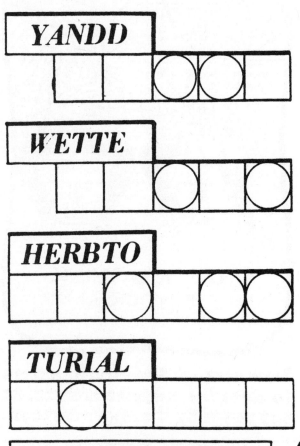

HOW TO OFFER THEM BETTER MEAT.

Now arrange the circled letters to form the surprise answer, as suggested by the above cartoon.

Print the SURPRISE ANSWER here

JUMBLE®

Unscramble these four Jumbles, one letter to each square, to form four ordinary words.

GOUNY

CANYF

NEPPAH

YIVELT

Regarding that shipment of underwear—

Oops! My wife!

MAKES MANY A SLIP!

Now arrange the circled letters to form the surprise answer, as suggested by the above cartoon.

Print the SURPRISE ANSWER here

JUMBLE®

Unscramble these four Jumbles,
one letter to each square, to
form four ordinary words.

TABEA

HARNC

INKIIB

UNPRIT

Go see him

Too much exertion

YOU WOULDN'T WANT
TO GO TO THE
DOCTOR IF YOU
SUFFERED FROM THIS.

Now arrange the circled letters
to form the surprise answer, as
suggested by the above cartoon.

Print the SURPRISE ANSWER here

JUMBLE®

Unscramble these four Jumbles,
one letter to each square, to
form four ordinary words.

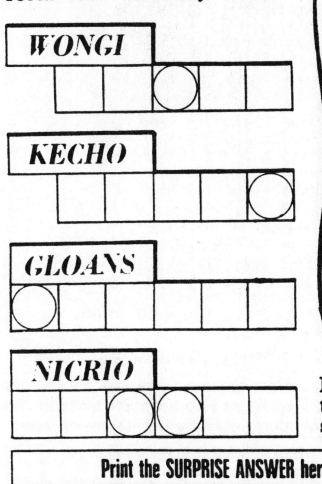

WONGI

KECHO

GLOANS

NICRIO

IT'S DEFINITELY
A RACKET!

Now arrange the circled letters
to form the surprise answer, as
suggested by the above cartoon.

Print the SURPRISE ANSWER here

JUMBLE®

Unscramble these four Jumbles, one letter to each square, to form four ordinary words.

CYREM

FITAH

INCLEY

TROIGE

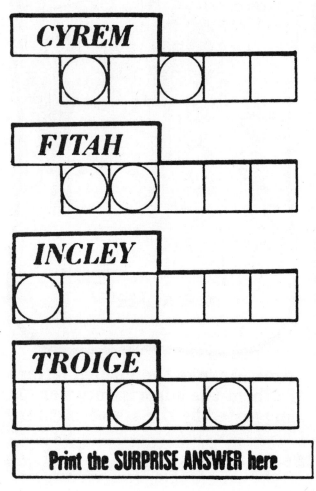

Hurry!

TELL THIS GUY TO GO TO BLAZES — AND YOU'LL GET A RESPONSE OUT OF HIM!

Now arrange the circled letters to form the surprise answer, as suggested by the above cartoon.

Print the SURPRISE ANSWER here

A

JUMBLE®

Unscramble these four Jumbles,
one letter to each square, to
form four ordinary words.

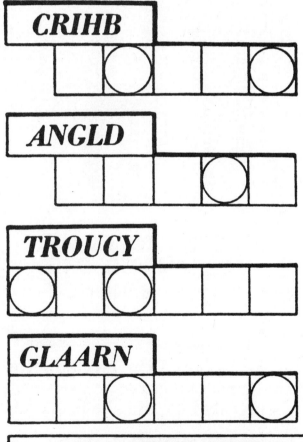

CRIHB

ANGLD

TROUCY

GLAARN

I gave at the office

Will
you
help?

THIS IS THE LEAST
YOU CAN DO!

Now arrange the circled letters
to form the surprise answer, as
suggested by the above cartoon.

Print the SURPRISE ANSWER here

JUMBLE.

Unscramble these four Jumbles,
one letter to each square, to
form four ordinary words.

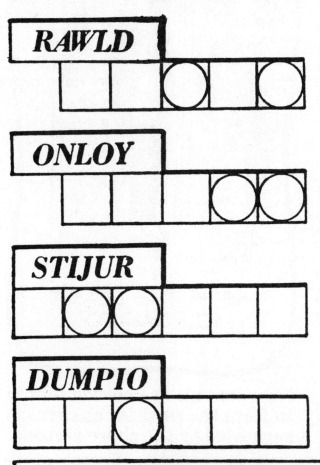

RAWLD

ONLOY

STIJUR

DUMPIO

For the last time—
did you do it?

MADE TO COME
CLEAN BEFORE
THE HANGING!

Now arrange the circled letters
to form the surprise answer, as
suggested by the above cartoon.

Print the SURPRISE ANSWER here

JUMBLE®

Unscramble these four Jumbles,
one letter to each square, to
form four ordinary words.

RUYLB

EGGOR

CANTIG

HETOLC

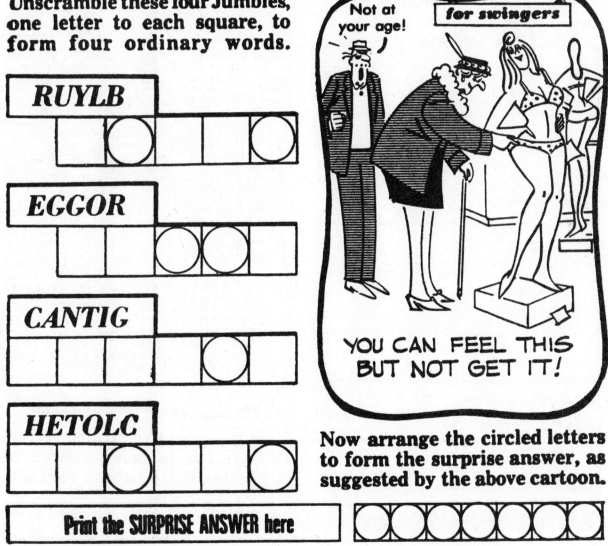

Not at your age!

for swingers

YOU CAN FEEL THIS
BUT NOT GET IT!

Now arrange the circled letters
to form the surprise answer, as
suggested by the above cartoon.

Print the SURPRISE ANSWER here

JUMBLE®

Unscramble these four Jumbles,
one letter to each square, to
form four ordinary words.

MALFE

HIKKA

DILEEY

LAFBLE

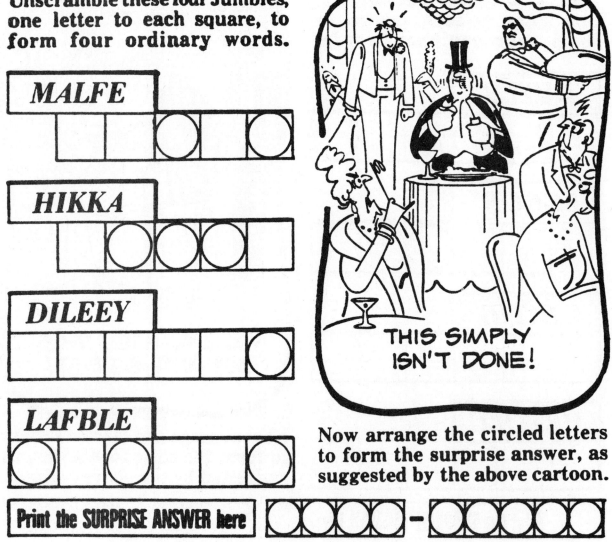

THIS SIMPLY
ISN'T DONE!

Now arrange the circled letters
to form the surprise answer, as
suggested by the above cartoon.

Print the SURPRISE ANSWER here ◯◯◯◯◯ - ◯◯◯◯◯◯

JUMBLE®

Unscramble these four Jumbles,
one letter to each square, to
form four ordinary words.

AZERC

SHUBY

PRITOM

ASHIMP

Boy—the way
those gods
carried on!

YOU MIGHT FIND "SPICE"
IN THESE POEMS.

Now arrange the circled letters
to form the surprise answer, as
suggested by the above cartoon.

Print the SURPRISE ANSWER here

JUMBLE®

Unscramble these four Jumbles,
one letter to each square, to
form four ordinary words.

LYKIS

SURBT

FEEDAM

MALFEE

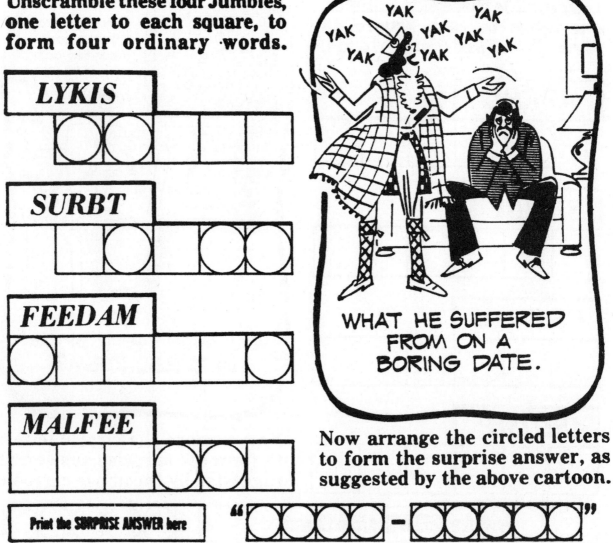

WHAT HE SUFFERED
FROM ON A
BORING DATE.

Now arrange the circled letters
to form the surprise answer, as
suggested by the above cartoon.

Print the SURPRISE ANSWER here

" ☐☐☐☐☐ - ☐☐☐☐☐☐ "

JUMBLE®

Unscramble these four Jumbles,
one letter to each square, to
form four ordinary words.

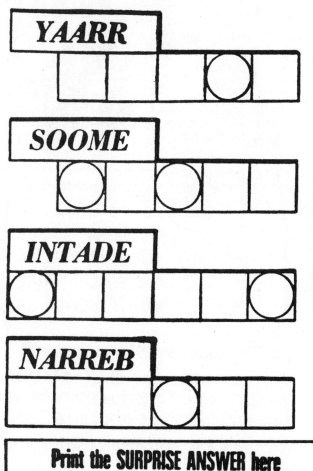

YAARR

SOOME

INTADE

NARREB

Remember when you gave me this?

WHAT YOU COULD
FIND IF YOU JUST
OPENED THE DICTIONARY
AT RANDOM.

Now arrange the circled letters
to form the surprise answer, as
suggested by the above cartoon.

Print the SURPRISE ANSWER here

JUMBLE®

Unscramble these four Jumbles,
one letter to each square, to
form four ordinary words.

MAGEL

ORNOH

LIDBOY

WAIRND

Low pay . . . don't
have much to
put in . . .

EH?

MIGHT BE A
SOUND INVESTMENT
FOR THOSE WHO DON'T
GET EVERYTHING.

Now arrange the circled letters
to form the surprise answer, as
suggested by the above cartoon.

Print the SURPRISE ANSWER here

A ◯◯◯◯◯◯◯◯ ◯◯◯

JUMBLE®

Unscramble these four Jumbles,
one letter to each square, to
form four ordinary words.

ALLIV

NORTS

THEIRE

UNCOBE

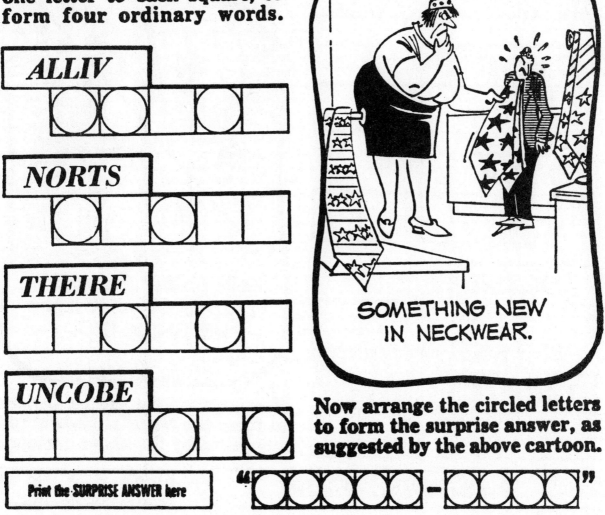

SOMETHING NEW
IN NECKWEAR.

Now arrange the circled letters
to form the surprise answer, as
suggested by the above cartoon.

Print the SURPRISE ANSWER here

" ◯◯◯◯◯ – ◯◯◯◯ "

JUMBLE.

Unscramble these four Jumbles, one letter to each square, to form four ordinary words.

DARNB

ZEFOR

LOCASE

YARWIA

VOLUNTEERS

LET'S BEAT HIM!

ONE *USED* TO BE THIS IN OR AT WHEN HE ENLISTED.

Now arrange the circled letters to form the surprise answer, as suggested by the above cartoon.

Print the SURPRISE ANSWER here

JUMBLE®

Unscramble these four Jumbles, one letter to each square, to form four ordinary words.

MORGO

CHITH

GIRFID

FRAITY

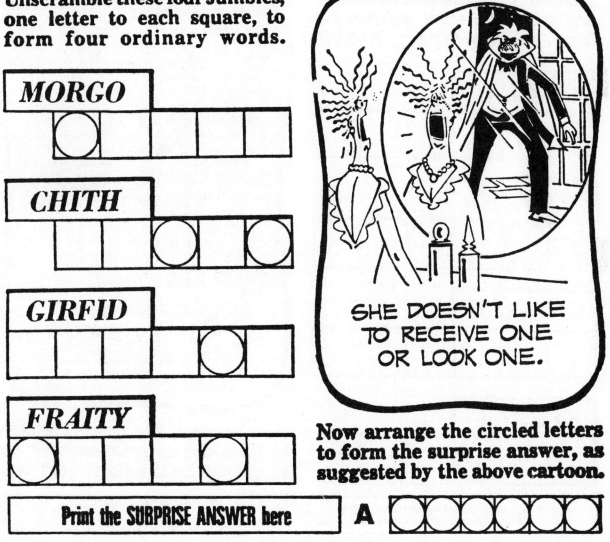

SHE DOESN'T LIKE TO RECEIVE ONE OR LOOK ONE.

Now arrange the circled letters to form the surprise answer, as suggested by the above cartoon.

Print the SURPRISE ANSWER here

A

JUMBLE®

Unscramble these four Jumbles, one letter to each square, to form four ordinary words.

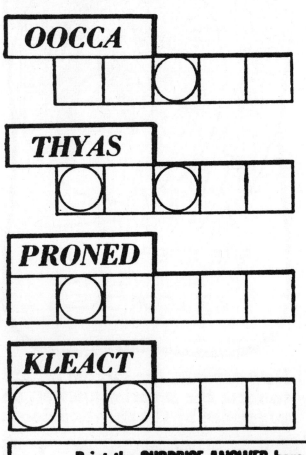

OOCCA

THYAS

PRONED

KLEACT

Have you heard the latest . . . ?

Drink up and shut up!

THIS DRINK MIGHT PUT AN END TO RUMORS.

Now arrange the circled letters to form the surprise answer, as suggested by the above cartoon.

Print the SURPRISE ANSWER here

JUMBLE®

Unscramble these four Jumbles,
one letter to each square, to
form four ordinary words.

ECHLE

MOBOL

GLENET

AMMBLE

BRIGADE HQS.

Lollipops for everybody!

SOUNDS LIKE A
BIT OF A NUT IN
THE ARMY.

Now arrange the circled letters
to form the surprise answer, as
suggested by the above cartoon.

Print the SURPRISE ANSWER here

JUMBLE.®

Unscramble these four Jumbles,
one letter to each square, to
form four ordinary words.

YINNF

SMAUE

ACTOLE

TUKJEN

What kind
do you use?

WE have a
machine!

FOR
DISHES

HARD ON THE HANDS!

Now arrange the circled letters
to form the surprise answer, as
suggested by the above cartoon.

Print the SURPRISE ANSWER here

JUMBLE®

Unscramble these four Jumbles, one letter to each square, to form four ordinary words.

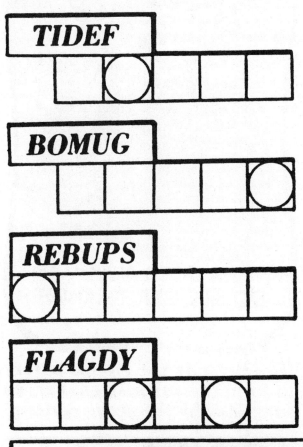

TIDEF

BOMUG

REBUPS

FLAGDY

So soon?

WHAT SHOES OFTEN ARE, AFTER BEING BOUGHT.

Now arrange the circled letters to form the surprise answer, as suggested by the above cartoon.

Print the SURPRISE ANSWER here

" ⭕⭕⭕⭕⭕⭕ "

JUMBLE®

Unscramble these four Jumbles,
one letter to each square, to
form four ordinary words.

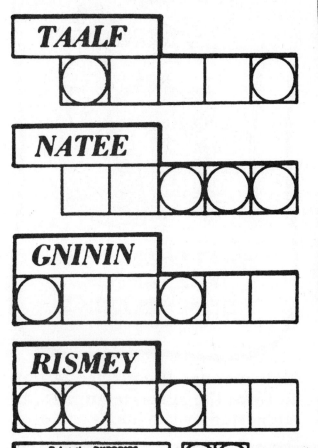

TAALF

NATEE

GNININ

RISMEY

YAK   YAK

YAK   YAK

YAK   YAK

YAK   YAK

How many more
years is this
going to last?

WHEN DOES A WOMAN
DO ALL HER TALKING?

Now arrange the circled letters
to form the surprise answer, as
suggested by the above cartoon.

Print the SURPRISE
ANSWER here

HER

JUMBLE.

Unscramble these four Jumbles, one letter to each square, to form four ordinary words.

HOALT

RADAW

TERRFE

LOSOCH

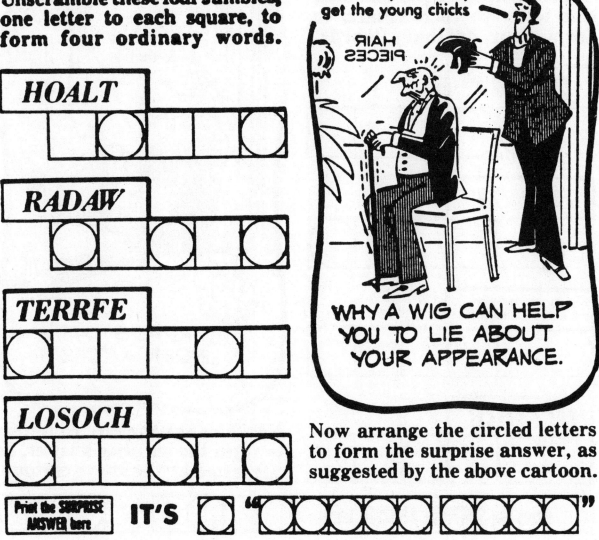

With this you'll really get the young chicks

HAIR PIECES

WHY A WIG CAN HELP YOU TO LIE ABOUT YOUR APPEARANCE.

Now arrange the circled letters to form the surprise answer, as suggested by the above cartoon.

Print the SURPRISE ANSWER here

IT'S ◯ " ◯◯◯◯◯◯ ◯◯◯◯ "

JUMBLE®

Unscramble these four Jumbles, one letter to each square, to form four ordinary words.

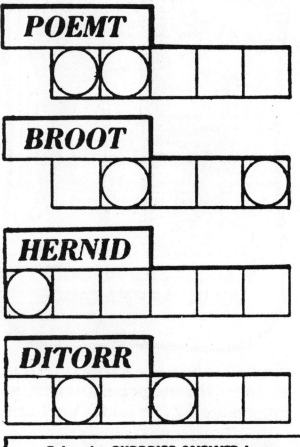

POEMT

BROOT

HERNID

DITORR

This is the life

SPREADS OUT UNDER A TREE.

Now arrange the circled letters to form the surprise answer, as suggested by the above cartoon.

Print the SURPRISE ANSWER here

JUMBLE®

Unscramble these four Jumbles,
one letter to each square, to
form four ordinary words.

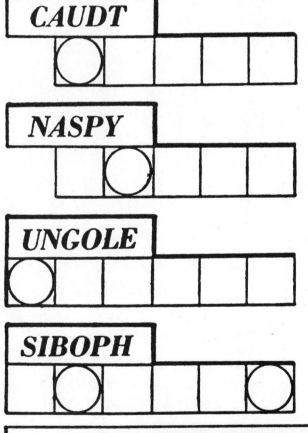

CAUDT

NASPY

UNGOLE

SIBOPH

Where are the
Scottish woolens?

DRY
GOODS

THIS MATERIAL
MUST BE CHECKED!

Now arrange the circled letters
to form the surprise answer, as
suggested by the above cartoon.

Print the SURPRISE ANSWER here

JUMBLE®

Unscramble these four Jumbles,
one letter to each square, to
form four ordinary words.

ENSOO

BELLI

LETHAH

GANNIA

Wait'll you see
OUR kid

CHILD PRODIGY
NIGHT

THEY SHOW SIGNS
OF BRILLIANCE.

Now arrange the circled letters
to form the surprise answer, as
suggested by the above cartoon.

Print the SURPRISE ANSWER here

JUMBLE®

Unscramble these four Jumbles, one letter to each square, to form four ordinary words.

VERIP

MYLAD

COLOTE

HYNDIG

WHAT AN UNEMPLOYED FILM STAR IS.

Yes, but what's he done lately?

Now arrange the circled letters to form the surprise answer, as suggested by the above cartoon.

Print the SURPRISE ANSWER here   A   ◯◯◯◯◯◯ ◯◯◯◯◯

JUMBLE®

Unscramble these four Jumbles,
one letter to each square, to
form four ordinary words.

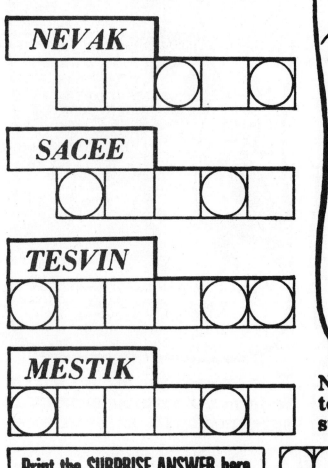

NEVAK

SACEE

TESVIN

MESTIK

Print the SURPRISE ANSWER here

How high?

With snow,
it's higher

THEY CONTAIN MORE
FEET IN WINTER
THAN IN SUMMER.

Now arrange the circled letters
to form the surprise answer, as
suggested by the above cartoon.

JUMBLE®

Unscramble these four Jumbles, one letter to each square, to form four ordinary words.

SWEHL

YACKT

FALOTA

DUBUSE

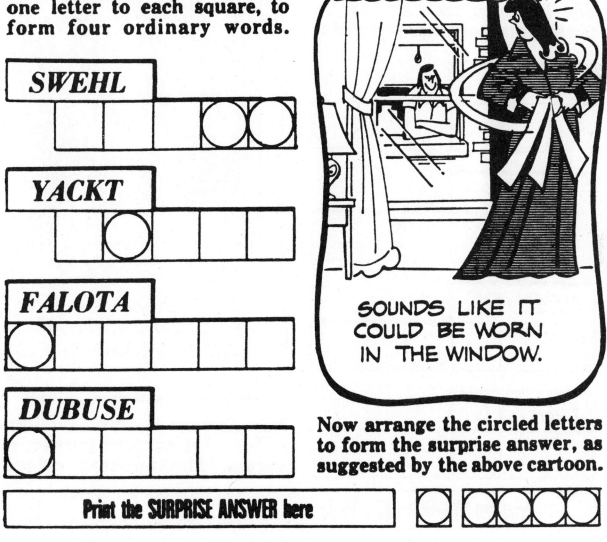

SOUNDS LIKE IT COULD BE WORN IN THE WINDOW.

Now arrange the circled letters to form the surprise answer, as suggested by the above cartoon.

Print the SURPRISE ANSWER here

JUMBLE.

Unscramble these four Jumbles, one letter to each square, to form four ordinary words.

DEEXU

ANAUF

CERUDE

LAAXYG

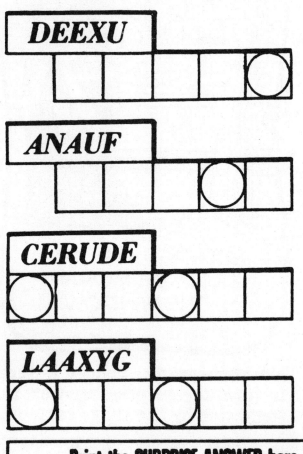

Give!

I'm inclined . . .

THIS COULD MAKE YOU FEEL YOU OUGHT TO DO SOMETHING.

Now arrange the circled letters to form the surprise answer, as suggested by the above cartoon.

Print the SURPRISE ANSWER here

JUMBLE®

Unscramble these four Jumbles,
one letter to each square, to
form four ordinary words.

BOYHB

LIWLT

ANFLOG

DACUDE

Print the SURPRISE ANSWER here

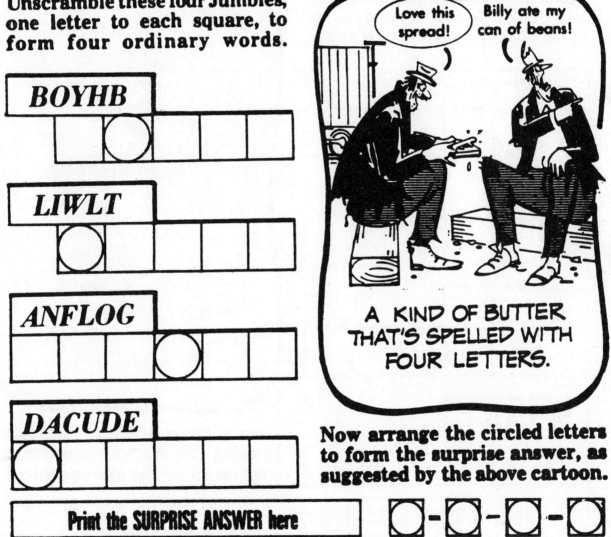

Love this spread!

Billy ate my can of beans!

A KIND OF BUTTER
THAT'S SPELLED WITH
FOUR LETTERS.

Now arrange the circled letters
to form the surprise answer, as
suggested by the above cartoon.

◯-◯-◯-◯

JUMBLE®

Unscramble these four Jumbles,
one letter to each square, to
form four ordinary words.

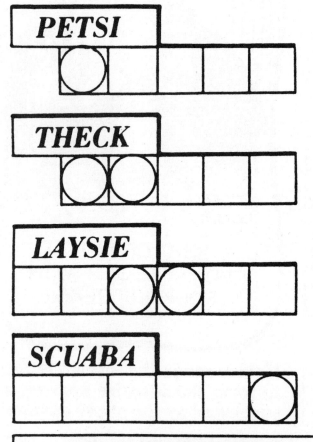

PETSI

THECK

LAYSIE

SCUABA

Hmph!

MIGHT MAKE YOU
CROSS AT THE END
OF A LETTER.

Now arrange the circled letters
to form the surprise answer, as
suggested by the above cartoon.

Print the SURPRISE ANSWER here

JUMBLE®

Unscramble these four Jumbles,
one letter to each square, to
form four ordinary words.

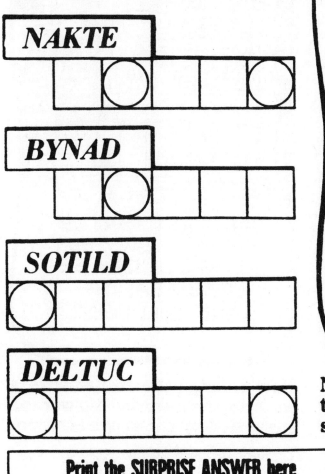

NAKTE

BYNAD

SOTILD

DELTUC

I maintain blah blah

Oh, yeah?

YOU WOULDN'T TAKE
THIS SITTING DOWN!!

Now arrange the circled letters
to form the surprise answer, as
suggested by the above cartoon.

Print the SURPRISE ANSWER here

JUMBLE®

Unscramble these four Jumbles,
one letter to each square, to
form four ordinary words.

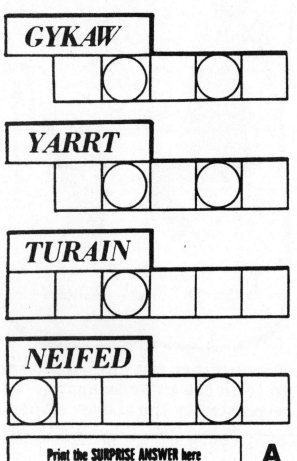

GYKAW

YARRT

TURAIN

NEIFED

Print the SURPRISE ANSWER here

PUB

THE FIRST PART IS
RATHER HEAVY, BUT
THE WHOLE CAN BE
LIFTED EASILY—
AND WILLINGLY!

Now arrange the circled letters
to form the surprise answer, as
suggested by the above cartoon.

A " ⬡⬡⬡⬡⬡ - ⬡⬡⬡ "

JUMBLE®

Unscramble these four Jumbles, one letter to each square, to form four ordinary words.

ADDEJ

BAWLY

KLUBEC

SHAUTI

This'll flush out the remainder

A MOPPING-UP OPERATION BY THE NAVY.

Now arrange the circled letters to form the surprise answer, as suggested by the above cartoon.

Print the SURPRISE ANSWER here

JUMBLE®

Unscramble these four Jumbles,
one letter to each square, to
form four ordinary words.

TOYUG

NIGTY

INGLEM

DOMECY

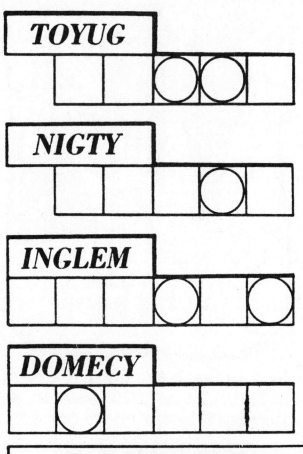

I submit this as Exhibit A

Keen!

OFTEN GROWS
SHARPER WITH USE.

Now arrange the circled letters
to form the surprise answer, as
suggested by the above cartoon.

Print the SURPRISE ANSWER here

A ⬭⬭⬭⬭⬭⬭

JUMBLE®

Unscramble these four Jumbles, one letter to each square, to form four ordinary words.

MAUCS

NOPER

YAVINT

TANIAT

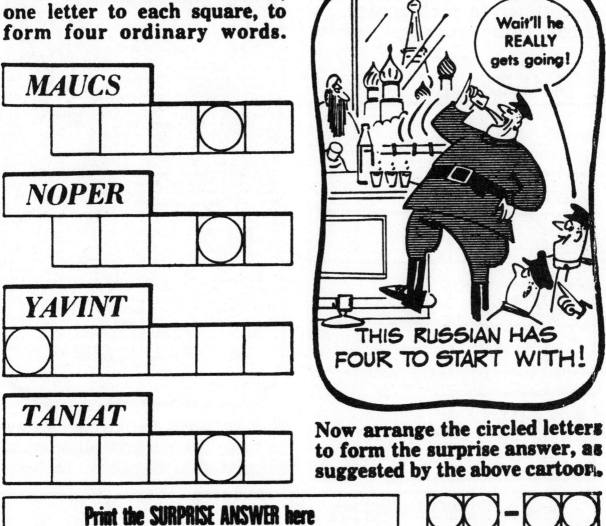

Wait'll he REALLY gets going!

THIS RUSSIAN HAS FOUR TO START WITH!

Now arrange the circled letters to form the surprise answer, as suggested by the above cartoon.

Print the SURPRISE ANSWER here

◯◯ - ◯◯

PUZZLE # 172

JUMBLE.®

Unscramble these four Jumbles, one letter to each square, to form four ordinary words.

VALEE

BOANT

SNULES

CATBUD

Print the SURPRISE ANSWER here

HOW TO COMPLAIN ABOUT A DULL KNIFE.

Now arrange the circled letters to form the surprise answer, as suggested by the above cartoon.

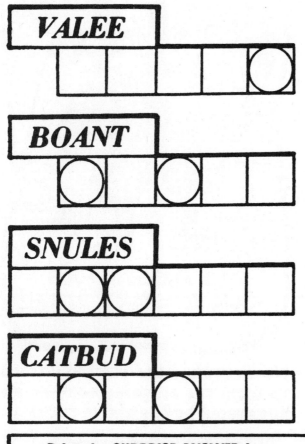

174

JUMBLE.®

Unscramble these four Jumbles,
one letter to each square, to
form four ordinary words.

YURLS

PUROG

VORPLE

HUNGOE

Aren't they cute?

Hurry! Hurry!

WHAT THE BARKER'S
OFFSPRING WERE CALLED.

Now arrange the circled letters
to form the surprise answer, as
suggested by the above cartoon.

Print the SURPRISE ANSWER here

JUMBLE®

Unscramble these four Jumbles,
one letter to each square, to
form four ordinary words.

TUBOA

GERAW

TIPMER

LYKING

Nice guy

But it cost you plenty!

HE HAD SOME
REDEEMING FEATURES.

Now arrange the circled letters
to form the surprise answer, as
suggested by the above cartoon.

Print the SURPRISE ANSWER here **THE**

JUMBLE®

Unscramble these four Jumbles,
one letter to each square, to
form four ordinary words.

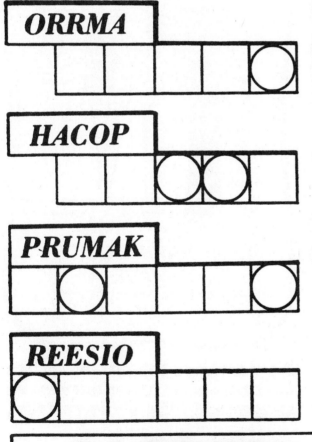

ORRMA

HACOP

PRUMAK

REESIO

Print the SURPRISE ANSWER here

This stuff
is mine!

COULD BE A
USELESS THING—
TO FIGHT OVER!

Now arrange the circled letters
to form the surprise answer, as
suggested by the above cartoon.

JUMBLE®

Unscramble these four Jumbles,
one letter to each square, to
form four ordinary words.

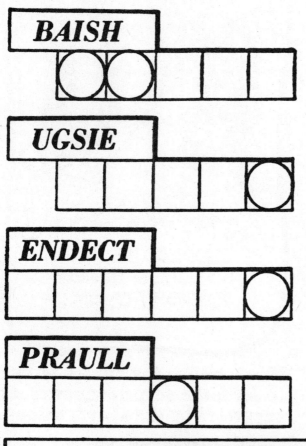

BAISH

UGSIE

ENDECT

PRAULL

Whatever
you want,
dear

THIS WARM LIQUID
CAN HAVE A
MELTING EFFECT.

Now arrange the circled letters
to form the surprise answer, as
suggested by the above cartoon.

Print the SURPRISE ANSWER here

JUMBLE®

Unscramble these four Jumbles, one letter to each square, to form four ordinary words.

SOSAB

HUVOC

EVIDID

LOYMED

"DROPPED" BY A NOSY PERSON.

Now arrange the circled letters to form the surprise answer, as suggested by the above cartoon.

Print the SURPRISE ANSWER here

" ◯◯◯◯◯ "

JUMBLE®

Unscramble these four Jumbles,
one letter to each square, to
form four ordinary words.

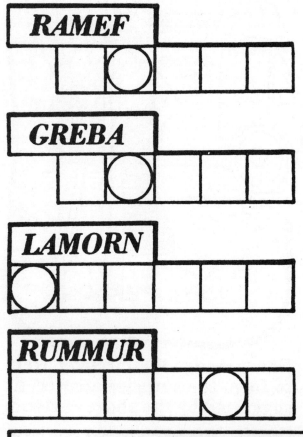

RAMEF

GREBA

LAMORN

RUMMUR

My jewels! I lost my key!

Bash it open— we're late!

YOU MIGHT BREAK
INTO THIS WHEN
IN A HURRY.

Now arrange the circled letters
to form the surprise answer, as
suggested by the above cartoon.

 Print the SURPRISE ANSWER here

JUMBLE.®

Unscramble these four Jumbles,
one letter to each square, to
form four ordinary words.

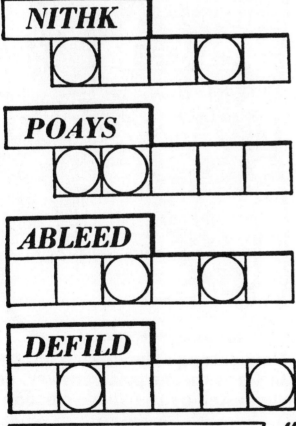

NITHK

POAYS

ABLEED

DEFILD

Must be nails
in your shoe!

BOOTS

Now arrange the circled letters
to form the surprise answer, as
suggested by the above cartoon.

Print the SURPRISE ANSWER here " ◯◯◯◯◯◯◯◯◯ "

JUMBLE®

Unscramble these four Jumbles,
one letter to each square, to
form four ordinary words.

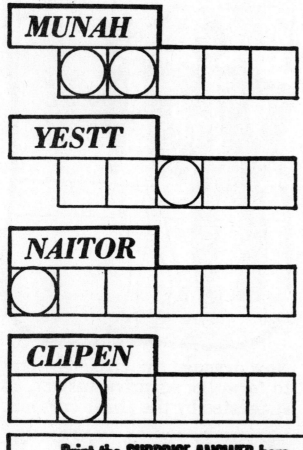

MUNAH

YESTT

NAITOR

CLIPEN

Could connect
us with that
woman!

Now arrange the circled letters
to form the surprise answer, as
suggested by the above cartoon.

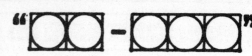

Print the SURPRISE ANSWER here

" ◯◯ - ◯◯◯ "

JUMBLE.

Unscramble these four Jumbles,
one letter to each square, to
form four ordinary words.

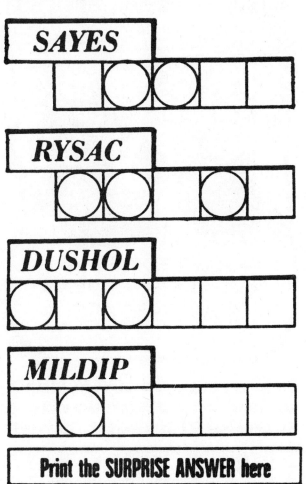

SAYES

RYSAC

DUSHOL

MILDIP

Print the SURPRISE ANSWER here

Break
it up!

DIVIDES BY UNITING
AND UNITES
BY DIVIDING.

Now arrange the circled letters
to form the surprise answer, as
suggested by the above cartoon.

JUMBLE®

Unscramble these four Jumbles,
one letter to each square, to
form four ordinary words.

YORFT

ARBIN

HIMSUL

ROPOLY

Print the SURPRISE ANSWER here

WHAT PEOPLE WHO
BOO AT PERFORMERS
SOMETIMES ARE.

Now arrange the circled letters
to form the surprise answer, as
suggested by the above cartoon.

"□□□-□□"

JUMBLE®

Unscramble these four Jumbles,
one letter to each square, to
form four ordinary words.

CADUL

TIFFY

MACENE

DIONIE

NOT TO BE PLAYED
WITH WHEN LOADED.

Now arrange the circled letters
to form the surprise answer, as
suggested by the above cartoon.

Print the SURPRISE ANSWER here

JUMBLE®

Unscramble these four Jumbles, one letter to each square, to form four ordinary words.

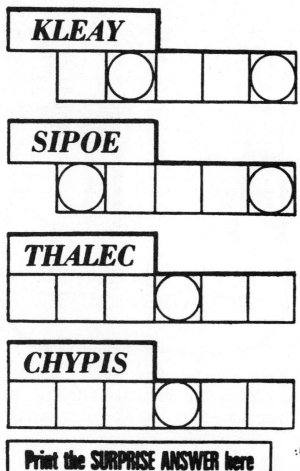

KLEAY

SIPOE

THALEC

CHYPIS

Print the SURPRISE ANSWER here

Don't try to fool me

FAR FROM ALERT BUT OUTWARDLY SLY.

Now arrange the circled letters to form the surprise answer, as suggested by the above cartoon.

" ⬜⬜ - ⬜⬜⬜ - ⬜ "

JUMBLE®

Unscramble these four Jumbles,
one letter to each square, to
form four ordinary words.

PREKO

CAIBS

LURCUN

SPOCER

A KIND OF EUROPEAN
CURTAIN MATERIAL.

Now arrange the circled letters
to form the surprise answer, as
suggested by the above cartoon.

Print the SURPRISE ANSWER here

JUMBLE.

Unscramble these four Jumbles,
one letter to each square, to
form four ordinary words.

DENEY

SURUP

REGEME

KOVINE

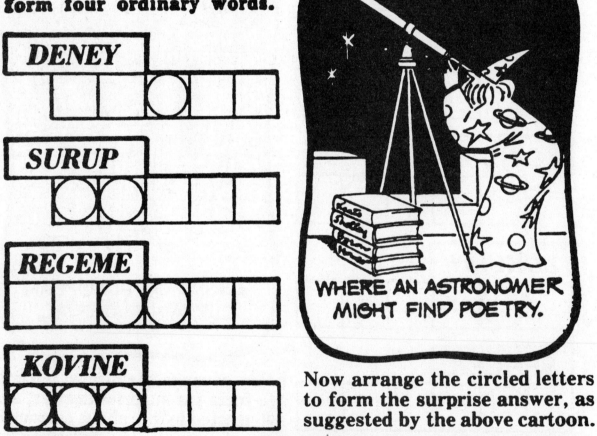

WHERE AN ASTRONOMER
MIGHT FIND POETRY.

Now arrange the circled letters
to form the surprise answer, as
suggested by the above cartoon.

IN THE "◯◯◯-◯◯◯◯◯"

JUMBLE®

Unscramble these four Jumbles,
one letter to each square, to
form four ordinary words.

GEWED

CITOX

LEMPOC

PANOWE

DRAGGED AWAY – TO
GET MARRIED.

Now arrange the circled letters
to form the surprise answer, as
suggested by the above cartoon.

Print the SURPRISE ANSWER here

" ◯◯ – ◯◯◯ "

JUMBLE.

Unscramble these four Jumbles,
one letter to each square, to
form four ordinary words.

ADGEL

GLEEY

DIMRAY

TURBAP

WHAT YOU'LL FIND IN
THE ROOM OF
YOUR DREAMS.

Now arrange the circled letters
to form the surprise answer, as
suggested by the above cartoon.

Print the SURPRISE ANSWER here

JUMBLE.

Unscramble these four Jumbles, one letter to each square, to form four ordinary words.

ELVOG

UPTYT

WILDEM

GRUBEO

HOW TO SELL AN
ELECTRICAL GADGET.

Now arrange the circled letters to form the surprise answer, as suggested by the above cartoon.

Print the SURPRISE ANSWER here

JUMBLE®

Unscramble these four Jumbles,
one letter to each square, to
form four ordinary words.

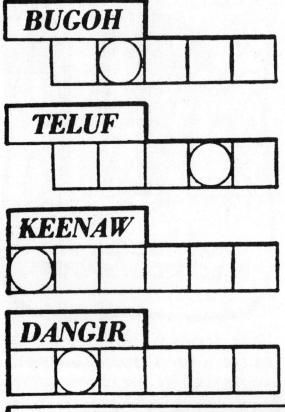

BUGOH

TELUF

KEENAW

DANGIR

Tsk! Tsk! Dead battery!

YOU MIGHT BE
POWERLESS
TO ACCEPT THIS.

Now arrange the circled letters
to form the surprise answer, as
suggested by the above cartoon.

Print the SURPRISE ANSWER here

JUMBLE.

Unscramble these four Jumbles, one letter to each square, to form four ordinary words.

INYAR

HALET

CALVEE

FLAUDE

Print the SURPRISE ANSWER here

I want 'em spotless!

WORKING HE GETS ALL *THE DIRTIER*.

Now arrange the circled letters to form the surprise answer, as suggested by the above cartoon.

JUMBLE®

Unscramble these four Jumbles,
one letter to each square, to
form four ordinary words.

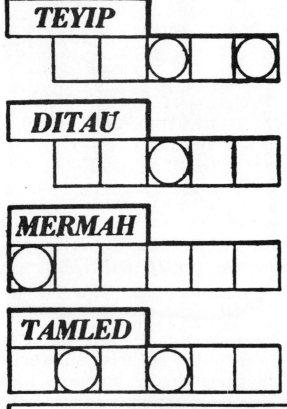

TEYIP

DITAU

MERMAH

TAMLED

Print the SURPRISE ANSWER here

Time to wash
up for dinner!

IT'S ALWAYS DONE
IN THE EVENING!

Now arrange the circled letters
to form the surprise answer, as
suggested by the above cartoon.

JUMBLE®

Unscramble these four Jumbles,
one letter to each square, to
form four ordinary words.

LAGEE

METHY

DOEKOH

SYTHAN

Print the SURPRISE ANSWER here

Snob!

WHAT "A MAN
OF LEISURE" MIGHT
LOOK DOWN AT.

Now arrange the circled letters
to form the surprise answer, as
suggested by the above cartoon.

JUMBLE®

Unscramble these four Jumbles,
one letter to each square, to
form four ordinary words.

NOICT

SNOBI

KOYDEN

LEWLOY

Print the SURPRISE ANSWER here

LOOT TAKEN FROM
A SHOE STORE.

Now arrange the circled letters
to form the surprise answer, as
suggested by the above cartoon.

" ☐☐☐☐ - ☐ "

JUMBLE®

Unscramble these four Jumbles,
one letter to each square, to
form four ordinary words.

ELZAH

LORGY

INOUSC

DRIAFA

He wants to attack

But how'll
he buy the
guns?

WHAT THE GENERAL
SAID WHEN THEY
RAN OUT OF MONEY
TO FIGHT THE WAR.

Now arrange the circled letters
to form the surprise answer, as
suggested by the above cartoon.

Print the SURPRISE ANSWER here

◯◯◯◯◯◯ !

JUMBLE®

Unscramble these four Jumbles,
one letter to each square, to
form four ordinary words.

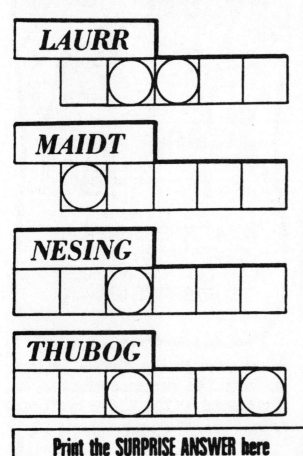

LAURR

MAIDT

NESING

THUBOG

Print the SURPRISE ANSWER here

Guess what it says about you for today!

WHAT HE SAID
ALL THAT ASTROLOGY
BULL WAS.

Now arrange the circled letters
to form the surprise answer, as
suggested by the above cartoon.

JUMBLE®

Unscramble these four Jumbles,
one letter to each square, to
form four ordinary words.

FLEAB

WYLLO

SCOMAT

GIDINO

Wodda ya
expect for
a buck?

THIN UPRIGHT
FIGURES.

Now arrange the circled letters
to form the surprise answer, as
suggested by the above cartoon.

Print the SURPRISE ANSWER here

"◯◯◯◯"

JUMBLE®

Unscramble these four Jumbles,
one letter to each square, to
form four ordinary words.

TUILB

GALOT

ENTODE

PRYNTA

What's it gonna be?

WHAT THE
CERAMICS WORKER
WAS DEVELOPING.

Now arrange the circled letters
to form the surprise answer, as
suggested by the above cartoon.

Print the SURPRISE ANSWER here

JUMBLE®

Unscramble these four Jumbles, one letter to each square, to form four ordinary words.

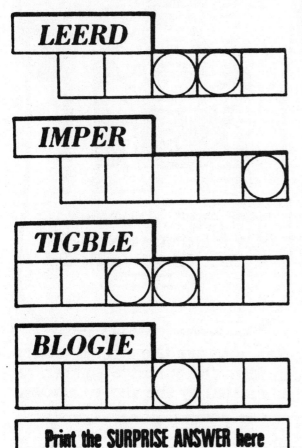

LEERD

IMPER

TIGBLE

BLOGIE

Print the SURPRISE ANSWER here

Breakfast is ready

Hope she doesn't burn the bacon again

YOU WOULDN'T EAT IT WHEN IN THIS!

Now arrange the circled letters to form the surprise answer, as suggested by the above cartoon.

" – – ⬡⬡⬡⬡⬡⬡⬡ "

JUMBLE®

Unscramble these four Jumbles, one letter to each square, to form four ordinary words.

MEZIA

THRAW

ROWDYS

GONEPS

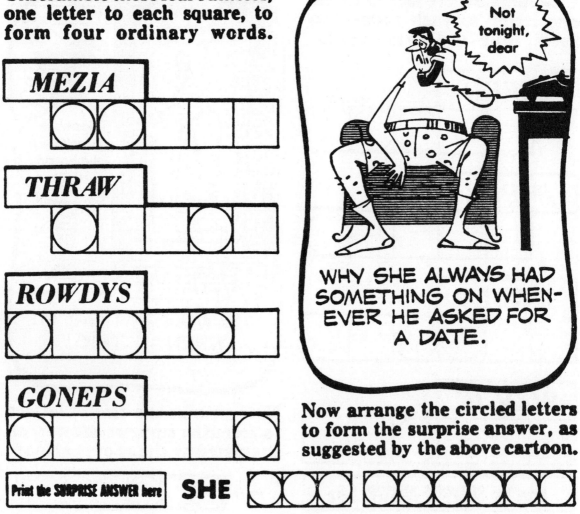

Not tonight, dear

WHY SHE ALWAYS HAD SOMETHING ON WHEN- EVER HE ASKED FOR A DATE.

Now arrange the circled letters to form the surprise answer, as suggested by the above cartoon.

Print the SURPRISE ANSWER here   SHE

JUMBLE®

Unscramble these four Jumbles,
one letter to each square, to
form four ordinary words.

GOLIC

LENEK

VINTEN

STIMCY

THIS LIGHT TOUCH
COULD PRODUCE
LAUGHTER IN THE
THEATER.

Now arrange the circled letters
to form the surprise answer, as
suggested by the above cartoon.

Print the SURPRISE ANSWER here

A ⬡⬡⬡⬡⬡⬡⬡

JUMBLE®

Unscramble these four Jumbles,
one letter to each square, to
form four ordinary words.

ARCTT

ESSOU

INJOAD

HISVAL

Sounds serious!

NOT THE SORT OF CASE
HE EXPECTED TO FIND
IN THE BUNGALOW.

Now arrange the circled letters
to form the surprise answer, as
suggested by the above cartoon.

Print the SURPRISE ANSWER here | A

JUMBLE®

Unscramble these four Jumbles, one letter to each square, to form four ordinary words.

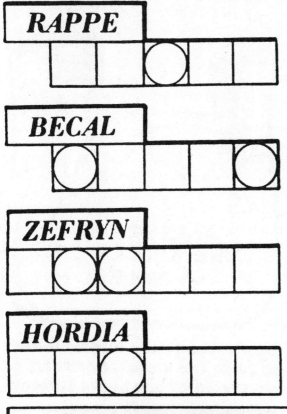

RAPPE

BECAL

ZEFRYN

HORDIA

Print the SURPRISE ANSWER here

I'm going to bake a cake

FOLLOWED IN THE KITCHEN.

Now arrange the circled letters to form the surprise answer, as suggested by the above cartoon.

A

JUMBLE.

Unscramble these four Jumbles,
one letter to each square, to
form four ordinary words.

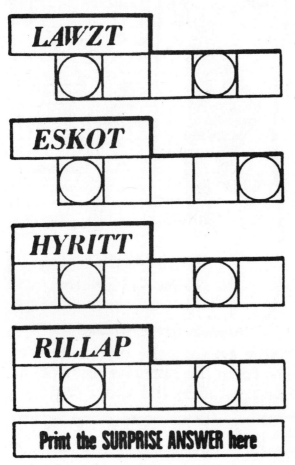

LAWZT

ESKOT

HYRITT

RILLAP

Print the SURPRISE ANSWER here

A FIGURE IN
THE MIDDLE OF
A FIGURE.

Now arrange the circled letters
to form the surprise answer, as
suggested by the above cartoon.

JUMBLE®

Unscramble these four Jumbles,
one letter to each square, to
form four ordinary words.

OUSLE

SESCH

PYTSHU

HOMARI

A PIECE OF
CHOPIN SUITABLE
AT DINNERTIME.

Now arrange the circled letters
to form the surprise answer, as
suggested by the above cartoon.

Print the SURPRISE ANSWER here

" ⟨ ◯ ◯ ◯ ◯ ⟩ "

JUMBLE®

Unscramble these four Jumbles, one letter to each square, to form four ordinary words.

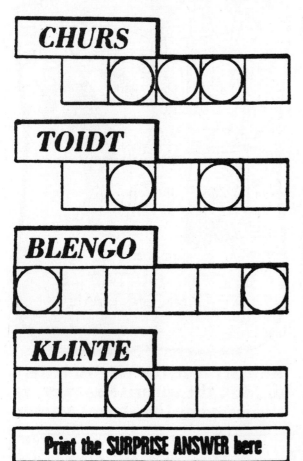

CHURS

TOIDT

BLENGO

KLINTE

Print the SURPRISE ANSWER here

Let's play with the new train

WHAT YOU MIGHT FEEL LIKE DOING AFTER DINNER.

Now arrange the circled letters to form the surprise answer, as suggested by the above cartoon.

JUMBLE®

Unscramble these four Jumbles, one letter to each square, to form four ordinary words.

YASTT

TULFE

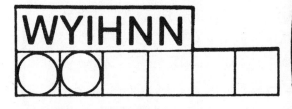

WYIHNN

GROINI

It's a flood!

THE TRAIN CARRYING THE LAUNDRYMEN TO WORK WAS DELAYED BECAUSE OF THIS.

Now arrange the circled letters to form the surprise answer, as suggested by the above cartoon.

Answer: " ◯◯◯◯ ◯◯◯ " ON THE ◯◯◯◯

JUMBLE®

Unscramble these four Jumbles, one letter to each square, to form four ordinary words.

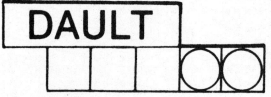
DAULT

ENNIL

CHOPON

FANNIT

I suppose he expects a big tip

WHAT YOU HAVE TO TAKE INTO CONSIDERATION THESE DAYS WHEN YOU HAVE YOUR TIRES PUMPED UP.

Now arrange the circled letters to form the surprise answer, as suggested by the above cartoon.

Print answer here:

JUMBLE.

Unscramble these four Jumbles, one letter to each square, to form four ordinary words.

SHECS

TRAFC

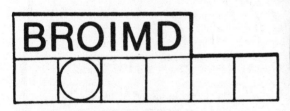

BROIMD

ENVARG

THREATENED TO RAIN ON THE ACTORS AT THE OUTDOOR THEATER.

Now arrange the circled letters to form the surprise answer, as suggested by the above cartoon.

Print answer here: "  "

JUMBLE.

Unscramble these four Jumbles,
one letter to each square, to form
four ordinary words.

NOAKE

SHWIK

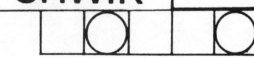

FLUTAR

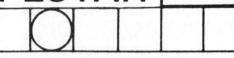

COSTAM

AGITATED WHERE
COCKTAILS ARE
CONCERNED.

Now arrange the circled letters to
form the surprise answer, as suggested by the above cartoon.

Print answer here: THE

JUMBLE®

Unscramble these four Jumbles, one letter to each square, to form four ordinary words.

ACNIP

RAMEK

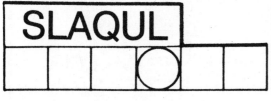
SLAQUL

LASSIA

How dare you!

A "CHASM" THAT MIGHT CREATE A DEEP GAP BE— TWEEN HUSBANDS AND WIVES.

Now arrange the circled letters to form the surprise answer, as suggested by the above cartoon.

Print answer here: "  "

JUMBLE.

Unscramble these four Jumbles,
one letter to each square, to form
four ordinary words.

DRUIL

YOVIR

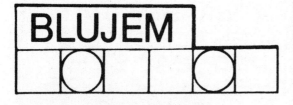
BLUJEM

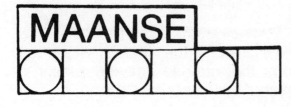
MAANSE

WHAT HE CALLED
HIS PRETTY FEMALE
ASSISTANT.

Now arrange the circled letters to
form the surprise answer, as suggested by the above cartoon.

Answer here: A

JUMBLE®

Unscramble these four Jumbles,
one letter to each square, to form
four ordinary words.

POAZT

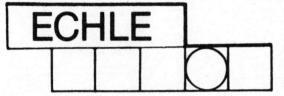

ECHLE

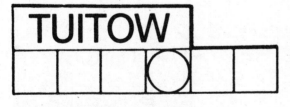

TUITOW

REPACT

WHAT THE GUY WHO
SWORE HE WAS GO-
ING TO LOSE WEIGHT
ENDED UP EATING.

Now arrange the circled letters to
form the surprise answer, as suggested by the above cartoon.

Print answer here:

JUMBLE®

Unscramble these four Jumbles,
one letter to each square, to form
four ordinary words.

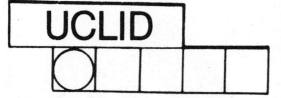

UCLID

MASCH

ONBOAB

QUIETY

Oh, dear

SHOULD YOU CUT
THEM AND THROW
THEM AWAY—OR
JUST FILE THEM?

Now arrange the circled letters to
form the surprise answer, as suggested by the above cartoon.

Print answer here:

JUMBLE®

Unscramble these four Jumbles,
one letter to each square, to form
four ordinary words.

UNDOP

HASUQ

UNGOLE

NARFIA

WHAT THEY CALLED
THE BEAUTICIAN.

Now arrange the circled letters to
form the surprise answer, as suggested by the above cartoon.

Answer: THE " ⬡⬡⬡ - ⬡⬡⬡⬡⬡⬡⬡ "

JUMBLE.

Unscramble these four Jumbles,
one letter to each square, to form
four ordinary words.

URRYC

GOBUH

DARIFA

FLUFEM

WHAT YOU MIGHT
SEE IF YOU REFUSE
HER REQUEST FOR
A MINK COAT.

Now arrange the circled letters to
form the surprise answer, as suggested by the above cartoon.

Print answer here: THE

JUMBLE®

Unscramble these four Jumbles, one letter to each square, to form four ordinary words.

ALQUI

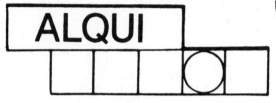
EMAHR

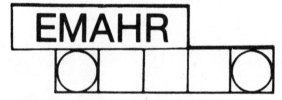
THARRE

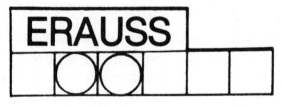
ERAUSS

⊙!★Noise!

But all the other kids have it!

WHAT THE BROKEN PHONOGRAPH RECORD MUST HAVE BEEN.

Now arrange the circled letters to form the surprise answer, as suggested by the above cartoon.

Print answer here: A

JUMBLE®

Unscramble these four Jumbles, one letter to each square, to form four ordinary words.

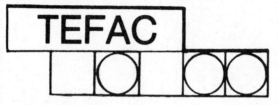
TEFAC

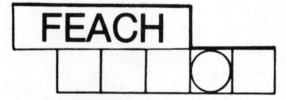
FEACH

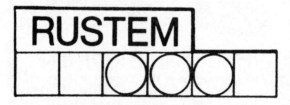
RUSTEM

LEEXAH

DENTIS FOOD MEAT DRUGS SHOES

MANY A "TRUE" WORD IS SPOKEN BETWEEN THEM.

Now arrange the circled letters to form the surprise answer, as suggested by the above cartoon.

Answer here:

JUMBLE.

Unscramble these four Jumbles,
one letter to each square, to form
four ordinary words.

ROWNC

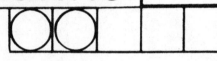

TEBER

SAILEY

ENTHIZ

WHAT THE MAD
CHEF WAS.

Now arrange the circled letters to
form the surprise answer, as suggested by the above cartoon.

Print answer here:

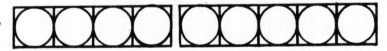

JUMBLE.

Unscramble these four Jumbles,
one letter to each square, to form
four ordinary words.

SUPIO

RAYPH

INNACE

WORDSY

WHAT TURTLE
SOUP IS.

Now arrange the circled letters to
form the surprise answer, as suggested by the above cartoon.

Answer here: A ⬡⬡⬡⬡⬡⬡ ⬡⬡⬡⬡

JUMBLE®

Unscramble these four Jumbles, one letter to each square, to form four ordinary words.

PINTE

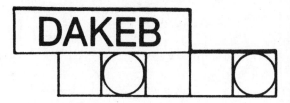

DAKEB

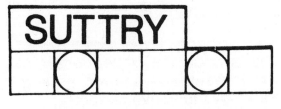

NIAMEA

SUTTRY

SALES RESISTANCE IS THE TRIUMPH OF THIS.

Now arrange the circled letters to form the surprise answer, as suggested by the above cartoon.

Answer: ☐☐☐☐ OVER ☐☐☐☐☐☐☐

JUMBLE®

Unscramble these four Jumbles, one letter to each square, to form four ordinary words.

URROF

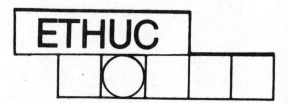

ETHUC

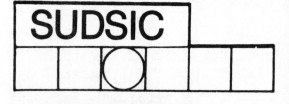

SUDSIC

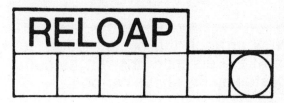

RELOAP

Now arrange the circled letters to form the surprise answer, as suggested by the above cartoon.

Print answer here:

JUMBLE.®

Unscramble these four Jumbles,
one letter to each square, to form
four ordinary words.

REWFE

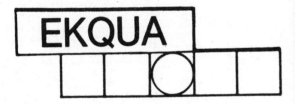

EKQUA

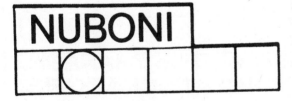

NUBONI

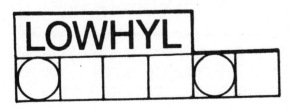

LOWHYL

My attorney will
communicate with you!

EVICTION
NOTICE

THIS IS TERRIBLE—
BUT A LETTER
WOULD MAKE
IT LEGAL.

Now arrange the circled letters to
form the surprise answer, as suggested by the above cartoon.

Print answer here:

JUMBLE.

Unscramble these four Jumbles,
one letter to each square, to form
four ordinary words.

YUMOS

MEERY

CHUNQE

LAMMAM

WHAT THE PHARAOH
WHO ATE CRACKERS
IN BED WAS.

Now arrange the circled letters to
form the surprise answer, as suggested by the above cartoon.

Answer: A ☐☐☐☐☐☐ ☐☐☐☐☐☐

JUMBLE.

Unscramble these four Jumbles, one letter to each square, to form four ordinary words.

WALOG

SIADY

REMMIO

HINSAV

WHAT YOU GET IF YOU EAT TOO MUCH.

Now arrange the circled letters to form the surprise answer, as suggested by the above cartoon.

Answer here: A "⬡⬡⬡⬡ ⬡⬡⬡⬡"

JUMBLE®

Unscramble these four Jumbles,
one letter to each square, to form
four ordinary words.

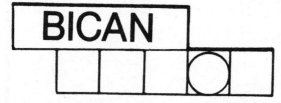

BICAN

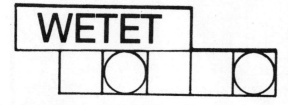

WETET

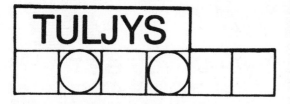

TULJYS

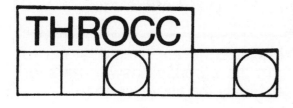

THROCC

No!

CAVIAR
TRUFFLES

WHAT YOU OFTEN
HAVE TO DO TO
STAY WITHIN
YOUR BUDGET.

Now arrange the circled letters to
form the surprise answer, as suggested by the above cartoon.

Print answer here:

JUMBLE®

Unscramble these four Jumbles,
one letter to each square, to form
four ordinary words.

ESTUG

KIHCT

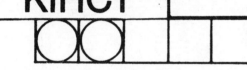
CERTIM

USDABE

I can see fine now, thanks to you

E

HOW THE EYE
DOCTOR MIGHT
MAKE YOUR LIFE.

Now arrange the circled letters to
form the surprise answer, as suggested by the above cartoon.

Answer: A "  "

JUMBLE®

Unscramble these four Jumbles,
one letter to each square, to form
four ordinary words.

RUZEA

TAYFF

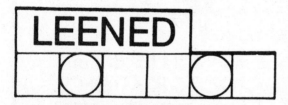

LEENED

MOUFAS

WHAT THE LAZY
BUTCHER WAS.

Now arrange the circled letters to
form the surprise answer, as suggested by the above cartoon.

Answer here: A

JUMBLE®

Unscramble these four Jumbles,
one letter to each square, to form
four ordinary words.

LYGUL

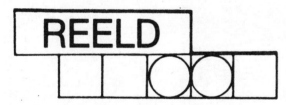

REELD

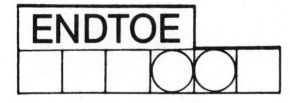

ENDTOE

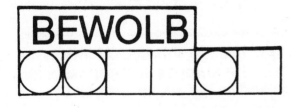

BEWOLB

THAT OIL TYCOON
SURE WAS THIS!

Now arrange the circled letters to
form the surprise answer, as suggested by the above cartoon.

Answer here: "◯◯◯◯◯" - ◯◯ - ◯◯

JUMBLE®

Unscramble these four Jumbles,
one letter to each square, to form
four ordinary words.

KYWAG

LEETA

CLIOCA

MABGIT

WHAT YOU MIGHT
FIND PLENTY OF IN A
BURNED-OUT
POST OFFICE.

Now arrange the circled letters to
form the surprise answer, as suggested by the above cartoon.

Print answer here:

JUMBLE®

Unscramble these four Jumbles,
one letter to each square, to form
four ordinary words.

TAIMY

SARBS

ENSTEW

DELPOW

I'll do the lawn tomorrow

WHAT A
PROCRASTINATOR
HAS.

Now arrange the circled letters to
form the surprise answer, as suggested by the above cartoon.

Answer: A ☐☐☐☐☐ ☐☐☐☐☐☐☐☐

JUMBLE®

Unscramble these four Jumbles,
one letter to each square, to form
four ordinary words.

GYTAN

MAGDO

TADEEB

ZARBLE

WHAT THE DOCTOR
CHARGED TO FIX UP
THE GUY WHO
INJURED HIS ELBOW
AND KNEE.

Now arrange the circled letters to
form the surprise answer, as suggested by the above cartoon.

Print answer here: AN ◯◯◯ & A ◯◯◯

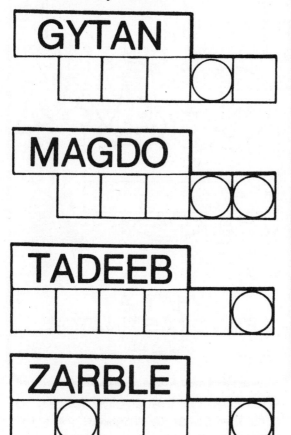

JUMBLE®

Unscramble these four Jumbles,
one letter to each square, to form
four ordinary words.

SWEHL

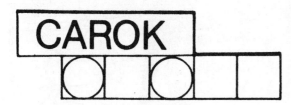

CAROK

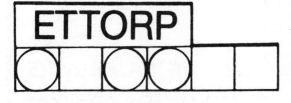

ETTORP

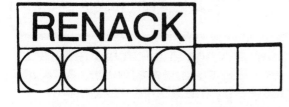

RENACK

JEWELRY

WHAT A GUY WHO
DOESN'T LIKE HAVING
TIME ON HIS
HANDS SHOULD GET.

Now arrange the circled letters to
form the surprise answer, as suggested by the above cartoon.

Answer: A ⬭⬭⬭⬭⬭⬭⬭ ⬭⬭⬭⬭⬭

JUMBLE®

Unscramble these four Jumbles,
one letter to each square, to form
four ordinary words.

POTIV

ROHON

IMUSSE
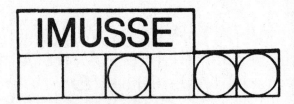

KINIBI
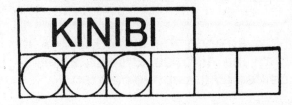

But. . .
but. . .

WHAT THE GAMBLING
ADDICT HAD TROUBLE
BALANCING.

Now arrange the circled letters to
form the surprise answer, as suggested by the above cartoon.

Answer here:

JUMBLE.

Unscramble these four Jumbles,
one letter to each square, to form
four ordinary words.

REVNY

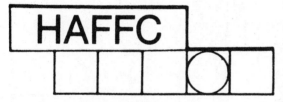

HAFFC

GAZZIG

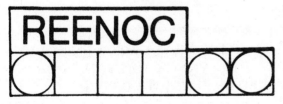

REENOC

WHAT YOU MIGHT
DO IF YOU TRY TO
PAINT A GIRL
IN THE NUDE.

Now arrange the circled letters to
form the surprise answer, as suggested by the above cartoon.

Print answer here:

JUMBLE®

Unscramble these four Jumbles, one letter to each square, to form four ordinary words.

MUTAG

ORXYP

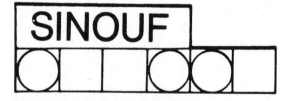

SINOUF

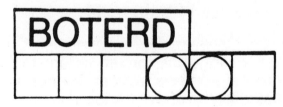

BOTERD

THEY DECIDED TO APPOINT HIM CHIEF COOK BECAUSE HE HAD THIS.

Now arrange the circled letters to form the surprise answer, as suggested by the above cartoon.

Answer: THE "⬭⬭⬭⬭" ⬭⬭⬭⬭ ⬭⬭

JUMBLE®

Unscramble these four Jumbles, one letter to each square, to form four ordinary words.

RUPOC

VARAL

RAWHOR

BOLGEN

HOW MANY POUNDS OF LIMBURGER CHEESE DO YOU WANT?

Now arrange the circled letters to form the surprise answer, as suggested by the above cartoon.

Print answer here:

JUMBLE.

Unscramble these four Jumbles,
one letter to each square, to form
four ordinary words.

ULARR

LABAN

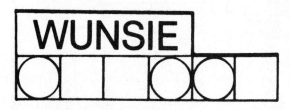

WUNSIE

PORTIM

A FEELING YOU GET
WHEN YOU OPEN YOUR
MAIL ON THE FIRST
OF THE MONTH.

Now arrange the circled letters to
form the surprise answer, as suggested by the above cartoon.

Answer here: " 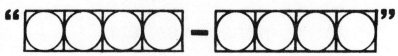 "

JUMBLE®

Unscramble these four Jumbles, one letter to each square, to form four ordinary words.

BODUT

YAMOF

VEEVOL

MUDINS

JEWELRY

WHEN SHE ASKED FOR A DIAMOND, HE TURNED THIS.

Now arrange the circled letters to form the surprise answer, as suggested by the above cartoon.

Answer here: "⬡⬡⬡⬡⬡" ⬡⬡⬡⬡

JUMBLE®

Unscramble these four Jumbles,
one letter to each square, to form
four ordinary words.

KEREC

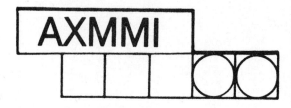

AXMMI

SAYMUL

EXLANF

Stop!

WHAT THE ROBBER
SAID AS HE MADE
HIS GETAWAY.

Now arrange the circled letters to
form the surprise answer, as suggested by the above cartoon.

Answer: " ⬡⬡⬡⬡ " BY A ⬡⬡⬡⬡

JUMBLE.

Unscramble these four Jumbles,
one letter to each square, to form
four ordinary words.

GOGSY

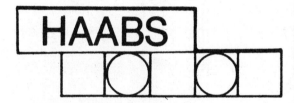

HAABS

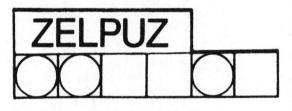

ZELPUZ

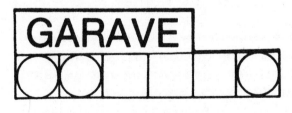

GARAVE

WHAT HE SAID
THAT SO-CALLED
BARLEY SOUP WAS.

Now arrange the circled letters to
form the surprise answer, as suggested by the above cartoon.

Answer here:

JUMBLE.

Unscramble these four Jumbles,
one letter to each square, to form
four ordinary words.

KEJOR

YEMON

RAYPER

DEVAUL

WHAT THE
DOWN-AND-OUT
POET DID.

Now arrange the circled letters to
form the surprise answer, as suggested by the above cartoon.

Answer: " ⬡⬡⬡ " ⬡⬡⬡⬡⬡⬡⬡⬡⬡

JUMBLE®

Unscramble these four Jumbles, one letter to each square, to form four ordinary words.

VINGE

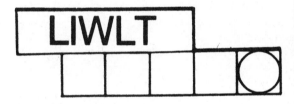

LIWLT

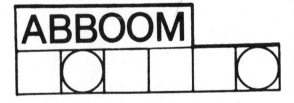

ABBOOM

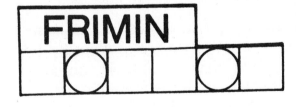

FRIMIN

How about joining us?

No . . . not for me

WHAT THE SOLITARY PAWNBROKER UNDOUBTEDLY WAS.

Now arrange the circled letters to form the surprise answer, as suggested by the above cartoon.

Print answer here: A "  "

JUMBLE®

Unscramble these four Jumbles,
one letter to each square, to form
four ordinary words.

LOJYL

GLIYN

MANALY

SYMFIL

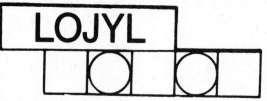

This so-called tenderloin
sure is tough

ANOTHER NAME
FOR HORSE MEAT.

Now arrange the circled letters to
form the surprise answer, as suggested by the above cartoon.

Answer:

JUMBLE®

Unscramble these four Jumbles,
one letter to each square, to form
four ordinary words.

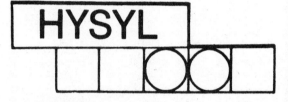
HYSYL

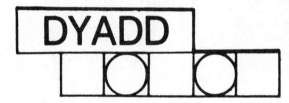
DYADD

GURTED

HILERS

WHY SHE DECIDED
TO WATCH
HER FIGURE.

Now arrange the circled letters to
form the surprise answer, as suggested by the above cartoon.

Answer: ◯◯◯ THE ◯◯◯◯◯ ◯◯◯

JUMBLE®

Unscramble these four Jumbles,
one letter to each square, to form
four ordinary words.

DUXEE

STUMY

RELILK

INTEWG

You said you were going
to hurry up and finish
the lawn today

THE ONLY THING
HE DID FAST
WAS THIS.

Now arrange the circled letters to
form the surprise answer, as suggested by the above cartoon.

Print answer here: ◯◯◯ ◯◯◯◯◯◯

JUMBLE®

Unscramble these four Jumbles,
one letter to each square, to form
four ordinary words.

LODEY

BATHI

ROBUGE

GISMOE

Achoo!

WHAT THAT NUT
WHO CAUGHT A
COLD MUST
HAVE BEEN.

Now arrange the circled letters to
form the surprise answer, as suggested by the above cartoon.

Answer: ⬡⬡⬡⬡⬡⬡ & ⬡⬡⬡⬡⬡⬡

JUMBLE®

Unscramble these four Jumbles,
one letter to each square, to form
four ordinary words.

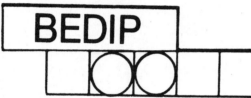

BEDIP

ESTED

VIKONE

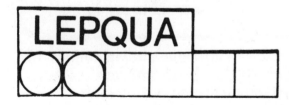

LEPQUA

WHAT IT WAS
WHEN THE PRISONER
ESCAPED.

Now arrange the circled letters to
form the surprise answer, as suggested by the above cartoon.

Answer: A ⬡⬡⬡⬡⬡ OF THE " ⬡⬡⬡ "

JUMBLE®

Unscramble these four Jumbles,
one letter to each square, to form
four ordinary words.

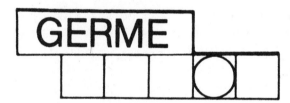
NIHKT

GERME

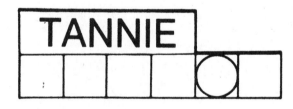
TANNIE

RETIGO

THAT DOCTOR
DECIDED TO "PRACTICE"
MEDICINE UNTIL
HE GOT—

Now arrange the circled letters to
form the surprise answer, as suggested by the above cartoon.

Print answer here:

JUMBLE®

Unscramble these four Jumbles,
one letter to each square, to form
four ordinary words.

TABBO

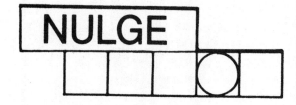

NULGE

ONNACY

ZULZEG

Spent it all on women

TMENT STORE

THE HARD PART OF
BEING BROKE IS
WATCHING THE REST
OF THE WORLD
DO THIS.

Now arrange the circled letters to
form the surprise answer, as suggested by the above cartoon.

Print answer here: "  "

JUMBLE.

Unscramble these four Jumbles, one letter to each square, to form four ordinary words.

BYRIN

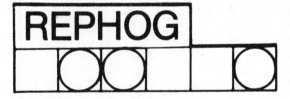
DIXEO

REPHOG

FEYGIF

Oh, well—what did you expect?

CLANG CLANG!

WHAT THE BOSS'S SON WAS, NATURALLY.

Now arrange the circled letters to form the surprise answer, as suggested by the above cartoon.

Answer here: "⬡⬡⬡⬡ ⬡⬡⬡⬡⬡"

JUMBLE®

Unscramble these four Jumbles, one letter to each square, to form four ordinary words.

CHAVO
⬭⬭□⬭□

INGAR
⬭⬭□□

JENTIC
⬭□□⬭□⬭

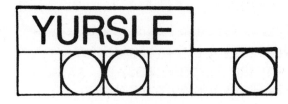

YURSLE
□⬭⬭□⬭

WHAT A TALKATIVE BARBER MIGHT DO.

Now arrange the circled letters to form the surprise answer, as suggested by the above cartoon.

Answer: ⬭⬭⬭ IN ⬭⬭⬭⬭ ⬭⬭⬭⬭

JUMBLE®

Unscramble these four Jumbles,
one letter to each square, to form
four ordinary words.

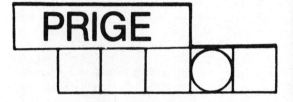
PRIGE

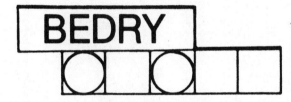
BEDRY

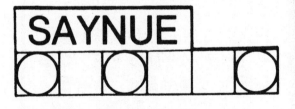
SAYNUE

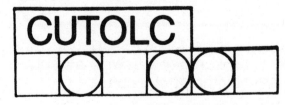
CUTOLC

WHAT PEOPLE OFTEN
DO AT THE
BEAUTY PARLOR.

Now arrange the circled letters to
form the surprise answer, as suggested by the above cartoon.

Answer here:

JUMBLE.

Unscramble these four Jumbles,
one letter to each square, to form
four ordinary words.

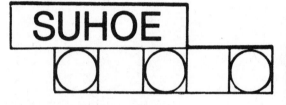

SUHOE

FARIE

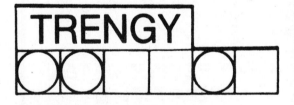

TRENGY

PINDAK

He doesn't have any
real authority

WHAT THE CHAIRMAN
OF THE MATHEMATICS
DEPARTMENT WAS
CALLED.

Now arrange the circled letters to
form the surprise answer, as suggested by the above cartoon.

Answer: THE ⬡⬡⬡⬡⬡⬡⬡⬡⬡⬡⬡⬡⬡

JUMBLE ®

Unscramble these four Jumbles,
one letter to each square, to form
four ordinary words.

RUGAU

OTTOH

NYWIRT

CARILA

WHAT THE PATIENT
SAID WHEN HIS
DOCTOR TOLD HIM
TO DIET.

Now arrange the circled letters to
form the surprise answer, as suggested by the above cartoon.

Answer here:  ?

JUMBLE®

Unscramble these four Jumbles, one letter to each square, to form four ordinary words.

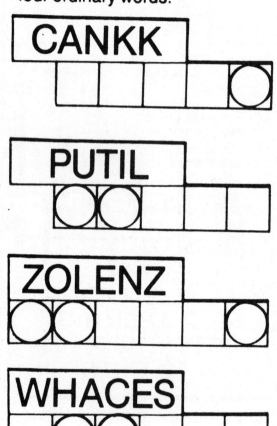

CANKK

PUTIL

ZOLENZ

WHACES

WHAT SOME PEOPLE DO AT SNEAK PREVIEWS.

Now arrange the circled letters to form the surprise answer, as suggested by the above cartoon.

Print answer here:

JUMBLE®

Unscramble these four Jumbles,
one letter to each square, to form
four ordinary words.

RECEL

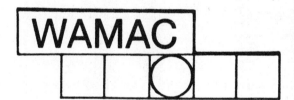

WAMAC

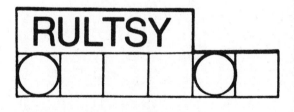

RULTSY

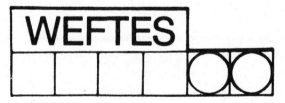

WEFTES

ALCOHOL WILL
PRESERVE ALMOST
EVERYTHING
EXCEPT THIS.

Now arrange the circled letters to
form the surprise answer, as suggested by the above cartoon.

Print answer here:

JUMBLE®

Unscramble these four Jumbles,
one letter to each square, to form
four ordinary words.

YOOBT

DUMIO

ORTETT

GUMPSY

Brother—can you spare
a dime?

IF IT'S DRACULA WHOM
YOU MEET ON THE
STREET, HE'LL SURE
KNOW HOW TO
DO THIS.

Now arrange the circled letters to
form the surprise answer, as suggested by the above cartoon.

Answer: ⬡⬡⬡ THE ⬡⬡⬡⬡⬡ ON ⬡⬡⬡

JUMBLE®

Unscramble these four Jumbles, one letter to each square, to form four ordinary words.

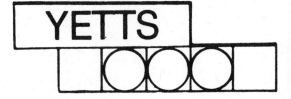

YETTS

DEBIA

LIERIX

NIGLAC

IN ORDER TO SELECT THE FINEST WINE, EXAMINE THIS.

Now arrange the circled letters to form the surprise answer, as suggested by the above cartoon.

Answer: THE ⬡⬡⬡⬡ - ⬡⬡⬡⬡⬡⬡⬡ LIST

JUMBLE.

Unscramble these four Jumbles,
one letter to each square, to form
four ordinary words.

TINJO

BICCU

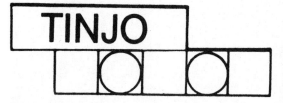

ROCCEE

THERE'S PLENTY OF
THIS WHEN A MAN
DOESN'T PAY
ALIMONY.

SIMYAD

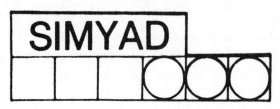

Now arrange the circled letters to
form the surprise answer, as suggested by the above cartoon.

Print answer here:

JUMBLE®

Unscramble these four Jumbles, one letter to each square, to form four ordinary words.

NABOR

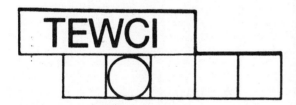

TEWCI

WEDDEG

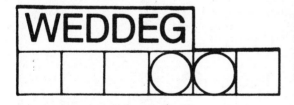

FALLUW

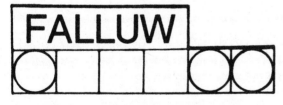

He's always botching things up

WHAT THAT INCOMPETENT POLITICIAN SEEMED TO LIVE BY.

Now arrange the circled letters to form the surprise answer, as suggested by the above cartoon.

Answer: THE ⬡⬡⬡ OF THE "⬡⬡⬡⬡⬡⬡"

JUMBLE®

Unscramble these four Jumbles, one letter to each square, to form four ordinary words.

DUGEN
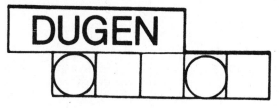

KNARC

DERAIV

ROVACT

WHEN YOU'RE IN IT, YOU NEVER KNOW.

Now arrange the circled letters to form the surprise answer, as suggested by the above cartoon.

Print answer here:

JUMBLE®

Unscramble these four Jumbles, one letter to each square, to form four ordinary words.

VERBA

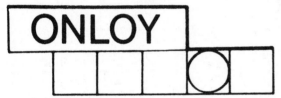

ONLOY

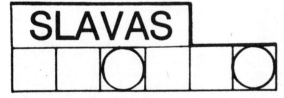

SLAVAS

MUCPIE

NO TALKING

Shh!

Shh!

WHAT THE POLITE CROOK USED WHEN HE HELD UP THE PUBLIC LIBRARY.

Now arrange the circled letters to form the surprise answer, as suggested by the above cartoon.

Print answer here: A

JUMBLE.

Unscramble these four Jumbles, one letter to each square, to form four ordinary words.

UDGIE

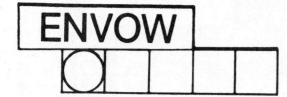

ENVOW

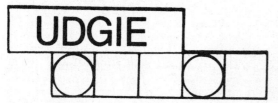

NITTEY

VOCLEN

MY HUSBAND FOUND A NEW POSITION—

RACING

Now arrange the circled letters to form the surprise answer, as suggested by the above cartoon.

Answer here: " ⭘⭘⭘⭘⭘ ⭘⭘⭘⭘ "

JUMBLE.

Unscramble these four Jumbles,
one letter to each square, to form
four ordinary words.

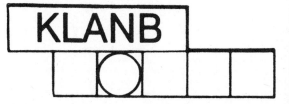
KLANB

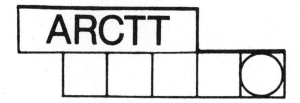
ARCTT

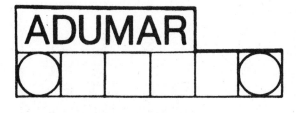
ADUMAR

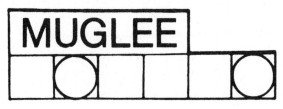
MUGLEE

WHAT HAPPENED TO THE
PLASTIC SURGEON WHO
WAS WORKING IN AN
OVERHEATED
OPERATING ROOM?

Now arrange the circled letters to
form the surprise answer, as suggested by the above cartoon.

Print answer here: HE

JUMBLE.®

Unscramble these four Jumbles,
one letter to each square, to form
four ordinary words.

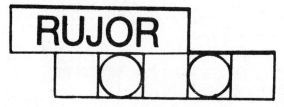

RUJOR

YIXTS

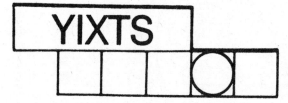

LYNKIG

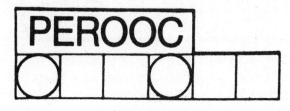

PEROOC

WHAT YOU'RE LIKELY
TO TAKE WHEN YOU'RE
INVITED TO DINNER
BY WITCHES.

Now arrange the circled letters to
form the surprise answer, as suggested by the above cartoon.

Print answer here:

JUMBLE®

Unscramble these four Jumbles, one letter to each square, to form four ordinary words.

LASIE

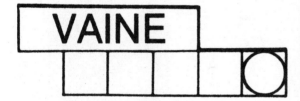

VAINE

DUBUSE

TUPIRD

I love game

WHY IS VENISON SO EXPENSIVE?

Now arrange the circled letters to form the surprise answer, as suggested by the above cartoon.

Print answer here:

JUMBLE.

Unscramble these four Jumbles,
one letter to each square, to form
four ordinary words.

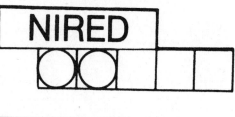

NIRED

YUCIJ

REEPAM

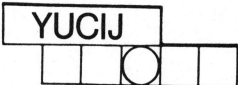

WHAT THE
FRIGHTENED
ROCK WAS.

NIFTIE

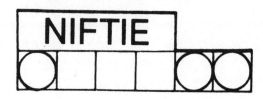

Now arrange the circled letters to
form the surprise answer, as suggested by the above cartoon.

Answer here: "⬡⬡⬡⬡⬡⬡⬡⬡⬡"

JUMBLE®

Unscramble these four Jumbles,
one letter to each square, to form
four ordinary words.

SHOWE

HECKE

DRIZAL

LIZZES

WHAT HIS RICH
UNCLE WHO WAS A
FAMOUS ARTIST KNEW
HOW TO DRAW BEST.

Now arrange the circled letters to
form the surprise answer, as suggested by the above cartoon.

Print answer here:

JUMBLE®

Unscramble these four Jumbles,
one letter to each square, to form
four ordinary words.

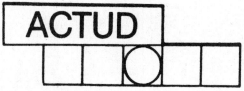

ACTUD

ESSOU

FRYTAC

TYKONT

BANG!

WHAT TO DO
WHEN A PLUG
DOESN'T FIT.

Now arrange the circled letters to
form the surprise answer, as suggested by the above cartoon.

Print answer here: "  "

JUMBLE®

Unscramble these four Jumbles, one letter to each square, to form four ordinary words.

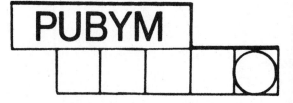

PUBYM

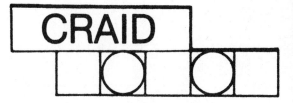

CRAID

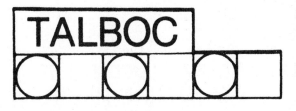

TALBOC

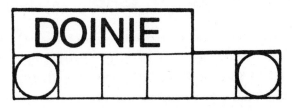

DOINIE

Guess I won't go to work today

Hurray, no school!

HOW DOES JACK FROST GET TO WORK?

Now arrange the circled letters to form the surprise answer, as suggested by the above cartoon.

Answer here:

JUMBLE.

Unscramble these four Jumbles,
one letter to each square, to form
four ordinary words.

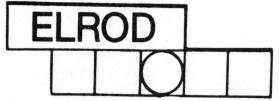
ELROD

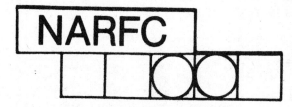
NARFC

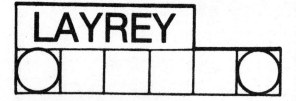
LAYREY

AUSANE

Can't take too many
precautions

WHAT THE
UMBRELLA MERCHANT
WAS SAVING HIS
MONEY FOR.

Now arrange the circled letters to
form the surprise answer, as suggested by the above cartoon.

Print answer here: A

JUMBLE.

Unscramble these four Jumbles,
one letter to each square, to form
four ordinary words.

WARLD

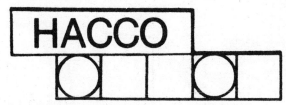

HACCO

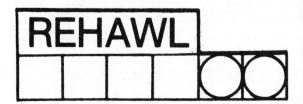

REHAWL

SKUTEM

BAR   TATTOOS

THE SHIP DOCKED
NEAR THE BARBERSHOP
BECAUSE THEY ALL
NEEDED THIS.

Now arrange the circled letters to
form the surprise answer, as suggested by the above cartoon.

Print answer here: "  "

JUMBLE®

Unscramble these four Jumbles, one letter to each square, to form four ordinary words.

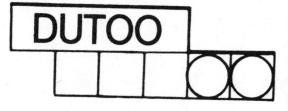

DUTOO

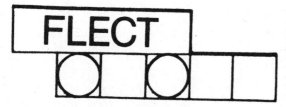

FLECT

EDGERD

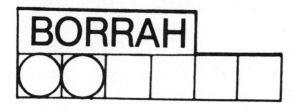

BORRAH

CRYPTOGRAPHY ROOM

WHAT THE SECRET AGENT WAS COMPLAINING OF.

Now arrange the circled letters to form the surprise answer, as suggested by the above cartoon.

Answer: A "◯◯◯◯" IN THE ◯◯◯◯

JUMBLE.

Unscramble these four Jumbles,
one letter to each square, to form
four ordinary words.

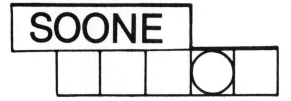

SOONE

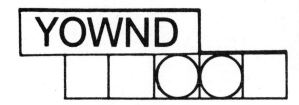

YOWND

BLUBEA

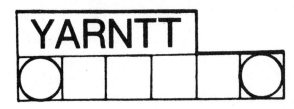

YARNTT

LOONY
BIN

WHY THEY HAD
TO PUT THE
VAMPIRE AWAY.

Now arrange the circled letters to
form the surprise answer, as suggested by the above cartoon.

Print answer here: HE

JUMBLE.

Unscramble these four Jumbles,
one letter to each square, to form
four ordinary words.

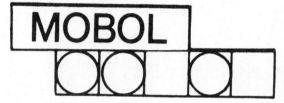

MOBOL

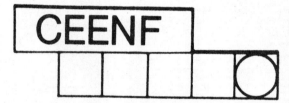

CEENF

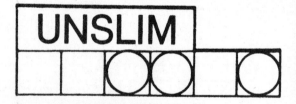

UNSLIM

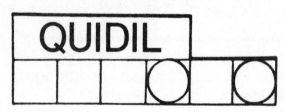

QUIDIL

WHAT THE DOCTOR
SAID WHEN THE
PATIENT COMPLAINED
OF RINGING IN
HIS EARS.

Now arrange the circled letters to
form the surprise answer, as suggested by the above cartoon.

Answer: YOU'RE ⬡⬡⬡⬡⬡ AS A ⬡⬡⬡⬡

JUMBLE®

Unscramble these four Jumbles,
one letter to each square, to form
four ordinary words.

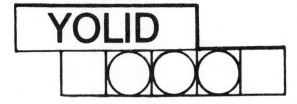

YOLID

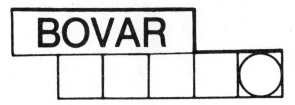

BOVAR

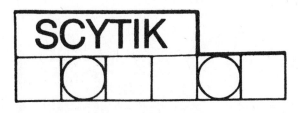

SCYTIK

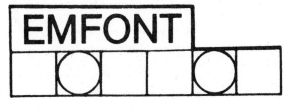

EMFONT

WHEN A VANDAL MADE
A HOLE IN THE FENCE
AT THE NUDIST CAMP,
THE COPS SAID
THEY'D DO THIS.

Now arrange the circled letters to
form the surprise answer, as suggested by the above cartoon.

Print answer here:  IT

JUMBLE.

Unscramble these four Jumbles, one letter to each square, to form four ordinary words.

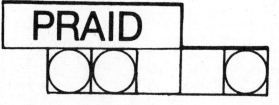

PRAID

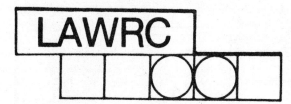

LAWRC

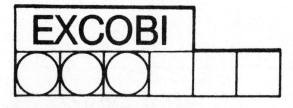

EXCOBI

NYLARX

WHAT HE GOT WHEN HE READ THE STORY ABOUT THOSE BODY SNATCHERS.

Now arrange the circled letters to form the surprise answer, as suggested by the above cartoon.

Answer:

JUMBLE®

Unscramble these four Jumbles,
one letter to each square, to form
four ordinary words.

ELVOG

PORDO

TAJUNY

MINGOH

HE DECIDED TO BECOME
AN ASTRONAUT WHEN
HIS WIFE TOLD HIM
HE WAS THIS.

Now arrange the circled letters to
form the surprise answer, as suggested by the above cartoon.

Answer: NO

JUMBLE®

Unscramble these four Jumbles,
one letter to each square, to form
four ordinary words.

PINYP

SABIN

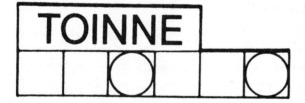

TOINNE

DRAFIT

HEALTH
CENTER

IF YOU WANT TO
START LOSING WEIGHT,
YOU CAN GET
INITIATED FROM THIS.

Now arrange the circled letters to
form the surprise answer, as suggested by the above cartoon.

Answer here: A " ◯◯◯◯◯◯◯◯◯ "

JUMBLE®

Unscramble these four Jumbles,
one letter to each square, to form
four ordinary words.

THIGE

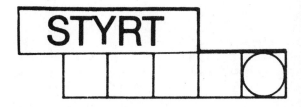

STYRT

YEUFLE

REGOUM

WHEN IS THE
CHEAPEST TIME TO
PHONE YOUR FRIENDS
BY LONG DISTANCE?

Now arrange the circled letters to
form the surprise answer, as suggested by the above cartoon.

Answer: WHEN ⬡⬡⬡⬡'⬡⬡ ⬡⬡⬡

JUMBLE.

Unscramble these four Jumbles,
one letter to each square, to form
four ordinary words.

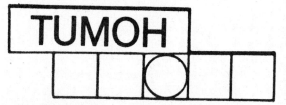

TUMOH

KYACT

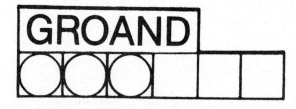

GROAND

SMEFLY

THE MAN WHO
STOLE A PUDDING
WAS TAKEN
INTO THIS.

Now arrange the circled letters to
form the surprise answer, as suggested by the above cartoon.

Print answer here: "  "

JUMBLE.

Unscramble these four Jumbles,
one letter to each square, to form
four ordinary words.

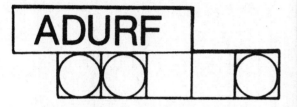

ADURF

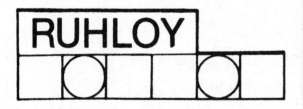

WANTY

RUHLOY

VAHLIS

WHAT HE SAID WHEN
TEACHER GAVE HIM
AN "F" ON THE
VOCABULARY TEST.

Now arrange the circled letters to
form the surprise answer, as suggested by the above cartoon.

Answer here: ⬡⬡⬡⬡⬡ ⬡⬡⬡⬡ ME

JUMBLE.

Unscramble these four Jumbles,
one letter to each square, to form
four ordinary words.

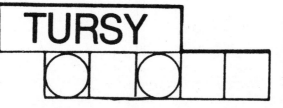

TURSY

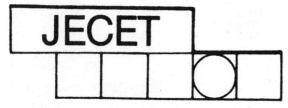

JECET

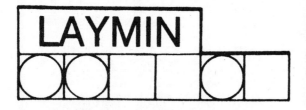

LAYMIN

SEPPOO

WHERE YOU
MIGHT FIND THE
SCHOOLMASTER.

Now arrange the circled letters to
form the surprise answer, as suggested by the above cartoon.

Answer: IN "THE ⬡⬡⬡⬡⬡⬡⬡⬡⬡⬡ "

JUMBLE®

Unscramble these four Jumbles,
one letter to each square, to form
four ordinary words.

MARAD

FOBEG

DIASUN

GUMMAN

FROM THE SURGEON
CAME THESE WORDS.

Now arrange the circled letters to
form the surprise answer, as suggested by the above cartoon.

Print answer here:

JUMBLE®

Unscramble these four Jumbles, one letter to each square, to form four ordinary words.

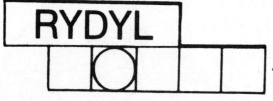
RYDYL

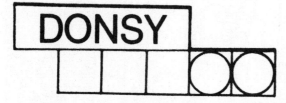
DONSY

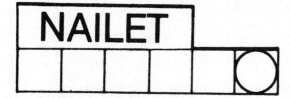
NAILET

BELNAG

WHAT HER IDEAL BECAME AFTER SHE MARRIED HIM.

Now arrange the circled letters to form the surprise answer, as suggested by the above cartoon.

Print answer here: AN

JUMBLE®

Unscramble these four Jumbles,
one letter to each square, to form
four ordinary words.

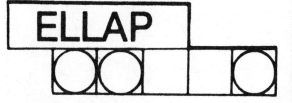
ELLAP

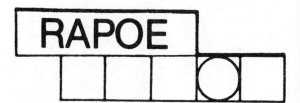
RAPOE

INSOUC

CAPTEK

Oh, not again!

WHAT THAT OLD-
TIME GARAGE
MECHANIC WAS
BOTHERED WITH.

Now arrange the circled letters to
form the surprise answer, as suggested by the above cartoon.

Answer: "  "

JUMBLE.

Unscramble these four Jumbles, one letter to each square, to form four ordinary words.

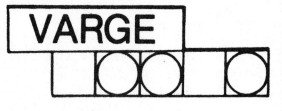
VARGE

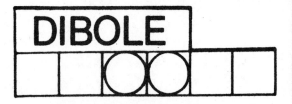
DIEFT

DIBOLE

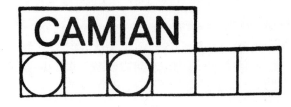
CAMIAN

HE THOUGHT HIS NEW COMPUTER WAS GOING TO GIVE HIM THIS KIND OF AN ILLNESS.

Now arrange the circled letters to form the surprise answer, as suggested by the above cartoon.

Answer: A " ◯◯◯◯◯◯◯◯ " ONE

JUMBLE.

Unscramble these four Jumbles,
one letter to each square, to form
four ordinary words.

GALOT

SMUCA

CUDINE

SAHDIR

WHAT THAT CRAZY
ARTIST MADE OF
HIS MODEL.

Now arrange the circled letters to
form the surprise answer, as suggested by the above cartoon.

Print answer here:

JUMBLE®

Unscramble these four Jumbles, one letter to each square, to form four ordinary words.

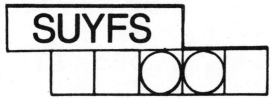

SUYFS

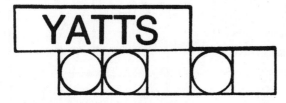

YATTS

SPEEXO

HAREMM

A real pro

WHAT A GOOD HISTORY TEACHER SHOULD BE.

Now arrange the circled letters to form the surprise answer, as suggested by the above cartoon.

Answer: A " ☐☐☐☐ " ☐☐☐☐☐☐

JUMBLE®

Unscramble these four Jumbles,
one letter to each square, to form
four ordinary words.

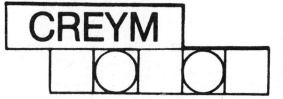

CREYM

YULST

GREATT

PANNKI

Here's a
penny for
you, my
good man

WHAT A CENT TIP
WOULD CERTAINLY
MAKE THESE DAYS.

Now arrange the circled letters to
form the surprise answer, as suggested by the above cartoon.

Answer here: A " ◯◯◯◯◯◯◯◯◯ "

JUMBLE.

Unscramble these four Jumbles, one letter to each square, to form four ordinary words.

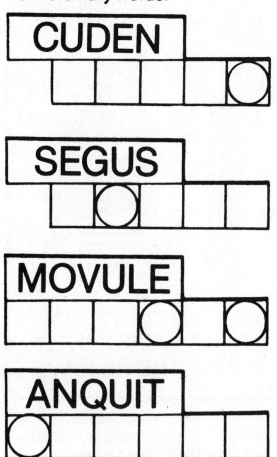

CUDEN

SEGUS

MOVULE

ANQUIT

I'm hungry

How much longer?

A WORD OF FIVE LETTERS THE LAST FOUR OF WHICH ARE UNNECESSARY.

Now arrange the circled letters to form the surprise answer, as suggested by the above cartoon.

Print answer here:

JUMBLE®

Unscramble these four Jumbles,
one letter to each square, to form
four ordinary words.

GELBI

DEPIT

THENUR

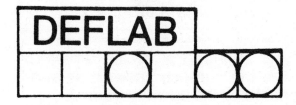

DEFLAB

Should I or
shouldn't I?

WHAT TO DO
WHEN YOU GET THE
FEELING THAT YOU
WANT TO SPLURGE.

Now arrange the circled letters to
form the surprise answer, as suggested by the above cartoon.

Answer: ⟨◯◯◯⟩ IT IN " ⟨◯◯◯⟩ - ⟨◯◯◯⟩ "
THE

JUMBLE®

Unscramble these four Jumbles,
one letter to each square, to form
four ordinary words.

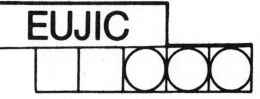

EUJIC

JAROM

PENXED

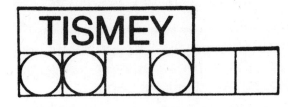

TISMEY

There's a slight discrepancy
in your account!

IRS

WHAT THE GOVERN-
MENT EXPECTS TO
GET FROM INCOME
TAXES.

Now arrange the circled letters to
form the surprise answer, as suggested by the above cartoon.

Answer: " ◯◯◯◯◯ ◯◯◯◯◯◯◯ "

JUMBLE.

Unscramble these four Jumbles,
one letter to each square, to form
four ordinary words.

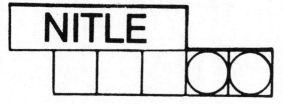
NITLE

INWET

ENFRYZ

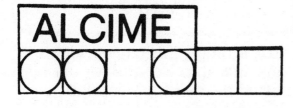
ALCIME

He's certainly becoming
well-known

WHAT THE AUTHOR'S
PSEUDONYM WAS.

Now arrange the circled letters to
form the surprise answer, as suggested by the above cartoon.

Answer: HIS "◯◯◯◯◯◯" ◯◯◯◯

JUMBLE.

Unscramble these four Jumbles,
one letter to each square, to form
four ordinary words.

ORFUL

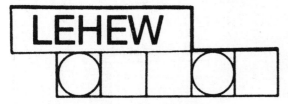
LEHEW

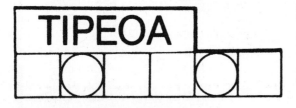
TIPEOA

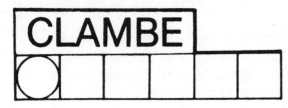
CLAMBE

Can't do a thing with it

WHAT SHE DID
EVERY TIME SHE
WASHED HER
HAIR.

Now arrange the circled letters to
form the surprise answer, as suggested by the above cartoon.

Print answer here:  HER

JUMBLE®

Unscramble these four Jumbles,
one letter to each square, to form
four ordinary words.

IRYAH

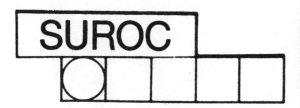

SUROC

MUJERP

DARAMA

There he goes again

WHAT A SLEEP-
WALKER'S HABIT
USUALLY IS.

Now arrange the circled letters to
form the surprise answer, as suggested by the above cartoon.

Print answer here:

JUMBLE.

Unscramble these four Jumbles,
one letter to each square, to form
four ordinary words.

YINKK

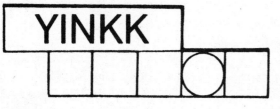
ZAWLT

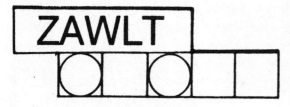
LURIAB

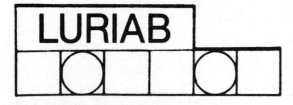
ACDAFE

WHAT A QUACK
DOCTOR USUALLY
TRIES TO DO.

Now arrange the circled letters to
form the surprise answer, as suggested by the above cartoon.

Print answer here:  THE

JUMBLE®

Unscramble these four Jumbles,
one letter to each square, to form
four ordinary words.

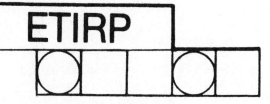

ETIRP

BOYHB

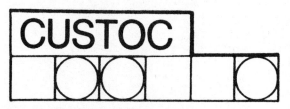

CUSTOC

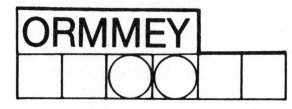

ORMMEY

HOW YOU HAVE TO
LEARN TO TAKE
CARE OF A BABY.

Now arrange the circled letters to
form the surprise answer, as suggested by the above cartoon.

Answer: FROM THE

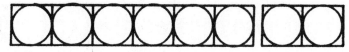

301

JUMBLE®

Unscramble these four Jumbles,
one letter to each square, to form
four ordinary words.

FORVA

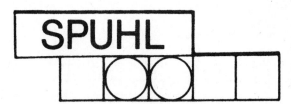

SPUHL

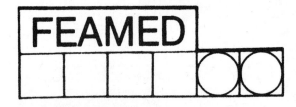

FEAMED

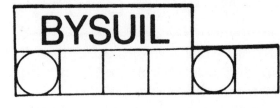

BYSUIL

HELD UP IN
BAD WEATHER.

Now arrange the circled letters to
form the surprise answer, as suggested by the above cartoon.

Print answer here: AN

302

JUMBLE®

Unscramble these four Jumbles,
one letter to each square, to form
four ordinary words.

TANGE

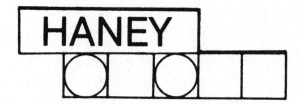

HANEY

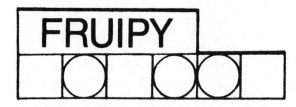

FRUIPY

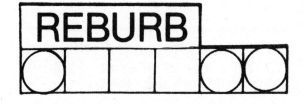

REBURB

Gorgeous!

WHAT A FASHION
MODEL MIGHT
FIGURE ON.

Now arrange the circled letters to
form the surprise answer, as suggested by the above cartoon.

Print answer here:

JUMBLE.

Unscramble these four Jumbles, one letter to each square, to form four ordinary words.

INGGA

YORFE

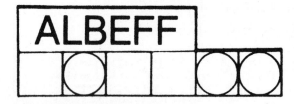

ALBEFF

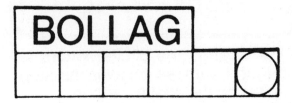

BOLLAG

DOES IT ALL COME FROM AN ALLERGY?

Now arrange the circled letters to form the surprise answer, as suggested by the above cartoon.

Print answer here: "

"

JUMBLE.

Unscramble these four Jumbles, one letter to each square, to form four ordinary words.

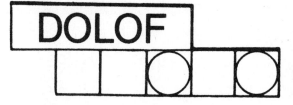

DOLOF

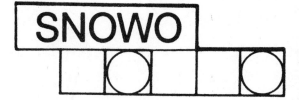

SNOWO

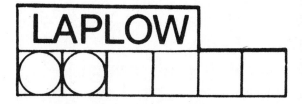

LAPLOW

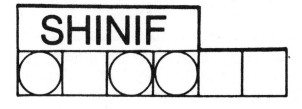

SHINIF

WHAT THAT PEEPING TOM WAS.

Now arrange the circled letters to form the surprise answer, as suggested by the above cartoon.

Answer here: A

JUMBLE®

Unscramble these four Jumbles,
one letter to each square, to form
four ordinary words.

TIDOT

WETHA

RYCKIT

WHALLO

HOW CHILDREN
ARRIVE AT YOUR
DOOR TONIGHT.

Now arrange the circled letters to
form the surprise answer, as suggested by the above cartoon.

Answer here: EVERY " ⃝⃝⃝⃝⃝ " ⃝⃝⃝

JUMBLE®

Unscramble these four Jumbles, one letter to each square, to form four ordinary words.

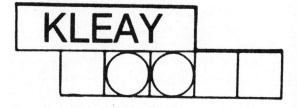

KLEAY

SAREE

VINTIE

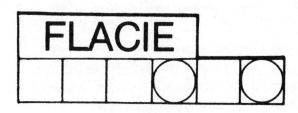

FLACIE

He believes everything he hears

But it's in one ear and out the other

WHAT TOO MUCH OF AN OPEN MIND MIGHT BE LIKE.

Now arrange the circled letters to form the surprise answer, as suggested by the above cartoon.

Print answer here:

JUMBLE®

Unscramble these four Jumbles,
one letter to each square, to form
four ordinary words.

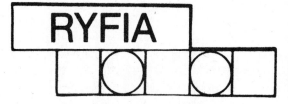

RYFIA

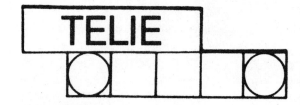

TELIE

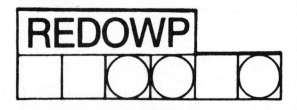

REDOWP

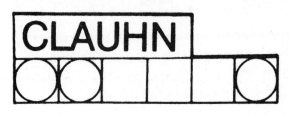

CLAUHN

Here—have some pills

WHAT THEY CALLED
THAT CROOKED
POLITICIAN
TURNED DOCTOR.

Now arrange the circled letters to
form the surprise answer, as suggested by the above cartoon.

Answer: THE [⃝⃝⃝⃝] " [⃝⃝⃝⃝⃝⃝] "

JUMBLE®

Unscramble these four Jumbles, one letter to each square, to form four ordinary words.

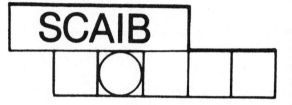
SCAIB

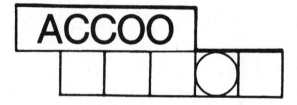
ACCOO

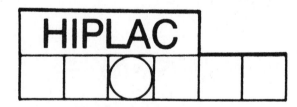
HIPLAC

ZEERIF

Always makes me nervous

IT'S "SAID" TO BE A TEST.

Now arrange the circled letters to form the surprise answer, as suggested by the above cartoon.

Print answer here:

JUMBLE®

Unscramble these four Jumbles,
one letter to each square, to form
four ordinary words.

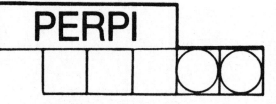

PERPI

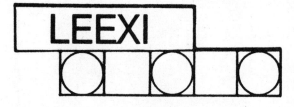

LEEXI

KAUMPE

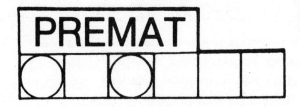

PREMAT

ANOTHER NAME
FOR A
PAWNBROKER.

Now arrange the circled letters to
form the surprise answer, as suggested by the above cartoon.

Answer: A "  "

JUMBLE®

Unscramble these four Jumbles,
one letter to each square, to form
four ordinary words.

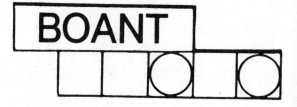

BOANT

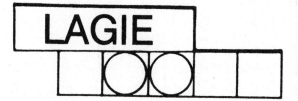

LAGIE

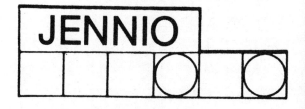

JENNIO

RITHEH

She's never had to
worry about money

WHAT TO DO IN
ORDER TO HAVE
SOFT WHITE HANDS.

Now arrange the circled letters to
form the surprise answer, as suggested by the above cartoon.

Print answer here:

JUMBLE.

Unscramble these four Jumbles,
one letter to each square, to form
four ordinary words.

ORMUF

ZUGEA

TENTAX

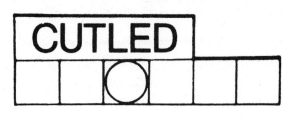

CUTLED

And I thought I was
doing great!

IRS

THE REASON
SO MANY OF US
ARE DISCONTENTED
WITH OUR LOT
THESE DAYS IS THAT
IT'S NO LONGER THIS.

Now arrange the circled letters to
form the surprise answer, as suggested by the above cartoon.

Print answer here:

JUMBLE®

Unscramble these four Jumbles,
one letter to each square, to form
four ordinary words.

ROVLE

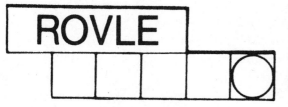
YOANN

TOOSHE

CUDREE

VOTE

HOW THE POP
SINGER TURNED
POLITICIAN RAN.

Now arrange the circled letters to
form the surprise answer, as suggested by the above cartoon.

Print answer here: HIS

JUMBLE®

Unscramble these four Jumbles, one letter to each square, to form four ordinary words.

RISUV

CLEEX

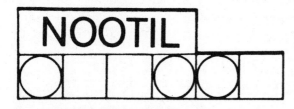

NOOTIL

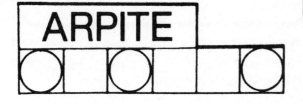

ARPITE

Oops!

WHAT AN ALIBI USUALLY IS.

Now arrange the circled letters to form the surprise answer, as suggested by the above cartoon.

Answer here: A " ⬡⬡⬡⬡⬡ " ⬡⬡⬡⬡⬡⬡

JUMBLE.

Unscramble these four Jumbles,
one letter to each square, to form
four ordinary words.

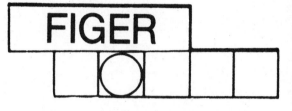

FIGER

LASIA

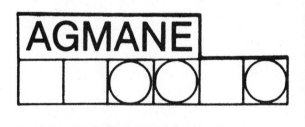

AGMANE

RIMPER

THE *MARINES*
WERE "ARRANGED"
AS A STUDY GROUP.

Now arrange the circled letters to
form the surprise answer, as suggested by the above cartoon.

Print answer here: "  "

JUMBLE®

Unscramble these four Jumbles, one letter to each square, to form four ordinary words.

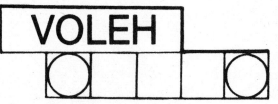

VOLEH

NISOB

CAMEZE

URBBUS

WHAT A GARBAGE TRUCK IS.

Now arrange the circled letters to form the surprise answer, as suggested by the above cartoon.

Answer here: A  "  "

JUMBLE®

Unscramble these four Jumbles,
one letter to each square, to form
four ordinary words.

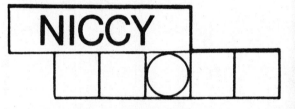

NICCY

TAREF

DOAZIC

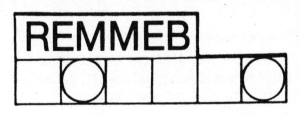

REMMEB

CONVENIENCE
DINNERS

WHAT THE PRICES
OF SOME OF
THOSE FROZEN FOODS
DEFINITELY WEREN'T.

Now arrange the circled letters to
form the surprise answer, as suggested by the above cartoon.

Print answer here:

JUMBLE.

Unscramble these four Jumbles,
one letter to each square, to form
four ordinary words.

PUMIO

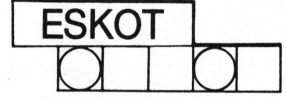
ESKOT

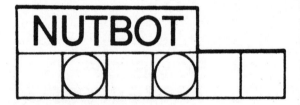
NUTBOT

TALUCA

They say she's a snob

WHAT PINUP GIRLS
SOMETIMES ARE.

Now arrange the circled letters to
form the surprise answer, as suggested by the above cartoon.

Print answer here: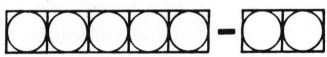

JUMBLE®

Unscramble these four Jumbles, one letter to each square, to form four ordinary words.

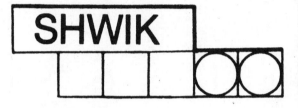

SHWIK

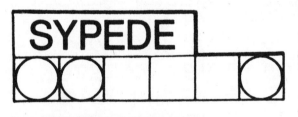

DARAW

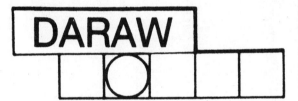

SYPEDE

NEEGIN

WHAT THE CHURCH SEXTON MINDS.

Now arrange the circled letters to form the surprise answer, as suggested by the above cartoon.

Answer here: HIS ⬡⬡⬡⬡ & ⬡⬡⬡⬡

JUMBLE®

Unscramble these four Jumbles,
one letter to each square, to form
four ordinary words.

RUFIT

ARBIN

NAUVEE

SLIMAD

WHILE SHE WAS
GETTING A FACEFUL
OF MUD SHE WAS
ALSO GETTING THIS.

Now arrange the circled letters to
form the surprise answer, as suggested by the above cartoon.

Answer: AN ⬡⬡⬡⬡⬡⬡⬡ OF "⬡⬡⬡⬡"

JUMBLE®

Unscramble these four Jumbles, one letter to each square, to form four ordinary words.

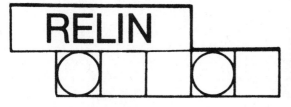

RELIN

HATIF

NAPHOR

TALKEN

WHAT A SNOWBALL MIGHT BE.

Now arrange the circled letters to form the surprise answer, as suggested by the above cartoon.

Answer: A "⬚⬚⬚⬚⬚" ⬚⬚⬚⬚⬚⬚⬚

JUMBLE.

Unscramble these four Jumbles, one letter to each square, to form four ordinary words.

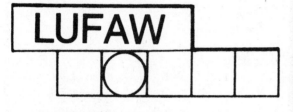
LUFAW

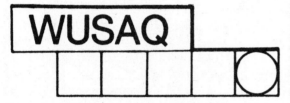
WUSAQ

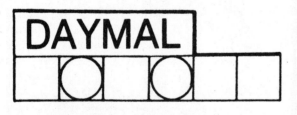
DAYMAL

DELIJA

WHAT THERE SEEMED TO BE IN THAT NOISY COURTROOM.

Now arrange the circled letters to form the surprise answer, as suggested by the above cartoon.

Answer: MORE " ◯◯◯ " THAN ◯◯◯

JUMBLE ®

Unscramble these four Jumbles,
one letter to each square, to form
four ordinary words.

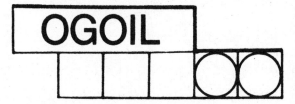

OGOIL

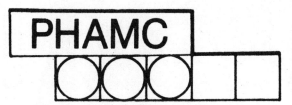

PHAMC

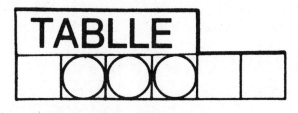

TABLLE

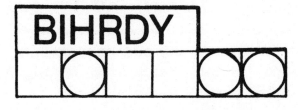

BIHRDY

AULD LANG SYNE

Good they're
not driving
tonight

WHAT NEW YEAR'S
EVE MIGHT BE
FOR SOME PEOPLE.

Now arrange the circled letters to
form the surprise answer, as suggested by the above cartoon.

Answer: AN " ⬡⬡⬡⬡⬡⬡⬡⬡⬡⬡⬡⬡ "

JUMBLE.

Unscramble these four Jumbles,
one letter to each square, to form
four ordinary words.

TULGI

OVEBA

THYROW

LURTIA

WHAT DOES A
SMALL INLAY
COST THESE DAYS?

Now arrange the circled letters to
form the surprise answer, as suggested by the above cartoon.

Answer here: A

JUMBLE®

Unscramble these four Jumbles, one letter to each square, to form four ordinary words.

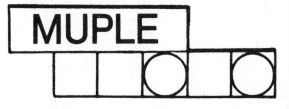

MUPLE

HARBO

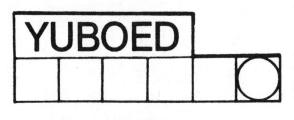

YUBOED

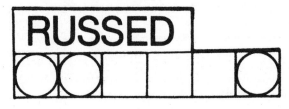

RUSSED

WHAT THAT
DUDE BECAME
AFTER MARRIAGE.

Now arrange the circled letters to form the surprise answer, as suggested by the above cartoon.

Print answer here:

JUMBLE.

Unscramble these four Jumbles, one letter to each square, to form four ordinary words.

HYSIF

UGGOE

GUYSAR

FRYBLE

OIL STOCKS

PROFIT FOR ME: $ ....

CONTRACT

FIGURES DON'T LIE — BUT LIARS DO THIS.

Now arrange the circled letters to form the surprise answer, as suggested by the above cartoon.

Print answer here:

JUMBLE®

Unscramble these four Jumbles,
one letter to each square, to form
four ordinary words.

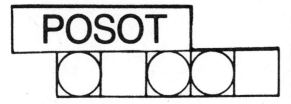

POSOT

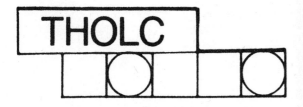

THOLC

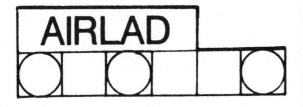

AIRLAD

GHURNY

A FABULOUSLY
SUCCESSFUL BAKER
MIGHT BRING THESE
WORDS TO MIND.

Now arrange the circled letters to
form the surprise answer, as suggested by the above cartoon.

Answer here:  IN

JUMBLE.

Unscramble these four Jumbles,
one letter to each square, to form
four ordinary words.

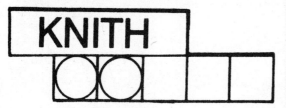

KNITH

OAKEW

CEDROF

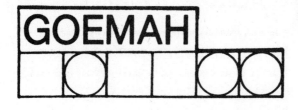

GOEMAH

SOME GUYS
DON'T KNOW WHEN
TO STOP UNTIL
THEY'RE TOLD THIS.

Now arrange the circled letters to
form the surprise answer, as suggested by the above cartoon.

Answer here:

JUMBLE®

Unscramble these four Jumbles,
one letter to each square, to form
four ordinary words.

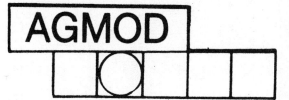
AGMOD

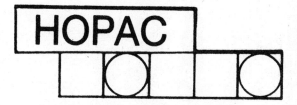
HOPAC

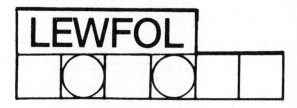
LEWFOL

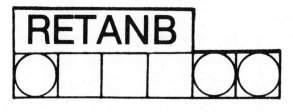
RETANB

WHAT A YAWN
OFTEN IS.

Now arrange the circled letters to
form the surprise answer, as suggested by the above cartoon.

Answer: A ⬡⚬⚬⚬⚬⬡ MADE
BY A ⬡⚬⚬⚬⬡

JUMBLE.

Unscramble these four Jumbles, one letter to each square, to form four ordinary words.

WILEH

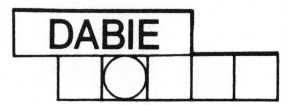
DABIE

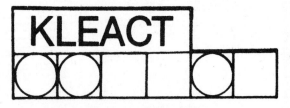
KLEACT

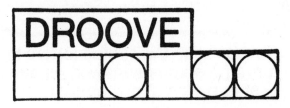
DROOVE

WHAT THE BLACK-SMITH DID TO HIS INCOMPETENT APPRENTICE.

Now arrange the circled letters to form the surprise answer, as suggested by the above cartoon.

Answer: ⬡⬡⬡⬡⬡⬡⬡⬡⬡ ⬡⬡⬡ HIM

JUMBLE®

Unscramble these four Jumbles,
one letter to each square, to form
four ordinary words.

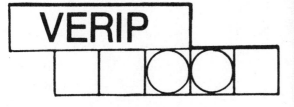

VERIP

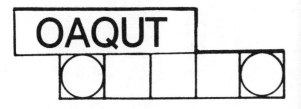

OAQUT

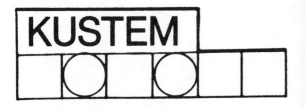

KUSTEM

DEGLUC

Cures bunions, baldness,
athlete's foot. . .

MEDICINE MEN
ARE SELDOM WHAT
THEY'RE THIS.

Now arrange the circled letters to
form the surprise answer, as suggested by the above cartoon.

Answer: "⬡⬡⬡⬡⬡⬡⬡⬡" ⬡⬡⬡ TO
BE

JUMBLE®

Unscramble these four Jumbles,
one letter to each square, to form
four ordinary words.

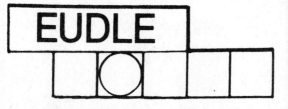

EUDLE

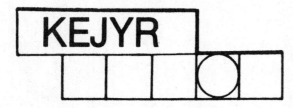

KEJYR

TRALFE

LIRIXE

WHAT THE SCOTSMAN
WHO RETURNED
HOME LATE ONE
NIGHT ALMOST GOT.

Now arrange the circled letters to
form the surprise answer, as suggested by the above cartoon.

Print answer here: "  "

JUMBLE.

Unscramble these four Jumbles,
one letter to each square, to form
four ordinary words.

LESIA

HUSBY

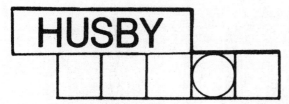
LANTUF

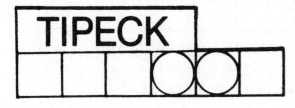
TIPECK

THOSE CARS
NEVER RUN AS
SMOOTHLY AS THIS.

Now arrange the circled letters to
form the surprise answer, as suggested by the above cartoon.

Print answer here:

JUMBLE®

Unscramble these four Jumbles,
one letter to each square, to form
four ordinary words.

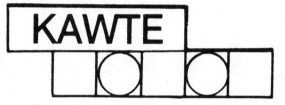

KAWTE

ROJEK

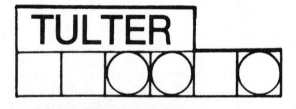

TULTER

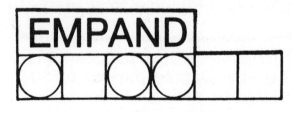

EMPAND

First fill these
out in triplicate

Then take them to. . .

APPLICATIONS
ACCEPTED HERE

WHAT A
BUREAUCRAT IS.

Now arrange the circled letters to
form the surprise answer, as suggested by the above cartoon.

Answer: A

JUMBLE.®

Unscramble these four Jumbles,
one letter to each square, to form
four ordinary words.

RACCK

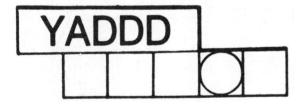

YADDD

TIMLEG

SHOIBY

IRS

WHAT THE
TAX COLLECTOR
DID FOR THE
MAN WHO THOUGHT
HE WAS SAVING UP
FOR A RAINY DAY.

Now arrange the circled letters to
form the surprise answer, as suggested by the above cartoon.

Answer here: " ◯◯◯◯◯◯ " ◯◯◯

JUMBLE.

Unscramble these four Jumbles, one letter to each square, to form four ordinary words.

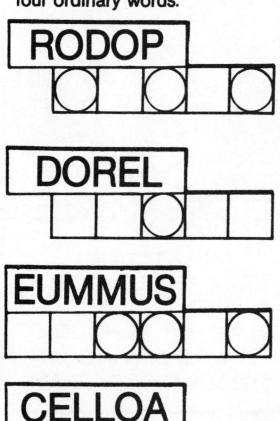

RODOP

DOREL

EUMMUS

CELLOA

HOW SOME SO-CALLED "MUSIC" THAT'S BEING COMPOSED THESE DAYS SOUNDS TO SOME PEOPLE.

Now arrange the circled letters to form the surprise answer, as suggested by the above cartoon.

Answer: " ☐☐ - ☐☐☐☐☐☐☐☐ "

JUMBLE.

Unscramble these four Jumbles, one letter to each square, to form four ordinary words.

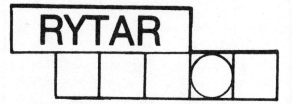

RYTAR

EDGUF

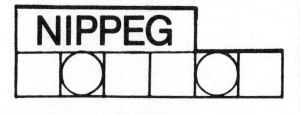

NIPPEG

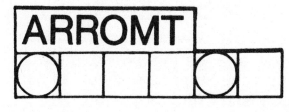

ARROMT

Who would have thought?

THAT BACTERIOLOGIST MADE HIS FAMOUS DISCOVERY BY START-ING OUT WITH THIS.

Now arrange the circled letters to form the surprise answer, as suggested by the above cartoon.

Answer here: THE ⬡⬡⬡⬡⬡ OF AN ⬡⬡⬡⬡⬡

JUMBLE.

Unscramble these four Jumbles,
one letter to each square, to form
four ordinary words.

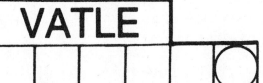

VATLE

TYDIT

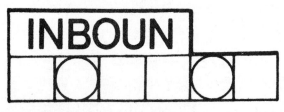

INBOUN

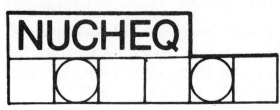

NUCHEQ

WHAT HE DID
AFTER STEALING A
PAIR OF SCISSORS.

Now arrange the circled letters to
form the surprise answer, as suggested by the above cartoon.

Print answer here:

JUMBLE®

Unscramble these four Jumbles,
one letter to each square, to form
four ordinary words.

GANYM

LIVAL

DOLFYN

CLOPEM

He'll never get anywhere
with that attitude!

A GUY WHO'S
BUSY COPING HAS
NO TIME FOR THIS.

Now arrange the circled letters to
form the surprise answer, as suggested by the above cartoon.

Print answer here:

JUMBLE.

Unscramble these four Jumbles,
one letter to each square, to form
four ordinary words.

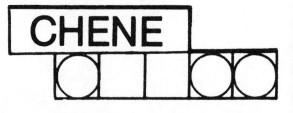

CHENE

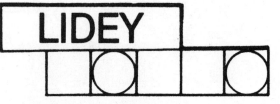

LIDEY

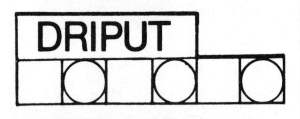

DRIPUT

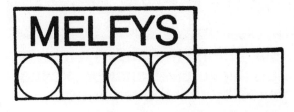

MELFYS

WHAT THE
MILLIONAIRE
LEFT.

Now arrange the circled letters to
form the surprise answer, as suggested by the above cartoon.

Answer:

TO
BE

JUMBLE.

Unscramble these four Jumbles,
one letter to each square, to form
four ordinary words.

CUTOS

GANTY

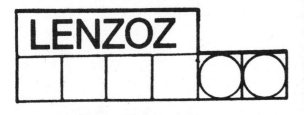
LENZOZ

MOOGLY

Will you let me get a
word in edgewise?

WHAT A CONVER-
SATION BETWEEN
HUSBAND AND
WIFE SOMETIMES IS.

Now arrange the circled letters to
form the surprise answer, as suggested by the above cartoon.

Answer here: A

JUMBLE.

Unscramble these four Jumbles, one letter to each square, to form four ordinary words.

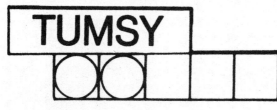

TUMSY

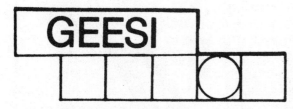

GEESI

LIVERD

SLAPOT

CANDY

But you promised!

WHAT TEARS ARE.

Now arrange the circled letters to form the surprise answer, as suggested by the above cartoon.

Answer here: "  "

JUMBLE®

Unscramble these four Jumbles, one letter to each square, to form four ordinary words.

GREEM

NARCH

CAFFEE

TABMIG
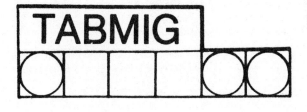

OUR
ANCESTORS

HOW SOME
PROMINENT
FAMILY TREES
WERE STARTED.

Now arrange the circled letters to form the surprise answer, as suggested by the above cartoon.

Answer here: BY " ◯◯◯◯◯◯◯◯◯ "

JUMBLE.

Unscramble these four Jumbles, one letter to each square, to form four ordinary words.

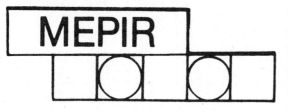

MEPIR

BLEEL

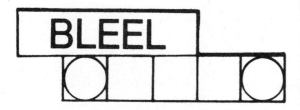

EXFRIP

TRAMOF

THE ONLY THING HE HAD AGAINST THE YOUNGER GENER-ATION WAS THAT HE WAS NOT THIS.

Now arrange the circled letters to form the surprise answer, as suggested by the above cartoon.

Answer here: A  IT

JUMBLE.

Unscramble these four Jumbles,
one letter to each square, to form
four ordinary words.

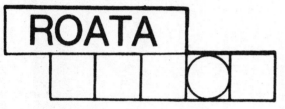

ROATA

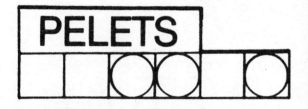

BYDAN

PELETS

DEELEN

HOW THE STUDENTS
FELT ABOUT
THE EXAMINATION.

Now arrange the circled letters to
form the surprise answer, as suggested by the above cartoon.

Answer: THEY "◯◯ - ◯◯◯◯◯ - ◯◯" IT

JUMBLE.

Unscramble these four Jumbles,
one letter to each square, to form
four ordinary words.

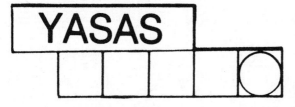

YASAS

TYPAR

GRUNNE

DAILIN

WHAT HE
QUIT DOING
IN TRYING TIMES.

Now arrange the circled letters to
form the surprise answer, as suggested by the above cartoon.

Print answer here:

JUMBLE®

Unscramble these four Jumbles,
one letter to each square, to form
four ordinary words.

DYGUP

PUMBY

MIOGES

YIFNER

WHAT IT WAS
WHEN THE
DOCTOR SAID,
"THIS WON'T HURT."

Now arrange the circled letters to
form the surprise answer, as suggested by the above cartoon.

Answer: AN "◯.◯." ◯◯◯◯◯◯◯◯

JUMBLE.

Unscramble these four Jumbles,
one letter to each square, to form
four ordinary words.

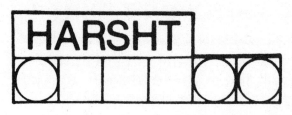

AMMIX

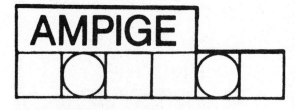

FEWAR

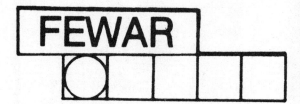

AMPIGE

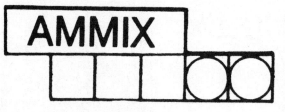

HARSHT

THE WAITER
FINALLY
COMES TO THIS.

Now arrange the circled letters to
form the surprise answer, as suggested by the above cartoon.

Answer here: ◯◯◯ WHO ◯◯◯◯◯

JUMBLE.

Unscramble these four Jumbles, one letter to each square, to form four ordinary words.

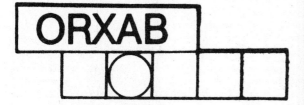

ORXAB

RAFIE

FENTOM

WARBOR

HE WAS THE TYPE OF MAN SOME WOMEN TAKE TO — AND ALSO THIS.

Now arrange the circled letters to form the surprise answer, as suggested by the above cartoon.

Print answer here:

JUMBLE.

Unscramble these four Jumbles,
one letter to each square, to form
four ordinary words.

TAING

URUGA

KRODEF

CHINTS

WHAT THEY CALLED
THE STAR OF
THE MONSTER SHOW.

Now arrange the circled letters to
form the surprise answer, as suggested by the above cartoon.

Answer: A ◯◯◯◯◯ " ◯◯◯◯◯◯◯ "

JUMBLE.

Unscramble these four Jumbles,
one letter to each square, to form
four ordinary words.

GOUNY

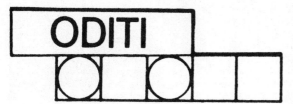

ODITI

REDDEG

LADVAN

A BEAUTY SALON
IS A PLACE WHERE
THIS MIGHT HAPPEN.

Now arrange the circled letters to
form the surprise answer, as suggested by the above cartoon.

Answer: THE ⬡⬡⬡⬡⬡⬡⬡ GO " ⬡⬡⬡ "
TO

JUMBLE.

Unscramble these four Jumbles,
one letter to each square, to form
four ordinary words.

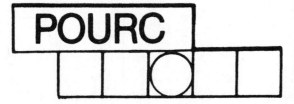
POURC

RABEG

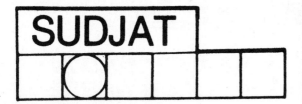
SUDJAT

YOUGLE

M.D.

Hypochondriac

HOW HE
FELT ABOUT
FEELING BAD.

Now arrange the circled letters to
form the surprise answer, as suggested by the above cartoon.

Print answer here:

JUMBLE.

Unscramble these four Jumbles, one letter to each square, to form four ordinary words.

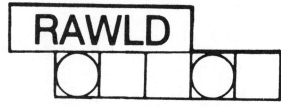

RAWLD

HEGIT

TICPED

ASANUE

Wait'll the gang hears about THIS!

IF YOU'RE GOING TO ACT LIKE A SKUNK JUST MAKE SURE THAT NOBODY DOES THIS.

Now arrange the circled letters to form the surprise answer, as suggested by the above cartoon.

Answer here:  OF IT

JUMBLE.

Unscramble these four Jumbles, one letter to each square, to form four ordinary words.

LOYKE

POTVI

BINLEB

EMBLAG

Kid brother was crying all night...

WHAT SOME COLLEGE STUDENTS MAJOR IN.

Now arrange the circled letters to form the surprise answer, as suggested by the above cartoon.

Answer: "◯◯◯◯◯◯ - ◯◯◯◯◯◯"

JUMBLE.

Unscramble these four Jumbles, one letter to each square, to form four ordinary words.

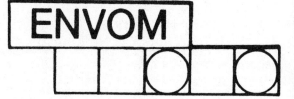

ENVOM

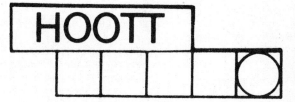

HOOTT

BONGEY

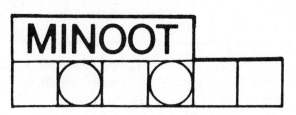

MINOOT

HOW THOSE FOLKS WHO ENJOYED EATING GRITS SANG.

Now arrange the circled letters to form the surprise answer, as suggested by the above cartoon.

Print answer here: IN "  "

JUMBLE.

Unscramble these four Jumbles,
one letter to each square, to form
four ordinary words.

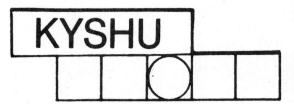

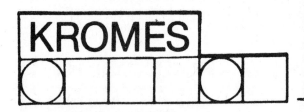

WHAT DO YOU THINK
OF THAT POET?

Now arrange the circled letters to
form the surprise answer, as suggested by the above cartoon.

Answer: I'VE

JUMBLE®

Unscramble these four Jumbles, one letter to each square, to form four ordinary words.

PARVO

RAMEF

MURBEN

LUSTYS

WHY THEY CALLED FOR THE CHIMNEY SWEEP.

Now arrange the circled letters to form the surprise answer, as suggested by the above cartoon.

Answer: IT WAS " ☐☐☐☐☐ " ☐☐☐☐☐☐☐
THE

JUMBLE®

Unscramble these four Jumbles, one letter to each square, to form four ordinary words.

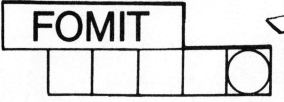
FOMIT

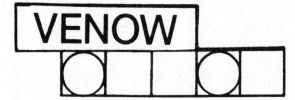
VENOW

LOPARR

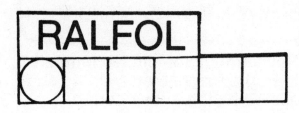
RALFOL

HOW HE FELT AFTER EATING TOO MANY PANCAKES.

Now arrange the circled letters to form the surprise answer, as suggested by the above cartoon.

Print answer here: "  "

JUMBLE.

Unscramble these four Jumbles, one letter to each square, to form four ordinary words.

GLITH

ORRIP

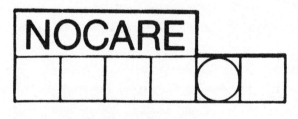
NOCARE

UDDEGI

Something's wrong

WHAT THE CARD GAME AT THE OIL FIELD MUST HAVE BEEN.

Now arrange the circled letters to form the surprise answer, as suggested by the above cartoon.

Print answer here: "  "

JUMBLE®

Unscramble these four Jumbles, one letter to each square, to form four ordinary words.

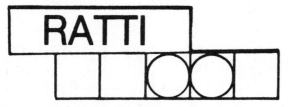
RATTI

NEFEC

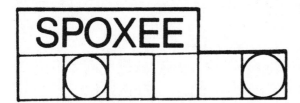
SPOXEE

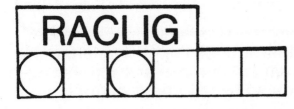
RACLIG

WHAT FIREWOOD USED TO BE.

Now arrange the circled letters to form the surprise answer, as suggested by the above cartoon.

Answer: ☐☐☐☐☐ FOR THE " ☐☐☐☐☐☐ "

JUMBLE.

Unscramble these four Jumbles, one letter to each square, to form four ordinary words.

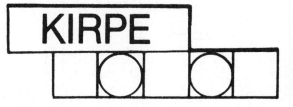

KIRPE

DUFAR

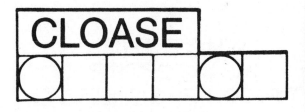

CLOASE

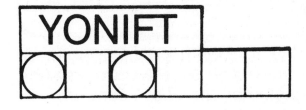

YONIFT

PIZZA

Willpower, willpower

THE BEST WAY TO WATCH CALORIES, IF YOU WANT TO LOSE WEIGHT.

Now arrange the circled letters to form the surprise answer, as suggested by the above cartoon.

Answer here: FROM A ⬭⬭⬭⬭⬭⬭⬭⬭

JUMBLE®

Unscramble these four Jumbles,
one letter to each square, to form
four ordinary words.

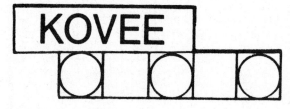

KOVEE

MASCK

PROWED

HEWPEN

DENTIST

CANDY

WHAT THE
HELICOPTER
TYCOON DECIDED TO
GET FOR HIMSELF.

Now arrange the circled letters to
form the surprise answer, as suggested by the above cartoon.

Answer: [ ][ ][ ]   [ ][ ][ ][ ][ ][ ][ ][ ][ ]

JUMBLE®

Unscramble these four Jumbles,
one letter to each square, to form
four ordinary words.

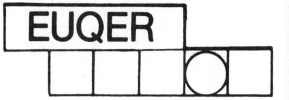

EUQER

SOUDE

NARTTY

SHEERY

WHAT THEY
SAID ABOUT THE
ANGRY GOVERNOR.

Now arrange the circled letters to
form the surprise answer, as suggested by the above cartoon.

Answer: WHAT "⬡⬡⬡⬡⬡⬡" ⬡⬡'⬡ IN !
A

JUMBLE®

Unscramble these four Jumbles, one letter to each square, to form four ordinary words.

OSHUE

VENIA

RUTIVE

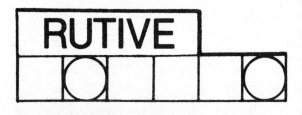

ARQUEV

I have an alibi

WHAT JUNIOR WAS WHEN MOM ACCUSED HIM OF BREAKING HER FAVORITE URN.

Now arrange the circled letters to form the surprise answer, as suggested by the above cartoon.

Answer here: "◯-◯◯◯◯◯-◯◯◯"

JUMBLE.

Unscramble these four Jumbles, one letter to each square, to form four ordinary words.

RINDE

CENIE

RAPOUR

UNPOOC

NO VACANCIES

HOW THE HOTEL ROOM CLERK APPEARED.

Now arrange the circled letters to form the surprise answer, as suggested by the above cartoon.

Answer: "  "

JUMBLE.

Unscramble these four Jumbles,
one letter to each square, to form
four ordinary words.

IRQUE

GOBUM

FOLFAY

CHURCO

PRICES REDUCED

DID THE
X-RATED MOVIE
MAKE ANY MONEY?

Now arrange the circled letters to
form the surprise answer, as suggested by the above cartoon.

Print answer here: " ⬡⬡⬡⬡⬡ – ⬡⬡ "

JUMBLE.

Unscramble these four Jumbles,
one letter to each square, to form
four ordinary words.

NAWGO

GORPY

UNBOCE

ZARWID

I think I know what to
get Junior for his
next birthday

WHAT BOYS DO WHEN
THEY GROW UP.

Now arrange the circled letters to
form the surprise answer, as suggested by the above cartoon.

Print answer here: ⬡⬡⬡⬡ " ⬡⬡⬡⬡ "

JUMBLE.

Unscramble these four Jumbles,
one letter to each square, to form
four ordinary words.

KLAYN

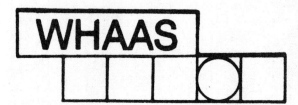

WHAAS

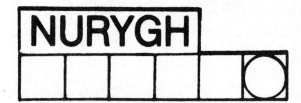

NURYGH

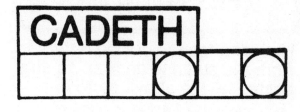

CADETH

Lives from
day to day

WHAT SORT OF
EXISTENCE DID THAT
CRAPSHOOTER LEAD?

Now arrange the circled letters to
form the surprise answer, as suggested by the above cartoon.

Print answer here: A "  " ONE

JUMBLE.

Unscramble these four Jumbles, one letter to each square, to form four ordinary words.

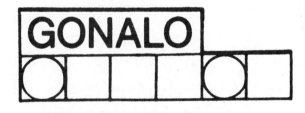

SEGIN

ROBOD

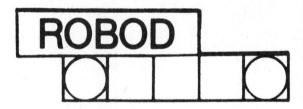

GONALO

SCUMEL

WHAT A GOOD BOOK USUALLY IS.

Now arrange the circled letters to form the surprise answer, as suggested by the above cartoon.

Answer: " ⬡⬡⬡⬡⬡ " TO ⬡⬡⬡⬡⬡

JUMBLE.

Unscramble these four Jumbles,
one letter to each square, to form
four ordinary words.

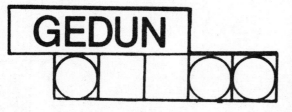

GEDUN

USSEO

THERAH

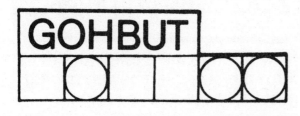

GOHBUT

HOW YOU HAVE
TO PAY FOR
SOME KINDS OF
PLASTIC SURGERY.

Now arrange the circled letters to
form the surprise answer, as suggested by the above cartoon.

Answer: ⬡⬡⬡⬡⬡⬡⬡ THE ⬡⬡⬡⬡

JUMBLE®

Unscramble these four Jumbles, one letter to each square, to form four ordinary words.

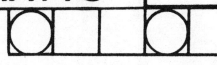

IXTYS

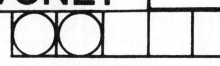

VONEY

CAINAM

KALLIA

A MAN WHO TAKES YOU INTO HIS "CONFIDENCE" OFTEN DOES THIS AFTERWARDS.

Now arrange the circled letters to form the surprise answer, as suggested by the above cartoon.

Answer here: JUST  YOU

371

JUMBLE.

Unscramble these four Jumbles, one letter to each square, to form four ordinary words.

SLARN

CRAFS

REECCO

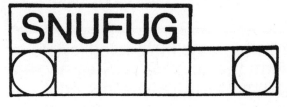

SNUFUG

Well, I wouldn't say yes and I wouldn't say no

POLITICAL CANDIDATES OFTEN STAY ON THE FENCE IN ORDER TO AVOID GIVING THIS.

Now arrange the circled letters to form the surprise answer, as suggested by the above cartoon.

Print answer here: " ☐☐ – ☐☐☐☐☐☐ "

JUMBLE

Unscramble these four Jumbles,
one letter to each square, to form
four ordinary words.

REVVE
⬜⬜⬜⬜⬜◯

APITO
◯⬜⬜◯⬜

KESNIC
◯◯⬜◯◯◯

SWACHE
⬜⬜◯◯⬜◯

SOME COLLEGE KIDS
WHO SPEND TOO
MUCH TIME WITH A
PIGSKIN SOMETIMES
FAIL TO GET THIS.

Now arrange the circled letters to
form the surprise answer, as suggested by the above cartoon.

Answer here: A ◯◯◯◯◯◯◯◯◯

JUMBLE®

Unscramble these four Jumbles,
one letter to each square, to form
four ordinary words.

NARCK

HYLYS

DOEKOH

ESCASC

BEFORE THEY'LL CASH
YOUR CHECK, THEY'LL
PROBABLY DO THIS.

Now arrange the circled letters to
form the surprise answer, as suggested by the above cartoon.

Answer: ⬡⬡⬡⬡⬡ YOUR ⬡⬡⬡⬡

JUMBLE.

Unscramble these four Jumbles,
one letter to each square, to form
four ordinary words.

BATOB

PYXOR

FLUNIX

MADAKS

He
wouldn't
hurt
a
flea

WHAT A CHIP
ON THE SHOULDER
USUALLY IS.

Now arrange the circled letters to
form the surprise answer, as suggested by the above cartoon.

Answer: JUST ⬡⬡⬡⬡⬡ "⬡⬡⬡⬡"

JUMBLE.

Unscramble these four Jumbles, one letter to each square, to form four ordinary words.

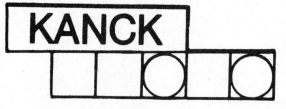
KANCK

BUCCI

ABANCA

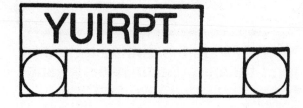
YUIRPT

How much do I owe you from last time?

WHAT MOST OF THE CHIROPRACTOR'S INCOME CAME FROM.

Now arrange the circled letters to form the surprise answer, as suggested by the above cartoon.

Print answer here:

JUMBLE.

Unscramble these four Jumbles,
one letter to each square, to form
four ordinary words.

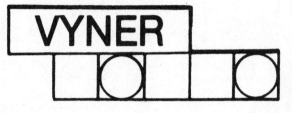

VYNER

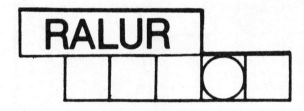

RALUR

DIMPOU

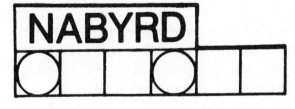

NABYRD

WHAT THE
COUNTERFEITER
WANTED.

Now arrange the circled letters to
form the surprise answer, as suggested by the above cartoon.

Answer here:

JUMBLE.

Unscramble these four Jumbles,
one letter to each square, to form
four ordinary words.

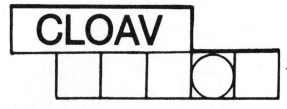

CLOAV

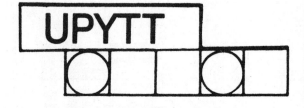

UPYTT

LENETS

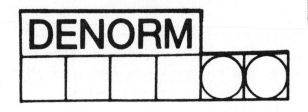

DENORM

A SMALL BOY
MIGHT WEAR OUT
EVERYTHING,
INCLUDING THIS.

Now arrange the circled letters to
form the surprise answer, as suggested by the above cartoon.

Print answer here: HIS

JUMBLE.

Unscramble these four Jumbles,
one letter to each square, to form
four ordinary words.

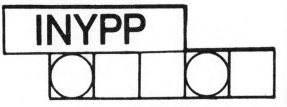

INYPP

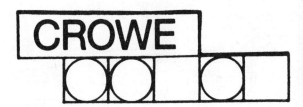

CROWE

RETAUN

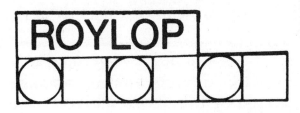

ROYLOP

Those big shots
are always
making a
killing

A CALCULATOR
IS A DEVICE
USED BY THESE.

Now arrange the circled letters to
form the surprise answer, as suggested by the above cartoon.

Answer: ⬡⬡⬡⬡⬡⬡ WHO ⬡⬡⬡⬡⬡

JUMBLE®

Unscramble these four Jumbles,
one letter to each square, to form
four ordinary words.

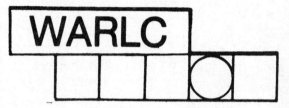
WARLC

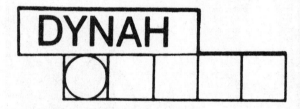
DYNAH

UNJELG

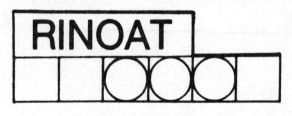
RINOAT

It's going to take a lot of time

HEALTH CLUB

You can put up with the inconvenience

WHERE YOU MIGHT GO IN ORDER TO MAKE YOURSELF MORE ATTRACTIVE.

Now arrange the circled letters to
form the surprise answer, as suggested by the above cartoon.

Answer: ☐☐☐☐ OF YOUR "☐☐☐☐☐☐"

JUMBLE.

Unscramble these four Jumbles,
one letter to each square, to form
four ordinary words.

PRAAT

SHEWO

NUGMIP

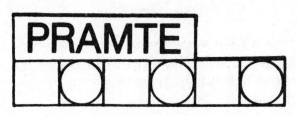

PRAMTE

SOME PEOPLE
WITH THE GIFT OF
GAB NEVER KNOW
WHEN TO DO THIS.

Now arrange the circled letters to
form the surprise answer, as suggested by the above cartoon.

Print answer here:

JUMBLE®

Unscramble these four Jumbles,
one letter to each square, to form
four ordinary words.

CALLI

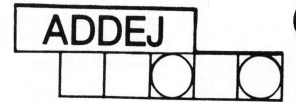

ADDEJ

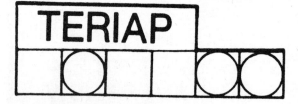

TERIAP

VINTER

Enjoy!

HE FELT THE ONLY
WAY TO MULTIPLY
HAPPINESS
WAS THIS.

Now arrange the circled letters to
form the surprise answer, as suggested by the above cartoon.

Print answer here: TO

JUMBLE®

Unscramble these four Jumbles, one letter to each square, to form four ordinary words.

DRIAP

KIMPS

MADORR

LENKEN

WHAT HE SUFFERED FROM WHEN THE RELATIVES ARRIVED.

Now arrange the circled letters to form the surprise answer, as suggested by the above cartoon.

Answer here: ""

JUMBLE®

Unscramble these four Jumbles, one letter to each square, to form four ordinary words.

SATHY

HASAB

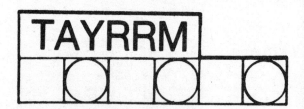

TAYRRM

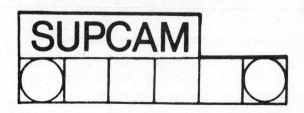

SUPCAM

WHAT ANY GOOD JUNKMAN KNOWS HOW TO CONVERT.

Now arrange the circled letters to form the surprise answer, as suggested by the above cartoon.

Answer:  INTO

JUMBLE®

Unscramble these four Jumbles, one letter to each square, to form four ordinary words.

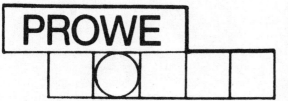

PROWE

PAKKO

LITGUY

QUIROL

SOME GIRLS CLOSE THEIR EYES WHILE KISSING, BUT OTHERS DO THIS.

Now arrange the circled letters to form the surprise answer, as suggested by the above cartoon.

 Answer: ☐☐☐☐☐ BEFORE  THEY "☐☐☐☐"

JUMBLE®

Unscramble these four Jumbles,
one letter to each square, to form
four ordinary words.

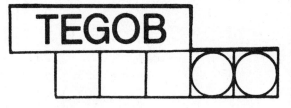

TEGOB

ROBIT

INSHIF

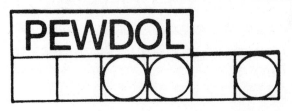

PEWDOL

THAT AFTER-DINNER
SPEAKER ALWAYS
KNEW WHEN TO RISE
TO THE OCCASION —
BUT SELDOM THIS.

Now arrange the circled letters to
form the surprise answer, as suggested by the above cartoon.

Answer: WHEN

JUMBLE®

Unscramble these four Jumbles, one letter to each square, to form four ordinary words.

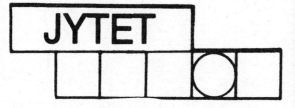

JYTET

SONEO

KRUTEY

TORREC

WHAT HE GOT WHEN HE BOUGHT THAT STOCK.

Now arrange the circled letters to form the surprise answer, as suggested by the above cartoon.

Print answer here:

JUMBLE®

Unscramble these four Jumbles, one letter to each square, to form four ordinary words.

SEBOE

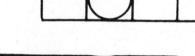
VENOL

UNJAYT
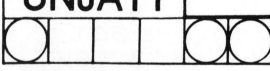

LIMSAD

Get to work!

WHAT HIS WIFE HAD A STEADY JOB TRYING TO KEEP HIM AT.

Now arrange the circled letters to form the surprise answer, as suggested by the above cartoon.

Answer here: A

JUMBLE.

Unscramble these four Jumbles, one letter to each square, to form four ordinary words.

YURST

WHASS

UNEEVA

GREDLE

Says one thing one day, and something else the next

Please vote for me

A POLITICAL PLAT-FORM IS SOMETHING A CANDIDATE NEEDS WHEN HE HASN'T THIS.

Now arrange the circled letters to form the surprise answer, as suggested by the above cartoon.

Answer here: A ☐☐☐ TO ☐☐☐☐☐ ON

JUMBLE®

Unscramble these four Jumbles, one letter to each square, to form four ordinary words.

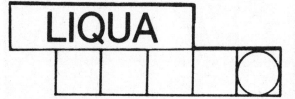

SLEHW

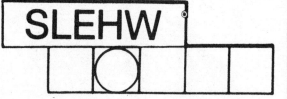

LIQUA

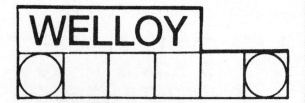

WELLOY

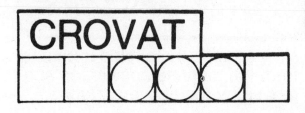

CROVAT

Sh-h-h-h!

WHAT SORT OF CONVERSATION WAS GOING ON AT THE LIBRARY?

Now arrange the circled letters to form the surprise answer, as suggested by the above cartoon.

Answer here: A  "  " ONE

JUMBLE®

Unscramble these four Jumbles,
one letter to each square, to form
four ordinary words.

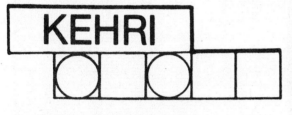

KEHRI

EXVIN

TOBUNT

RAZTUQ

Yeah—I
remember when
they were
all born

ANOTHER NAME
FOR THAT
MUCH TALKED
ABOUT BABY BOOM.

Now arrange the circled letters to
form the surprise answer, as suggested by the above cartoon.

Answer: THE "◯◯◯◯◯◯◯◯◯◯◯◯"

JUMBLE®

Unscramble these four Jumbles, one letter to each square, to form four ordinary words.

GIRRO

ENVAH

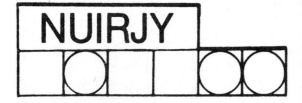

NUIRJY

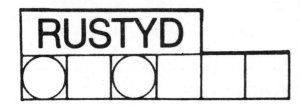

RUSTYD

OUCH!

A HANDY DEVICE FOR FINDING FURNITURE IN THE DARK.

Now arrange the circled letters to form the surprise answer, as suggested by the above cartoon.

Print answer here:

JUMBLE.

Unscramble these four Jumbles,
one letter to each square, to form
four ordinary words.

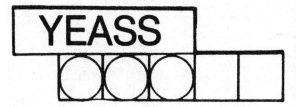
YEASS

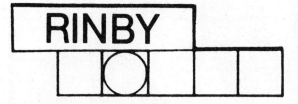
RINBY

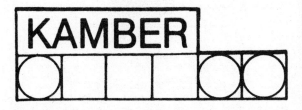
KAMBER

PLOUCE

WHAT A PERSON
WHO BELIEVES
IN FORTUNE-
TELLERS MIGHT BE.

Now arrange the circled letters to
form the surprise answer, as suggested by the above cartoon.

Answer: A "◯◯◯◯◯" ◯◯◯◯◯◯◯

JUMBLE.

Unscramble these four Jumbles, one letter to each square, to form four ordinary words.

RIHAC

ALMEY

YARTIF

DEXENP

Are you listening to all this?!

WHAT A STUFFED SHIRT OFTEN GOES WITH.

Now arrange the circled letters to form the surprise answer, as suggested by the above cartoon.

Answer here: AN ⬡⬡⬡⬡⬡⬡ ⬡⬡⬡⬡

JUMBLE.

Unscramble these four Jumbles, one letter to each square, to form four ordinary words.

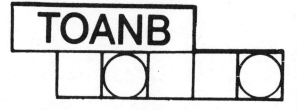

TOANB

POANI

KITSCY

GATHUC

WHEN DENTISTS AREN'T, THEIR PATIENTS ARE.

Now arrange the circled letters to form the surprise answer, as suggested by the above cartoon.

Answer:

JUMBLE.®

Unscramble these four Jumbles,
one letter to each square, to form
four ordinary words.

NILTE

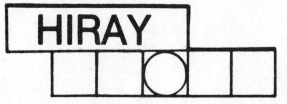

HIRAY

NISUFE

PINGRY

11-29

THE PIANIST
WAS A MUSICIAN
TO THIS.

Now arrange the circled letters to
form the surprise answer, as suggested by the above cartoon.

Answer: HIS ◯◯◯◯◯◯◯◯◯◯◯

JUMBLE.

Unscramble these four Jumbles, one letter to each square, to form four ordinary words.

CHUVO

AUFAN

EXVONC

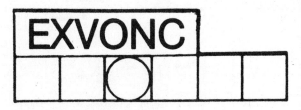

AREPPA

How ignorant can you get?

A PREJUDICED GUY IS DOWN ON ANYTHING HE'S NOT THIS.

Now arrange the circled letters to form the surprise answer, as suggested by the above cartoon.

Print answer here:

JUMBLE®

Unscramble these four Jumbles,
one letter to each square, to form
four ordinary words.

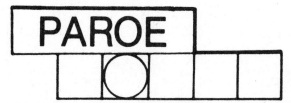
MAUSE

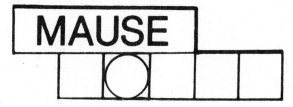
PAROE

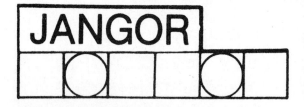
JANGOR

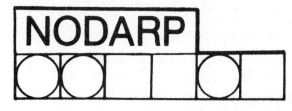
NODARP

WHAT THE TUBA
PLAYER'S KIDS
CALLED HIM.

Now arrange the circled letters to
form the surprise answer, as suggested by the above cartoon.

Answer here: " ◯◯◯◯ - ◯◯◯ - ◯◯◯ "

JUMBLE.

Unscramble these four Jumbles, one letter to each square, to form four ordinary words.

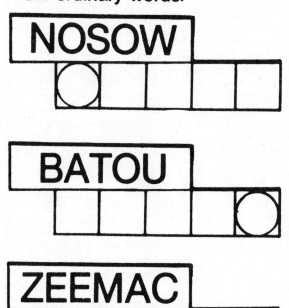

NOSOW

BATOU

ZEEMAC

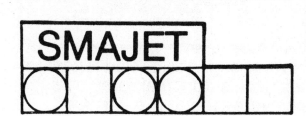

SMAJET

WHAT THAT PRACTICAL JOKER HAD.

Now arrange the circled letters to form the surprise answer, as suggested by the above cartoon.

Answer here: A  FOR

JUMBLE.

Unscramble these four Jumbles, one letter to each square, to form four ordinary words.

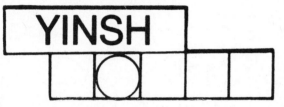
YINSH

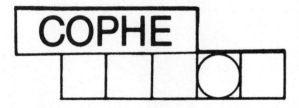
COPHE

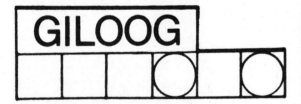
GILOOG

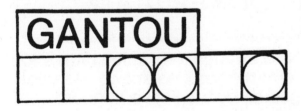
GANTOU

See you next summer

WITH THAT DEAD-BEAT, IT'S OFTEN A MATTER OF THIS.

Now arrange the circled letters to form the surprise answer, as suggested by the above cartoon.

Print answer here:  &

JUMBLE.

Unscramble these four Jumbles, one letter to each square, to form four ordinary words.

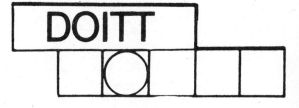

DOITT

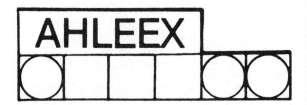

NOYOL

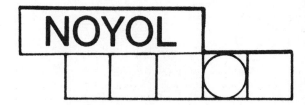

AHLEEX

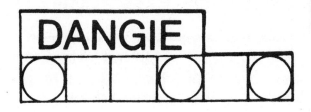

DANGIE

WHAT THEY WERE DOING AT THE SEWING CIRCLE.

Now arrange the circled letters to form the surprise answer, as suggested by the above cartoon.

Print answer here:

401

JUMBLE.

Unscramble these four Jumbles,
one letter to each square, to form
four ordinary words.

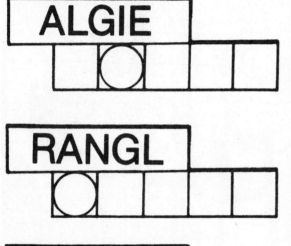

ALGIE

RANGL

NITMAR

CORNBO

HOW THE SO-
CALLED "COMING"
GENERATION SPENDS
MUCH OF ITS TIME.

Now arrange the circled letters to
form the surprise answer, as suggested by the above cartoon.

Print answer here: " ◯◯◯◯◯ "

JUMBLE®

Unscramble these four Jumbles, one letter to each square, to form four ordinary words.

UMPIO

NUDAT

CAVELE

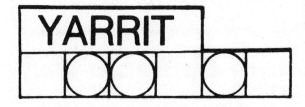
YARRIT

WHAT KIND OF MILK DOES AN INVISIBLE BABY GET, NATURALLY?

Now arrange the circled letters to form the surprise answer, as suggested by the above cartoon.

Answer here:

JUMBLE.

Unscramble these four Jumbles,
one letter to each square, to form
four ordinary words.

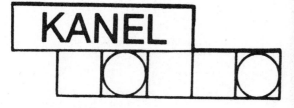

KANEL

OYLED

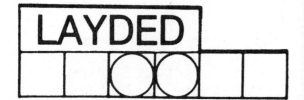

LAYDED

HEERIT

WHAT A CRIMINAL
WHO FALLS
INTO CEMENT
HAS TO BE.

Now arrange the circled letters to
form the surprise answer, as suggested by the above cartoon.

Answer here: A ⟨◯◯◯◯◯◯◯◯◯⟩ ONE

JUMBLE.

Unscramble these four Jumbles,
one letter to each square, to form
four ordinary words.

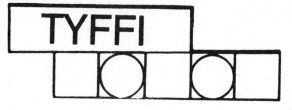
TYFFI

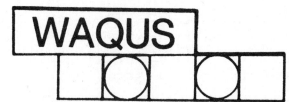
WAQUS

THORUG

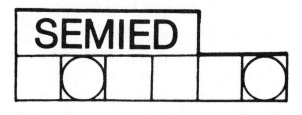
SEMIED

WHAT TANTRUMS
IN CHILDHOOD
APPEAR TO BE.

Now arrange the circled letters to
form the surprise answer, as suggested by the above cartoon.

Answer:  THE "  "

JUMBLE®

Unscramble these four Jumbles,
one letter to each square, to form
four ordinary words.

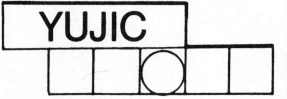

YUJIC

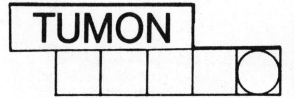

TUMON

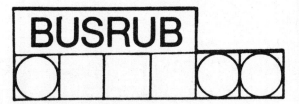

BUSRUB

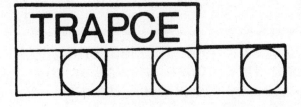

TRAPCE

Just you
wait and
see

WHAT DID THEY
GIVE DRACULA WHEN
HE FIRST WENT
TO HOLLYWOOD?

Now arrange the circled letters to
form the surprise answer, as suggested by the above cartoon.

Answer here: ""

JUMBLE®

Unscramble these four Jumbles, one letter to each square, to form four ordinary words.

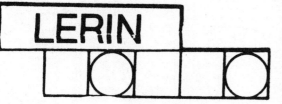

LERIN

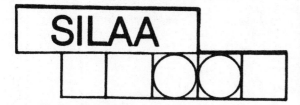

SILAA

WALLUF

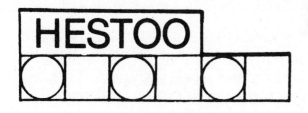

HESTOO

WHAT JOKES TOLD BY MOUNTAIN FOLK OFTEN ARE.

Now arrange the circled letters to form the surprise answer, as suggested by the above cartoon.

Answer: " ☐☐☐☐ – ☐☐☐☐☐☐ "

JUMBLE.

Unscramble these four Jumbles,
one letter to each square, to form
four ordinary words.

PETIR

BYGAG

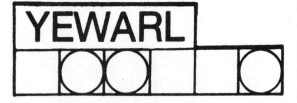

YEWARL

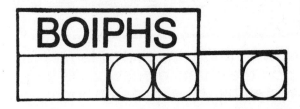

BOIPHS

WHAT TODAY'S
HANGOVER MIGHT BE
CONNECTED WITH.

Now arrange the circled letters to
form the surprise answer, as suggested by the above cartoon.

Answer: THE ⬡⬡⬡⬡⬡ OF ⬡⬡⬡⬡⬡⬡

JUMBLE®

Unscramble these four Jumbles, one letter to each square, to form four ordinary words.

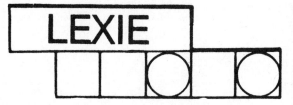

LEXIE

TENGA

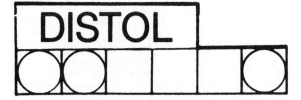

DISTOL

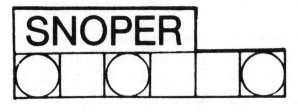

SNOPER

I'm exhausted

$

WHAT SHE WAS, AFTER A HARD DAY'S SHOPPING.

Now arrange the circled letters to form the surprise answer, as suggested by the above cartoon.

Answer: ◯◯◯◯◯ & " ◯◯◯◯◯◯ "

JUMBLE.

Unscramble these four Jumbles, one letter to each square, to form four ordinary words.

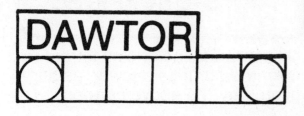
MILIT

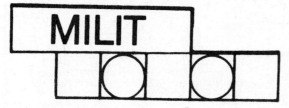
FIDUL

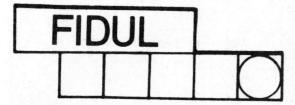
ENGRYT

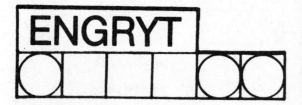
DAWTOR

I always speak my mind

WHAT A PERSON WHO CALLS A SPADE A SPADE IS PROBABLY ABOUT TO GIVE SOMEONE.

Now arrange the circled letters to form the surprise answer, as suggested by the above cartoon.

Answer here: A  "☐☐☐"

JUMBLE.

Unscramble these four Jumbles,
one letter to each square, to form
four ordinary words.

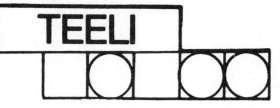

TEELI

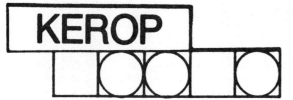

KEROP

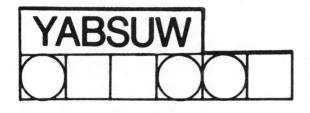

YABSUW

LENKER

He's always robbing
other people's ideas

ANOTHER
NAME FOR A
PLAGIARIST.

Now arrange the circled letters to
form the surprise answer, as suggested by the above cartoon.

Answer: A "⬡⬡⬡⬡⬡" ⬡⬡⬡⬡⬡⬡

JUMBLE.

Unscramble these four Jumbles, one letter to each square, to form four ordinary words.

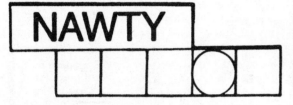
NAWTY

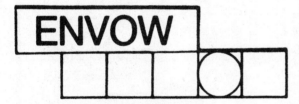
ENVOW

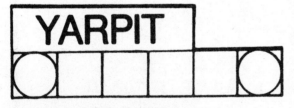
YARPIT

GOMURE

Another rejection

Why don't you go out and get a construction job?

WHAT AN UNTALENTED WRITER MIGHT EARN BY HIS PEN.

Now arrange the circled letters to form the surprise answer, as suggested by the above cartoon.

Print answer here: "◯◯◯ – ◯◯◯"

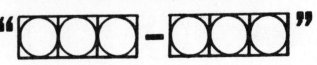

JUMBLE.

Unscramble these four Jumbles, one letter to each square, to form four ordinary words.

IXAMM

UPTYT

BOWELL

CRALIG

I can only give you a little clue, maybe more tomorrow

HOW THE SCANDAL-MONGER LET THE CAT OUT OF THE BAG.

Now arrange the circled letters to form the surprise answer, as suggested by the above cartoon.

Answer here: ONE ⟨◯◯◯◯⟩ AT A ⟨◯◯◯◯⟩

JUMBLE®

Unscramble these four Jumbles, one letter to each square, to form four ordinary words.

GAGBY

FRATE

SMIFAH

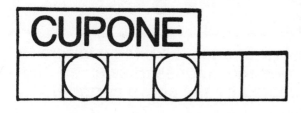

CUPONE

WALLPAPERING IS EASY ONCE YOU GET THIS.

Now arrange the circled letters to form the surprise answer, as suggested by the above cartoon.

Print answer here: THE   IT

JUMBLE®

Unscramble these four Jumbles,
one letter to each square, to form
four ordinary words.

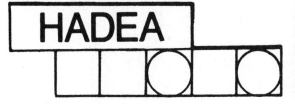

HADEA

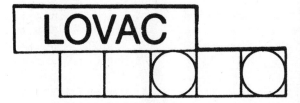

LOVAC

CEEDIT

TAKEGS

WHAT THE
POLITICIAN DID WHEN
HIS OPPONENT
"LAID AN EGG."

Now arrange the circled letters to
form the surprise answer, as suggested by the above cartoon.

Print answer here:

JUMBLE.

Unscramble these four Jumbles, one letter to each square, to form four ordinary words.

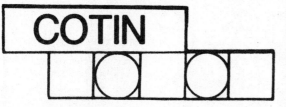

COTIN

MASCH

ROLARP

SURIAD

I know I'm going to hate the people there—I'm too good for them

THE EGOTIST FOUND FAULT WITH EVERYTHING EXCEPT THIS.

Now arrange the circled letters to form the surprise answer, as suggested by the above cartoon.

Print answer here:

JUMBLE ®

Unscramble these four Jumbles,
one letter to each square, to form
four ordinary words.

SWYNE

TAVIL

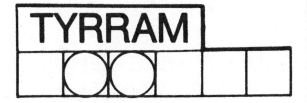

TYRRAM

VEECAL

SOME PEOPLE ARE
RICHER THAN OTHERS—
WHICH PROVES THAT
WEALTH MAY BE
ONLY THIS.

Now arrange the circled letters to
form the surprise answer, as suggested by the above cartoon.

Print answer here: "

"

JUMBLE.

Unscramble these four Jumbles,
one letter to each square, to form
four ordinary words.

LIXEE

STRUY

TRAGEY

GARCHE

He left nothing but debts

WHAT THE SPEND-
THRIFT ENDED UP
MAKING.

Now arrange the circled letters to
form the surprise answer, as suggested by the above cartoon.

Answer: HIS "⬭⬭⬭⬭⬭⬭" TURN ⬭⬭⬭⬭

JUMBLE.

Unscramble these four Jumbles,
one letter to each square, to form
four ordinary words.

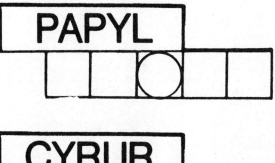
PAPYL

CYRUR

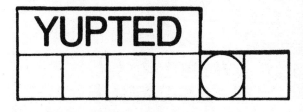
YUPTED

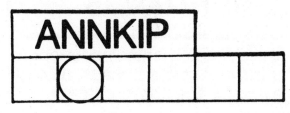
ANNKIP

WHAT KIND OF
ATTENTION DID THE
CHAIRMAN GET WHEN
HE RAPPED WITH
HIS GAVEL?

Now arrange the circled letters to
form the surprise answer, as suggested by the above cartoon.

Print answer here:

JUMBLE.

Unscramble these four Jumbles, one letter to each square, to form four ordinary words.

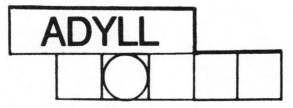
ADYLL

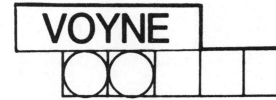
VOYNE

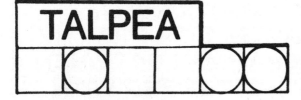
TALPEA

ECHTIC

Careful, you'll wrinkle my suit

WHAT AN IMPECCABLE CON MAN IS.

Now arrange the circled letters to form the surprise answer, as suggested by the above cartoon.

Answer here: A

JUMBLE.

Unscramble these four Jumbles,
one letter to each square, to form
four ordinary words.

GOSUB

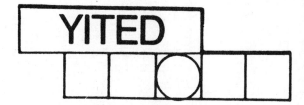

YITED

BYBURG

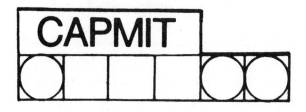

CAPMIT

She never asks
where I've been

WHAT A WIFE
WITHOUT CURIOSITY
COULD BE.

Now arrange the circled letters to
form the surprise answer, as suggested by the above cartoon.

Print answer here: A

JUMBLE.

Unscramble these four Jumbles,
one letter to each square, to form
four ordinary words.

NILER

MUPIO

TORRCE

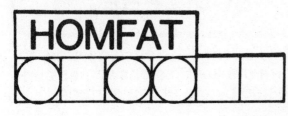

HOMFAT

Wish I had his
bank account

SOME PEOPLE
SCRATCH FOR MONEY;
OTHERS DO THIS.

Now arrange the circled letters to
form the surprise answer, as suggested by the above cartoon.

Print answer here:

JUMBLE.

Unscramble these four Jumbles,
one letter to each square, to form
four ordinary words.

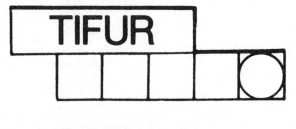

TIFUR

DUIHM

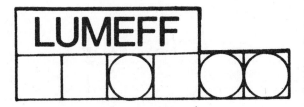

LUMEFF

CLAICO

WHY NO ONE
LAUGHED AT THAT
JOKE ABOUT THE
BROKEN HEATING
SYSTEM.

Now arrange the circled letters to
form the surprise answer, as suggested by the above cartoon.

Answer here: IT  THEM

JUMBLE.

Unscramble these four Jumbles,
one letter to each square, to form
four ordinary words.

LYMAN

REESA

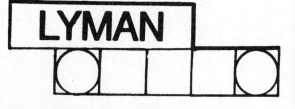

HOYBIS

WEENST

You're always right, J.P.!

HE OWES HIS
SUCCESS NOT TO
WHAT HE "KNOWS,"
BUT TO THIS.

Now arrange the circled letters to
form the surprise answer, as suggested by the above cartoon.

Answer: ⬭⬭⬭⬭ HE "⬭⬭⬭⬭⬭⬭"

JUMBLE®

Unscramble these four Jumbles,
one letter to each square, to form
four ordinary words.

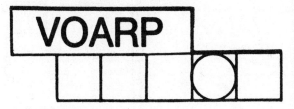
VOARP

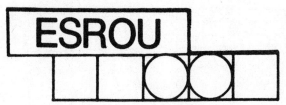
ESROU

HARMIO

WHAREK

THE LOAFER PUT
MORE HOURS IN
HIS WORK THAN
THIS.

Now arrange the circled letters to
form the surprise answer, as suggested by the above cartoon.

Answer here:  IN HIS

JUMBLE®

Unscramble these four Jumbles,
one letter to each square, to form
four ordinary words.

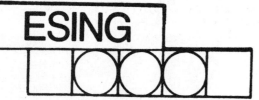

ESING

DYNOW

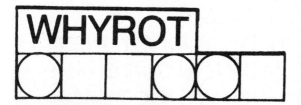

WHYROT

GYLINK

ANOTHER NAME
FOR A SUIT OF
ARMOR.

Now arrange the circled letters to
form the surprise answer, as suggested by the above cartoon.

Answer: A "◯◯◯◯◯◯ ◯◯◯◯◯"

JUMBLE.

Unscramble these four Jumbles, one letter to each square, to form four ordinary words.

VEVER

TUNDA

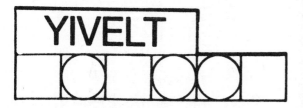

YIVELT

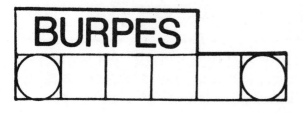

BURPES

WHAT THE ROBOT SURGEON OPERATED ON.

Now arrange the circled letters to form the surprise answer, as suggested by the above cartoon.

Print answer here:

427

JUMBLE®

Unscramble these four Jumbles, one letter to each square, to form four ordinary words.

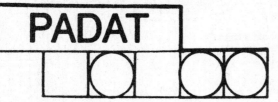

PADAT

TARFD

ROBRAW

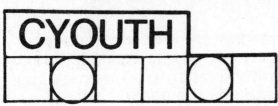

CYOUTH

WHY WAS HE SUCH A GREAT COOK?

Now arrange the circled letters to form the surprise answer, as suggested by the above cartoon.

Answer: HE ◯◯◯ THE ◯◯◯ ◯◯◯ IT

JUMBLE®

Unscramble these four Jumbles, one letter to each square, to form four ordinary words.

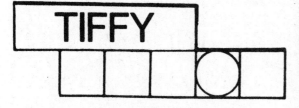
TIFFY

IRROG

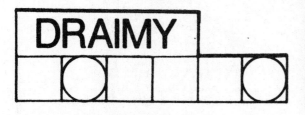
DRAIMY

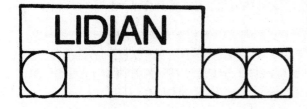
LIDIAN

I wish others would also be concerned about the neighborhood

SOMEBODY WHO CALLS A SPADE A SPADE MIGHT WANT TO GIVE YOU THIS.

Now arrange the circled letters to form the surprise answer, as suggested by the above cartoon.

 **Answer here:** A  " "

JUMBLE.

Unscramble these four Jumbles,
one letter to each square, to form
four ordinary words.

KULCC

LAQUI

UMDAAR

KEENAW

WHAT THE
ARTIST TURNED
COWBOY WAS.

Now arrange the circled letters to
form the surprise answer, as suggested by the above cartoon.

Answer: ◯◯◯◯◯◯ ON THE ◯◯◯◯◯

JUMBLE.

Unscramble these four Jumbles, one letter to each square, to form four ordinary words.

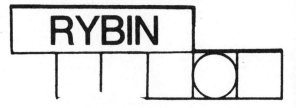
RYBIN

CAUTE

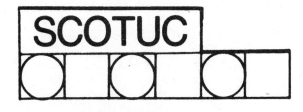
SCOTUC

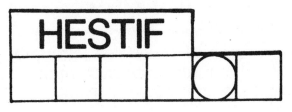
HESTIF

WHEN HIS WIFE GAVE BIRTH TO QUINTUPLETS, HE COULD HARDLY BELIEVE THIS.

Now arrange the circled letters to form the surprise answer, as suggested by the above cartoon.

Print answer here: HIS "  "

JUMBLE.

Unscramble these four Jumbles,
one letter to each square, to form
four ordinary words.

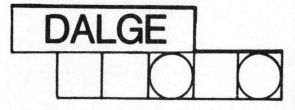

DALGE

YEEND

RENITE

NADDIC

WHERE DO ZOMBIES
LIKE TO SIT
WHEN THEY GO TO
THE MOVIES?

Now arrange the circled letters to
form the surprise answer, as suggested by the above cartoon.

Answer here:

JUMBLE®

Unscramble these four Jumbles,
one letter to each square, to form
four ordinary words.

UPTIL

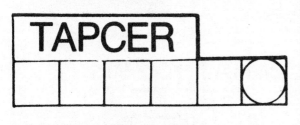

ASTUE

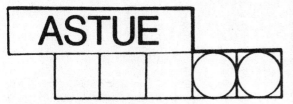

TAPCER

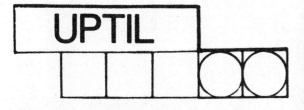

OOLANG

Maybe I'm too
tough on them

WHAT TEACHER
SAID WHEN HE SAT
ON A TACK.

Now arrange the circled letters to
form the surprise answer, as suggested by the above cartoon.

Print answer here: ◯◯◯ THE ◯◯◯◯◯◯

JUMBLE.

Unscramble these four Jumbles, one letter to each square, to form four ordinary words.

CHUGO

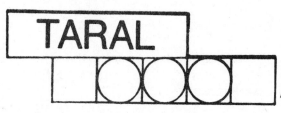

TARAL

SLARIO

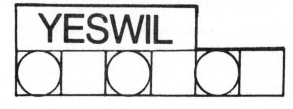

YESWIL

I hear it's terrific

WHAT YOU MIGHT SEE AT A PLANETARIUM.

Now arrange the circled letters to form the surprise answer, as suggested by the above cartoon.

Answer: AN ◯◯◯ - ◯◯◯◯◯ ◯◯◯◯◯

JUMBLE.

Unscramble these four Jumbles,
one letter to each square, to form
four ordinary words.

LOFOR

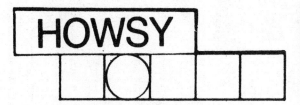

HOWSY

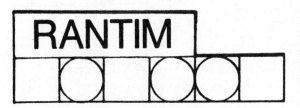

RANTIM

DORPAN

WHAT HE DID
EVERY TIME HE
BOUGHT A SUIT.

Now arrange the circled letters to
form the surprise answer, as suggested by the above cartoon.

Print answer here:

JUMBLE.

Unscramble these four Jumbles, one letter to each square, to form four ordinary words.

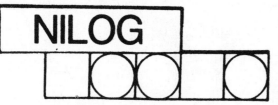

NILOG

CUIJY

ENMECT

HONGIM

Serves me right for hiring that shyster

WHAT A LAWYER SOMETIMES HELPS YOU GET.

Now arrange the circled letters to form the surprise answer, as suggested by the above cartoon.

Answer: WHAT'S ⬡⬡⬡⬡⬡⬡⬡ TO ⬡⬡⬡

JUMBLE®

Unscramble these four Jumbles,
one letter to each square, to form
four ordinary words.

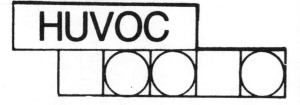
HUVOC

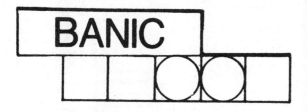
BANIC

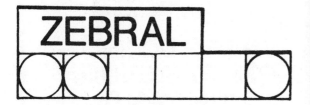
ZEBRAL

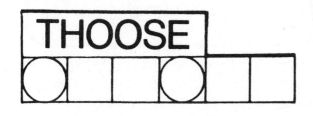
THOOSE

Don't pay any
attention to
any of that

WHAT WAS ALL
THAT TALK DOWN
AT THE GARBAGE
DUMP?

Now arrange the circled letters to
form the surprise answer, as suggested by the above cartoon.

Answer: A  OF

JUMBLE®

Unscramble these four Jumbles, one letter to each square, to form four ordinary words.

NAIPO

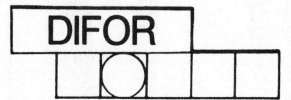

DIFOR

UNGOAT

RACCES

WHEN LOOKING FOR BARGAINS, YOU MIGHT GO THERE.

Now arrange the circled letters to form the surprise answer, as suggested by the above cartoon.

Answer: WHERE THE " ◯◯◯◯◯◯◯◯ " ◯◯

JUMBLE.

Unscramble these four Jumbles,
one letter to each square, to form
four ordinary words.

LOOGI

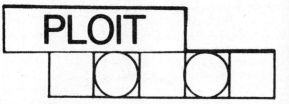
PLOIT

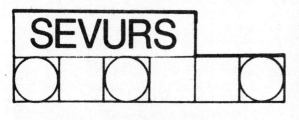
SEVURS

PUNACK

Those coins are meat
for that monster

WHAT THE BROKEN
SOFT DRINK
MACHINE WAS.

Now arrange the circled letters to
form the surprise answer, as suggested by the above cartoon.

Answer: " ◯◯◯◯ – ◯◯◯◯◯◯◯◯ "

JUMBLE.

Unscramble these four Jumbles,
one letter to each square, to form
four ordinary words.

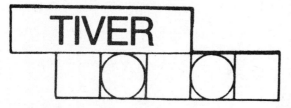

TIVER

WULAF

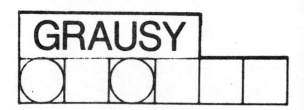

GRAUSY

CLISHE

I hope we're as smart
as we think we are

WHAT GOOD
CAMOUFLAGE IS.

Now arrange the circled letters to
form the surprise answer, as suggested by the above cartoon.

Print answer here:

JUMBLE®

Unscramble these four Jumbles, one letter to each square, to form four ordinary words.

RIQUE

ENSIO

CLEFEE

TERRAH

WHAT THAT GREAT HORROR FILM WAS.

Now arrange the circled letters to form the surprise answer, as suggested by the above cartoon.

Answer: "☐☐☐☐☐☐ - ☐☐☐☐"

JUMBLE.

Unscramble these four Jumbles,
one letter to each square, to form
four ordinary words.

BELZA

ORFYT

KLINTE

CURPSE

Move it!

WHAT TO DO
ABOUT SQUEAKY
FURNITURE WHEELS.

Now arrange the circled letters to
form the surprise answer, as suggested by the above cartoon.

Answer: USE "◯◯◯◯◯◯◯" ◯◯◯

JUMBLE®

Unscramble these four Jumbles,
one letter to each square, to form
four ordinary words.

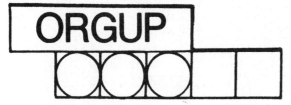

ORGUP

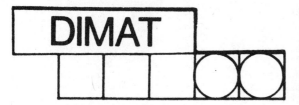

DIMAT

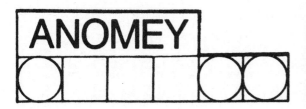

ANOMEY

CLUSKE

YAK YAK YAK YAK

A TIRESOME
PERSON ALWAYS
TAKES HIS TIME
DOING THIS.

Now arrange the circled letters to
form the surprise answer, as suggested by the above cartoon.

Answer here:

JUMBLE.

Unscramble these four Jumbles, one letter to each square, to form four ordinary words.

CHOPE

GATEA

AMMAND

LAGYAX

WHAT THE VICTIM THOUGHT WHEN THE ROBBER STUFFED HIS MOUTH WITH A DIRTY CLOTH.

Now arrange the circled letters to form the surprise answer, as suggested by the above cartoon.

Answer: " THAT'S   "

JUMBLE.

Unscramble these four Jumbles, one letter to each square, to form four ordinary words.

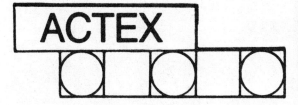

ACTEX

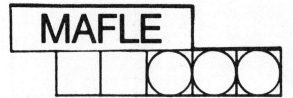

MAFLE

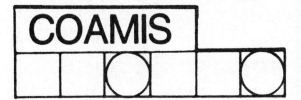

COAMIS

WHARRO

WHAT DO GHOSTS EAT FOR BREAKFAST?

Now arrange the circled letters to form the surprise answer, as suggested by the above cartoon.

Answer: ⬡⬡⬡⬡⬡⬡ OF ⬡⬡⬡⬡⬡

JUMBLE.

Unscramble these four Jumbles, one letter to each square, to form four ordinary words.

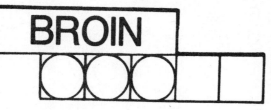

BROIN

PEELO

MYCLAB

ORSOUP

SEEMS TO GROW ABUNDANTLY IN THIS YARD.

Now arrange the circled letters to form the surprise answer, as suggested by the above cartoon.

Answer here: A

JUMBLE®

Unscramble these four Jumbles, one letter to each square, to form four ordinary words.

EUQUE

REBET

PHORGE

MEESID

He's as powerful as any ruler in history

WHAT THE ROPE TYCOON BUILT.

Now arrange the circled letters to form the surprise answer, as suggested by the above cartoon.

Answer here: A HUGE "◯◯◯◯ – ◯◯◯"

JUMBLE.

Unscramble these four Jumbles, one letter to each square, to form four ordinary words.

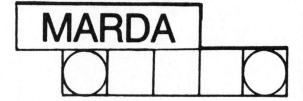

MARDA

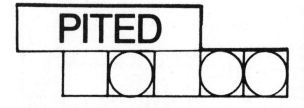

PITED

CRUSIC

INVOCE

I don't understand this

WHAT YOU SHOULD GET BEFORE IN- VESTING IN EXPENSIVE AUDIO EQUIPMENT.

Now arrange the circled letters to form the surprise answer, as suggested by the above cartoon.

Answer: " ⬡⬡⬡⬡⬡ " ⬡⬡⬡⬡⬡⬡

JUMBLE®

Unscramble these four Jumbles, one letter to each square, to form four ordinary words.

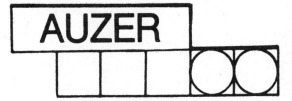

AUZER

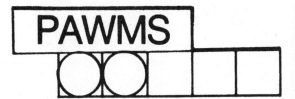

PAWMS

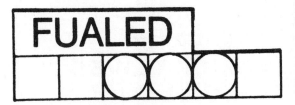

FUALED

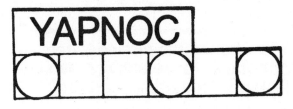

YAPNOC

He'd do a lot of good if he weren't so long-winded

WHAT MANY A PUBLIC SPEAKER DEVOTES HIS LIFE TO.

Now arrange the circled letters to form the surprise answer, as suggested by the above cartoon.

Answer: A "⬚⬚⬚⬚⬚⬚" ⬚⬚⬚⬚⬚⬚

JUMBLE.

Unscramble these four Jumbles, one letter to each square, to form four ordinary words.

SCUHR

AMMAD

ROCCEE

NICCIP

I'm getting hungry

Here's a quarter, go get me the special sandwich at that greasy spoon

A MISER LIVES POOR SO HE CAN DO THIS.

Now arrange the circled letters to form the surprise answer, as suggested by the above cartoon.

Print answer here:

JUMBLE®

Unscramble these four Jumbles,
one letter to each square, to form
four ordinary words.

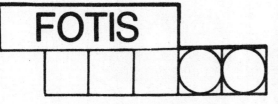

FOTIS

CIHRB

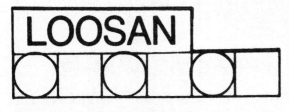

LOOSAN

SESAUR

We won—but after the
legal expenses, I
don't know...

THESE WORDS SOME-
TIMES DESCRIBE
A LAW SUIT.

Now arrange the circled letters to
form the surprise answer, as suggested by the above cartoon.

Print answer here: A

JUMBLE®

Unscramble these four Jumbles,
one letter to each square, to form
four ordinary words.

YONOL
☐☐◯☐☐

INBAR
☐◯◯☐☐

GUDEMS
◯◯☐☐☐◯☐

STOLCY
☐◯◯☐◯☐

WHERE YOU MIGHT
FIND THOSE OPTOMETRY
STUDENTS.

Now arrange the circled letters to
form the surprise answer, as suggested by the above cartoon.

Answer: IN THE " ◯◯◯◯◯◯ " ◯◯◯◯

Challenger

JUMBO

JUMBLE®

"I enjoy the
Jumble® books
and tell all my
friends about
them. What
better way
to enjoy life
than books."

**TONY LUCIANO
LIVERMORE FALLS, ME**

JUMBLE®

Unscramble these six Jumbles,
one letter to each square,
to form six ordinary words.

FLUTIE

TILPUF

RIMPER

CEVIED

HAWRTT

INDOOM

WHY ATLAS WAS
ARRESTED.

Now arrange the circled letters
to form the surprise answer, as
suggested by the above cartoon.

Print the
ANSWER here   HE ⬡⬡⬡⬡ ⬡⬡ THE ⬡⬡⬡⬡⬡

PUZZLE # 452

JUMBLE®

Unscramble these six Jumbles,
one letter to each square,
to form six ordinary words.

GINTRY

BOALIN

RUBBUS

FREBLY

TELLMA

CEDITE

A MAN WHO LIKES
YOU TO BE AT HIS
SERVICE.

Now arrange the circled letters
to form the surprise answer, as
suggested by the above cartoon.

Print the SURPRISE ANSWER here   THE ◯◯◯◯◯◯◯◯◯

JUMBLE®

Unscramble these six Jumbles,
one letter to each square,
to form six ordinary words.

HEHRST

ELFENN

YARRIT

KEEBAT

NEDDAW

CLAMBY

WHAT THE FEUDING
BRICKLAYERS
FINALLY DID.

Now arrange the circled letters
to form the surprise answer, as
suggested by the above cartoon.

Print the SURPRISE
ANSWER here

JUMBLE®

Unscramble these six Jumbles,
one letter to each square,
to form six ordinary words.

YESGER

NUCHEQ

WOCALL

CUSTOC

VAHLED

TOBUNT

WHAT HAPPENED WHEN
GOLIATH TRIED
SOME POT.

Now arrange the circled letters
to form the surprise answer, as
suggested by the above cartoon.

Print the SURPRISE ANSWER here   HE ☐☐☐ ☐☐☐☐☐☐

JUMBLE®

Unscramble these six Jumbles,
one letter to each square,
to form six ordinary words.

FLUWAL

WARIAY

BELUBB

PINGAY

GARNAH

NORGAD

You're
looking
better

WHAT A HUSBAND
WHO HAD RECENTLY
BEEN ILL SEEMED
TO BE DOING.

Now arrange the circled letters
to form the surprise answer, as
suggested by the above cartoon.

Print the SURPRISE
ANSWER here

JUMBLE®

Unscramble these six Jumbles, one letter to each square, to form six ordinary words.

COYTUR

HEEBAD

TISSAD

DEAGAN

NOSHET

ORDINO

THE FARMER RAISED HIS BOY TO BE A BOOTBLACK BECAUSE HE WANTED TO DO THIS.

Now arrange the circled letters to form the surprise answer, as suggested by the above cartoon.

ANSWER here   MAKE ⬜⭕⭕⭕ WHILE THE ⭕⭕⭕⭕ ⭕⭕⭕⭕⭕⭕⭕

JUMBLE®

Unscramble these six Jumbles,
one letter to each square,
to form six ordinary words.

LAYREY

STIGED

MEETOL

GANTEM

TAIREW

PARPEA

1970

46 . . .
47 . . .
48 . . .

WHAT 1969 PENNIES
ARE WORTH THIS YEAR.

Now arrange the circled letters
to form the surprise answer, as
suggested by the above cartoon.

ANSWER here   ALMOST

JUMBLE®

Unscramble these six Jumbles,
one letter to each square,
to form six ordinary words.

LINCEY

DORRIT

REMMEB

HESKAN

GAHOME

LAASSI

This'll
make
you
well!

HOW A WESTERN DOCTOR
MIGHT GIVE YOU
AN INOCULATION.

Now arrange the circled letters
to form the surprise answer, as
suggested by the above cartoon.

ANSWER
here WITH HIS ⬡⬡⬡⬡⬡ ⬡⬡⬡⬡⬡⬡⬡

JUMBLE®

Unscramble these six Jumbles,
one letter to each square,
to form six ordinary words.

FLAHBE

REVORF

GAMIPE

RAHDLE

YUNASE

LEPPUR

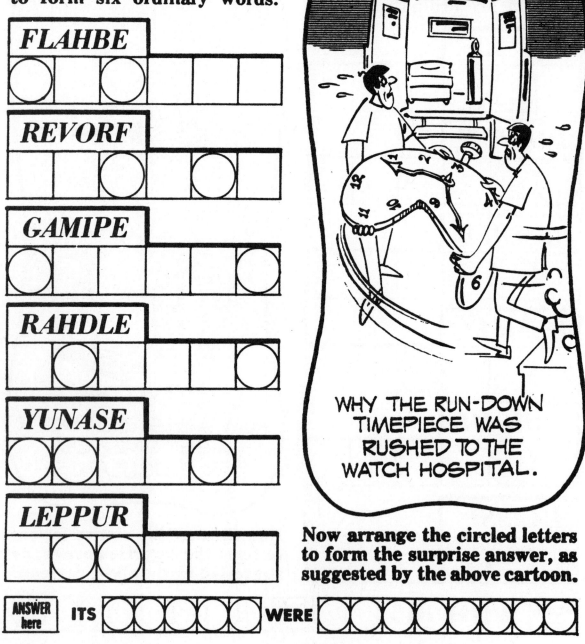

WHY THE RUN-DOWN
TIMEPIECE WAS
RUSHED TO THE
WATCH HOSPITAL.

Now arrange the circled letters
to form the surprise answer, as
suggested by the above cartoon.

ANSWER here   ITS ○○○○○ WERE ○○○○○○○○○

JUMBLE®

Unscramble these six Jumbles,
one letter to each square,
to form six ordinary words.

FICTEN

INTOOM

WRALEY

HOGUNE

PARULL

SILCHE

WHAT TO GET WHEN
YOUR DIET FAILS.

Now arrange the circled letters
to form the surprise answer, as
suggested by the above cartoon.

Print the SURPRISE ANSWER here

JUMBLE®

Unscramble these six Jumbles, one letter to each square, to form six ordinary words.

YUPRIF

STAFIE

CRYGLE

SENNIG

WOBETS

GESTAK

How much this time?

BILL

ONE OF THE MOST EXPENSIVE THINGS A HUSBAND HAS TO FACE.

Now arrange the circled letters to form the surprise answer, as suggested by the above cartoon.

ANSWER here ◯◯◯◯◯◯◯ **UP HIS** ◯◯◯◯◯'◯

JUMBLE®

Unscramble these six Jumbles,
one letter to each square,
to form six ordinary words.

YETTIN

GLINTE

ROHRRO

GRIBED

THACCY

MIRADS

DETERGENTS

WHAT YOU GENERALLY
GET BEFORE YOU DO
THE LAUNDRY.

Now arrange the circled letters
to form the surprise answer, as
suggested by the above cartoon.

Print the SURPRISE
ANSWER here

THE ◯◯◯◯◯◯◯ ◯◯◯◯◯

JUMBLE®

Unscramble these six Jumbles,
one letter to each square,
to form six ordinary words.

YIMWAD

DEXENP

BRENAT

TYNTOK

TORTOG

DISPUT

WHAT A HUSBAND WHO
WON'T STAND FOR HIS
WIFE'S EXTRAVAGANCE
WILL PROBABLY
HAVE TO DO.

Now arrange the circled letters
to form the surprise answer, as
suggested by the above cartoon.

ANSWER here ○○○○ IT ○○○○○○○○○ ○○○○

JUMBLE®

Unscramble these six Jumbles, one letter to each square, to form six ordinary words.

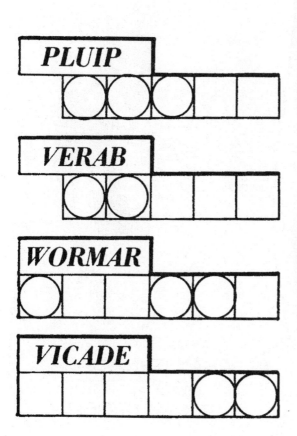

PLUIP

VERAB

WORMAR

VICADE

KEEP AMERICA BEAUTIFUL

THIS MIGHT GROW IN A JUNKYARD.

Now arrange the circled letters to form the surprise answer, as suggested by the above cartoon.

Print the SURPRISE ANSWER here

A

JUMBLE®

Unscramble these six Jumbles,
one letter to each square,
to form six ordinary words.

SHABIN

COSTAM

YADDLE

ARUSSE

NAUGIA

TILBEG

He must
know
PLENTY!

Next!

But he
won't
talk!

WHAT THEY SAID
ABOUT THE
PSYCHIATRIST.

Now arrange the circled letters
to form the surprise answer, as
suggested by the above cartoon.

ANSWER here "⬭⬭⬭⬭'⬭ **HIS** ⬭⬭⬭⬭⬭⬭⬭⬭⬭

JUMBLE®

Unscramble these six Jumbles, one letter to each square, to form six ordinary words.

FLIDED

DINTUC

HAIDAL

LOWELY

RITHEE

FRIEVY

No problem now

HOW TO STOP THAT NOISE IN YOUR CAR.

New arrange the circled letters to form the surprise answer, as suggested by the above cartoon.

ANSWER here [ ][ ][ ] **YOUR** [ ][ ][ ][ ][ ] [ ][ ][ ][ ][ ]

JUMBLE®

Unscramble these six Jumbles,
one letter to each square,
to form six ordinary words.

GOIBLE

SLUIBY

KINNAP

CHYSIP

BERKAM

COATIN

Horace, you're not
paying attention!

WHAT THE
ABSENTMINDED BOY
THOUGHT HE'D DO.

Now arrange the circled letters
to form the surprise answer, as
suggested by the above cartoon.

Print the SURPRISE ANSWER here

JUMBLE®

Unscramble these six Jumbles, one letter to each square, to form six ordinary words.

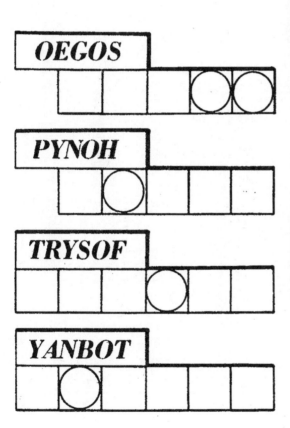

OEGOS

PYNOH

TRYSOF

YANBOT

I'm right!

DRUGS

No, I'm right!

ODD IF THEY'RE BOTH RIGHT!

Now arrange the circled letters to form the surprise answer, as suggested by the above cartoon.

 Print the ANSWER here

JUMBLE®

Unscramble these six Jumbles,
one letter to each square,
to form six ordinary words.

ENSCOD

GURFEE

SOWDRY

REDAIM

YULNOH

TESKAB

WHAT COLOR DID HE
PAINT THE SUN
AND THE WIND?

Now arrange the circled letters
to form the surprise answer, as
suggested by the above cartoon.

ANSWER here THE ⬚⬚⬚ ⬚⬚⬚⬚ , THE ⬚⬚⬚⬚ ⬚⬚⬚⬚

JUMBLE®

Unscramble these six Jumbles, one letter to each square, to form six ordinary words.

ENCLIP

TALCOE

DEBLOH

CLUDGE

BUCTAD

MEUMIN

WHAT THE SAILOR IN THE TOP BUNK WAS.

Now arrange the circled letters to form the surprise answer, as suggested by the above cartoon.

Print the SURPRISE ANSWER here

JUMBLE®

Unscramble these six Jumbles,
one letter to each square,
to form six ordinary words.

ZARQUT

TUSALE

SURSED

CATCEN

LICIAT

SLAQUL

WHAT TEARS ARE FOR
MANY A WIFE.

INVEST-
MENTS

Now arrange the circled letters
to form the surprise answer, as
suggested by the above cartoon.

Print the SURPRISE
ANSWER here

JUMBLE®

Unscramble these six Jumbles,
one letter to each square,
to form six ordinary words.

GALENT

BOTERD

LIKALA

HUNCAL

PHISOL

TUFACE

WHAT TO WEAR WHEN
YOU'RE GOING TO JUMP
OUT OF THE WINDOW.

Now arrange the circled letters
to form the surprise answer, as
suggested by the above cartoon.

Print the
ANSWER here   A

JUMBLE®

Unscramble these six Jumbles,
one letter to each square,
to form six ordinary words.

JUINER

THARGE

KEPCAT

BAAMEO

INTIEF

GAVESA

WHAT THE SPANISH
FISHERMAN TURNED
DANCER PLAYED.

Now arrange the circled letters
to form the surprise answer, as
suggested by the above cartoon.

Print the SURPRISE
ANSWER here

THE "⬡⬡⬡⬡ - ⬡ - ⬡⬡⬡"

JUMBLE®

Unscramble these six Jumbles, one letter to each square, to form six ordinary words.

THERAH

STEWID

CRYLEE

UNEAVE

MINDOO

HATTUG

WHAT THE THIEF GOT.

Now arrange the circled letters to form the surprise answer, as suggested by the above cartoon.

Print the SURPRISE ANSWER here

JUMBLE®

Unscramble these six Jumbles,
one letter to each square,
to form six ordinary words.

TUGONI

COHBOR

CAFEDE

RETHOM

PANKID

LIPOCE

MR. BIG

WHAT THE PRETZEL
KING MADE.

Now arrange the circled letters
to form the surprise answer, as
suggested by the above cartoon.

Print the SURPRISE
ANSWER here

JUMBLE®

Unscramble these six Jumbles,
one letter to each square,
to form six ordinary words.

STENOX

TOMSED

KRANET

FLUEYE

TONBEN

NEPAHP

WHAT THE MOTHER
GHOST SAID TO THE
BABY GHOST.

Now arrange the circled letters
to form the surprise answer, as
suggested by the above cartoon.

ANSWER here ◯◯◯◯◯◯ **YOUR** ◯◯◯◯◯◯ ◯◯◯◯

JUMBLE®

Unscramble these six Jumbles, one letter to each square, to form six ordinary words.

TYMARR

CLOIPY

MORNIF

YAMBIG

CLINOU

DUNBOA

Wow! That should reduce the cost of living!

WHAT GEORGE WASHINGTON MADE.

Now arrange the circled letters to form the surprise answer, as suggested by the above cartoon.

Print the SURPRISE ANSWER here

A

480

JUMBLE®

Unscramble these six Jumbles,
one letter to each square,
to form six ordinary words.

SWUINE

TENOPT

MODCEY

FRIMAF

CLAISO

TRUFUE

WHAT HE SAID WHEN
THE JUDGE INFORMED
HIM THAT HE'D BEEN
BROUGHT BEFORE THE
COURT FOR DRINKING.

Now arrange the circled letters
to form the surprise answer, as
suggested by the above cartoon.

Print the SURPRISE
ANSWER here ⬡⬡⬡'⬡ **GET** ⬡⬡⬡⬡⬡⬡⬡⬡

JUMBLE®

Unscramble these six Jumbles, one letter to each square, to form six ordinary words.

NORBEK

DARZIL

RELAFT

THROCC

PIRAMI

ALPECA

THEY GAVE THE CROOK A BATH SO HE COULD DO THIS.

Now arrange the circled letters to form the surprise answer, as suggested by the above cartoon.

Print the SURPRISE ANSWER here " ◯◯◯◯ ◯◯◯◯◯ "

JUMBLE®

Unscramble these six Jumbles, one letter to each square, to form six ordinary words.

PASTEC

THOGTE

DOWMIS

FLERBY

LONPEL

BAACAN

Darn!

WHY THE VAMPIRE AVOIDED HER.

Now arrange the circled letters to form the surprise answer, as suggested by the above cartoon.

Print the ANSWER here

JUMBLE®

Unscramble these six Jumbles,
one letter to each square,
to form six ordinary words.

TOESGO

PLUXED

CARCIT

RAYTLE

DROINO

GLYFAD

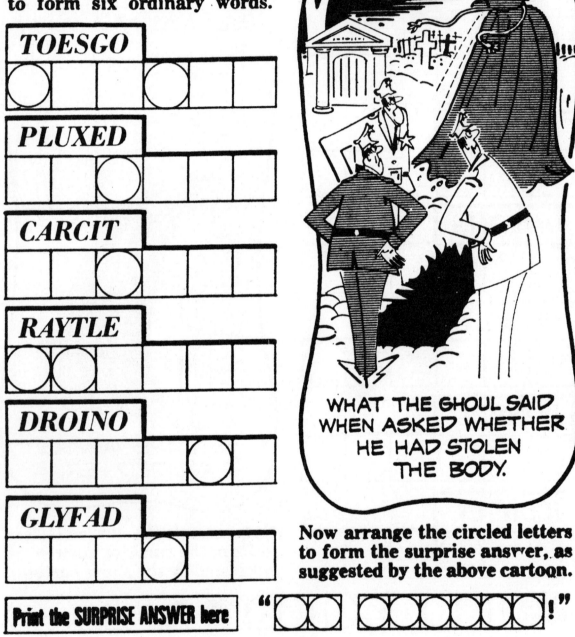

WHAT THE GHOUL SAID
WHEN ASKED WHETHER
HE HAD STOLEN
THE BODY.

Now arrange the circled letters
to form the surprise answer, as
suggested by the above cartoon.

Print the SURPRISE ANSWER here   " ⭕⭕ ⭕⭕⭕⭕⭕⭕⭕ ! "

JUMBLE®

Unscramble these six Jumbles, one letter to each square, to form six ordinary words.

SPOLGE

RIELOO

BOTHED

UNRATT

YIRAWA

BEEKAT

AN ALARM CLOCK CAN SCARE THIS.

Now arrange the circled letters to form the surprise answer, as suggested by the above cartoon.

ANSWER here **THE** ◯◯◯◯◯◯◯◯ ◯◯◯◯ **YOU**

485

JUMBLE®

Unscramble these six Jumbles,
one letter to each square,
to form six ordinary words.

CURPES

JEDGAG

LICTIE

ZULZEG

YUNCAL

SMOIGE

DIVORCES

WHY SOME COUPLES
GO TO "COURT."

Now arrange the circled letters
to form the surprise answer, as
suggested by the above cartoon.

Print the SURPRISE
ANSWER here TO

JUMBLE ®

Unscramble these six Jumbles,
one letter to each square,
to form six ordinary words.

ENTGAM

GROJAN

DAVULE

TOUTLE

WRAITE

LABBED

How
about
one of
your
famous
sandwiches?

IN OLDEN TIMES
THIS WAS OFTEN
TURNED OUT BY A
WELL-BRED MAID.

Now arrange the circled letters
to form the surprise answer, as
suggested by the above cartoon.

Print the SURPRISE
ANSWER here

◯◯◯◯ - ◯◯◯◯◯ ◯◯◯◯◯

JUMBLE.

Unscramble these six Jumbles, one letter to each square, to form six ordinary words.

DIPALL

CINTAG

HERTIE

COALJE

DEFUNC

OKOCIE

HEE HO

HOO HOO

WHY HE DIED LAUGHING.

Now arrange the circled letters to form the surprise answer, as suggested by the above cartoon.

ANSWER here HE WAS ⬚⬚⬚⬚⬚⬚⬚⬚ TO ⬚⬚⬚⬚⬚

JUMBLE®

Unscramble these six Jumbles, one letter to each square, to form six ordinary words.

RITTHY

HINSIF

ASCUBA

ENWAKE

REVABE

DRAPEA

EEK!

WHAT YOU GET WHEN YOU'RE KIDNAPPED BY A GHOST.

Now arrange the circled letters to form the surprise answer, as suggested by the above cartoon.

Print the SURPRISE ANSWER here

JUMBLE®

Unscramble these six Jumbles,
one letter to each square,
to form six ordinary words.

VEELEN

TRAULB

DINGHI

SHUBAM

UNDIPT

NECNAD

What
about
your
diet?

HE BLUSHED RIGHT
DOWN TO HIS
FINGERTIPS BECAUSE
HE WAS THIS.

Now arrange the circled letters
to form the surprise answer, as
suggested by the above cartoon.

ANSWER
here
⬡⬡⬡⬡⬡⬡ ⬡⬡⬡–⬡⬡⬡⬡⬡⬡

JUMBLE®

Unscramble these six Jumbles,
one letter to each square,
to form six ordinary words.

MARKEB

NOALOS

EXDOUT

DRIHNE

GLACEY

CHISPY

WHAT HE WAS WHEN
HE FOUND A PEARL
IN THE OYSTER.

Now arrange the circled letters
to form the surprise answer, as
suggested by the above cartoon.

Print the SURPRISE
ANSWER here

" ⃝⃝⃝⃝⃝⃝ " ⃝⃝⃝⃝⃝⃝⃝⃝⃝

JUMBLE®

Unscramble these six Jumbles,
one letter to each square,
to form six ordinary words.

FASTIE

UNGOTE

REEBOF

YEMITS

CYTHAC

TELPOI

REAL ESTATE

You now have full title to the house

DEED

YOU MIGHT HAVE A
VESTED INTEREST
IN THIS!

Now arrange the circled letters
to form the surprise answer, as
suggested by the above cartoon.

ANSWER here A ◯◯◯◯◯ - ◯◯◯◯◯◯ ◯◯◯◯

JUMBLE®

Unscramble these six Jumbles,
one letter to each square,
to form six ordinary words.

WECHEN

BOLGEN

SMIDOH

USEBUD

LOSFIS

ENLOUG

WHAT A GOOD
BODY SNATCHER WOULDN'T
BE WITHOUT ON A
NIGHT LIKE THIS.

Now arrange the circled letters
to form the surprise answer, as
suggested by the above cartoon.

Print the SURPRISE
ANSWER here

HIS "⬡⬡⬡⬡⬡⬡-⬡⬡⬡⬡⬡"

JUMBLE®

Unscramble these six Jumbles,
one letter to each square,
to form six ordinary words.

JINNOE

ROPPEH

SMARDI

LOUBES

GIZZAG

YINTTE

AT A PLACE LIKE THIS
EXPECT THEM AT
CLOSING TIME.

Now arrange the circled letters
to form the surprise answer, as
suggested by the above cartoon.

Print the SURPRISE ANSWER here

JUMBLE®

Unscramble these six Jumbles,
one letter to each square,
to form six ordinary words.

TRAWEY

FELBAF

YORCAN

GEOVAY

DEMANT

ENGINS

I refuse to
answer on the grounds . . .
(yak yak yak)

He doesn't say
much but he has
a tough
reputation

WHAT YOU WOULDN'T
EXPECT TO GET
FROM A MAN OF
FEW WORDS.

Now arrange the circled letters
to form the surprise answer, as
suggested by the above cartoon.

Print the SURPRISE
ANSWER here   A

JUMBLE®

Unscramble these six Jumbles,
one letter to each square,
to form six ordinary words.

ANOMEY

GASYRS

DROAFE

RITHED

CLARRO

PRAULB

ADMISSIONS

Darn it—this'll
do it!

WHERE YOU MIGHT TAKE
STEPS TO ENJOY YOUR-
SELF DURING THE
HOLIDAYS.

Now arrange the circled letters
to form the surprise answer, as
suggested by the above cartoon.

Print the SURPRISE ANSWER here

JUMBLE®

Unscramble these six Jumbles,
one letter to each square,
to form six ordinary words.

HOIDAR

TIPIED

BIMGAT

FELGUN

RAHWTT

SELAWE

PEOPLE WHO ARE
THIS HAVE SLIGHTLY
LOWER STANDING.

Now arrange the circled letters
to form the surprise answer, as
suggested by the above cartoon.

Print the
ANSWER here

JUMBLE®

Unscramble these six Jumbles,
one letter to each square, to form
six ordinary words.

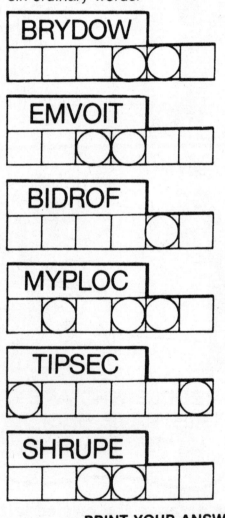

BRYDOW

EMVOIT

BIDROF

MYPLOC

TIPSEC

SHRUPE

WHAT YOU MIGHT
FIND AT A
HAUNTED COLLEGE.

Now arrange the circled letters to
form the surprise answer, as suggested by the above cartoon.

PRINT YOUR ANSWER IN THE CIRCLES BELOW

SOME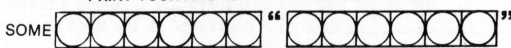

JUMBLE.

Unscramble these six Jumbles, one letter to each square, to form six ordinary words.

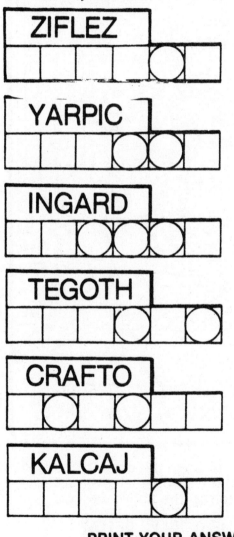

ZIFLEZ

YARPIC

INGARD

TEGOTH

CRAFTO

KALCAJ

You may kiss the bride

WHEN THE BRIDE AND GROOM STARTED QUARRELING, IT MUST HAVE BEEN THIS.

Now arrange the circled letters to form the surprise answer, as suggested by the above cartoon.

PRINT YOUR ANSWER IN THE CIRCLES BELOW

AN "⬡⬡⬡⬡⬡⬡ – ⬡⬡⬡⬡⬡⬡⬡"

JUMBLE.

Unscramble these six Jumbles, one letter to each square, to form six ordinary words.

BEJARB

YALSAW

DIRNEH

TRAUGI

HADILA

VACIDE

How do you like my new designer outfit?

$

WHAT CLOTHES MAKE A WOMAN.

Now arrange the circled letters to form the surprise answer, as suggested by the above cartoon.

PRINT YOUR ANSWER IN THE CIRCLES BELOW

" ⬡⬡⬡⬡⬡ " TO HER ⬡⬡⬡⬡⬡⬡⬡⬡

JUMBLE.

Unscramble these six Jumbles, one letter to each square, to form six ordinary words.

SAYMID

ANNOYE

GROAFE

BRUMPE

FLUINS

TYFARC

Must have had plenty of brains

But he wouldn't part with a penny

WHAT THAT CLEVER MISER WAS.

Now arrange the circled letters to form the surprise answer, as suggested by the above cartoon.

PRINT YOUR ANSWER IN THE CIRCLES BELOW

A ◯◯◯ OF ◯◯◯◯◯ ◯◯◯◯◯◯

JUMBLE®

Unscramble these six Jumbles,
one letter to each square, to form
six ordinary words.

MENECT

GROHPE

MARSID

LEZZUP

FLIECK

SHABIN

AN INSTANT
ON THE LIPS —

Now arrange the circled letters to
form the surprise answer, as suggested by the above cartoon.

PRINT YOUR ANSWER IN THE CIRCLES BELOW

A ⬡⬡⬡⬡⬡⬡⬡⬡⬡ ON THE ⬡⬡⬡⬡

JUMBLE.

Unscramble these six Jumbles,
one letter to each square, to form
six ordinary words.

VIYTLE

SCOMAT

GRANDO

STEMOD

REESHA

TAPECK

They say he's
the best!

MD

WHAT AN
OPHTHALMOLOGIST'S
OFFICE IS.

Now arrange the circled letters to
form the surprise answer, as suggested by the above cartoon.

PRINT YOUR ANSWER IN THE CIRCLES BELOW

A ⬡⬡⬡⬡ FOR ⬡⬡⬡⬡ ⬡⬡⬡⬡

JUMBLE®

Unscramble these six Jumbles,
one letter to each square, to form
six ordinary words.

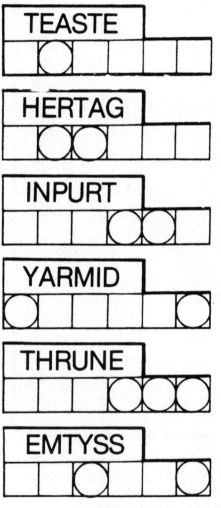

TEASTE

HERTAG

INPURT

YARMID

THRUNE

EMTYSS

Ugh . . . guess I'll
have to get through
another day

WHAT GETTING
UP EARLY
IN THE MORNING
IS A MATTER OF.

Now arrange the circled letters to
form the surprise answer, as suggested by the above cartoon.

PRINT YOUR ANSWER IN THE CIRCLES BELOW

OVER

JUMBLE.

Unscramble these six Jumbles,
one letter to each square, to form
six ordinary words.

CANTIG

UMLOVE

TYNTOK

PHISOL

JOBTEC

DRAISH

WHAT OVEREATING
MIGHT MAKE YOU.

Now arrange the circled letters to
form the surprise answer, as suggested by the above cartoon.

PRINT YOUR ANSWER IN THE CIRCLES BELOW

" ☐☐☐☐☐☐ " TO
YOUR ☐☐☐☐☐☐☐☐

JUMBLE.

Unscramble these six Jumbles, one letter to each square, to form six ordinary words.

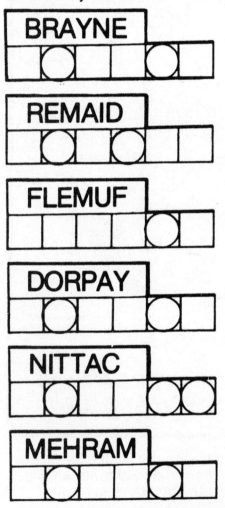

BRAYNE

REMAID

FLEMUF

DORPAY

NITTAC

MEHRAM

WHAT YOU MIGHT EAT AT A BUFFET DINNER.

Now arrange the circled letters to form the surprise answer, as suggested by the above cartoon.

A " ◯◯◯◯◯◯◯◯ " ◯◯◯◯

JUMBLE.

Unscramble these six Jumbles, one letter to each square, to form six ordinary words.

FLUEYE

TUBECK

CITOXE

INQUAT

INGLEM

NESSUC

Mind moving your feet, dear?

WHAT A BIG NOISE AT THE OFFICE OFTEN IS AT HOME.

Now arrange the circled letters to form the surprise answer, as suggested by the above cartoon.

PRINT YOUR ANSWER IN THE CIRCLES BELOW

A

JUMBLE®

Unscramble these six Jumbles,
one letter to each square, to form
six ordinary words.

TEAGEN

YEMILT

TINADY

LOOTIN

NISSIT

POWALL

WHAT AN ATTRACTIVE
SWEATER SOME—
TIMES PULLS.

Now arrange the circled letters to
form the surprise answer, as suggested by the above cartoon.

PRINT YOUR ANSWER IN THE CIRCLES BELOW

◯◯◯'◯◯◯◯◯ OVER THE ◯◯◯◯

JUMBLE.

Unscramble these six Jumbles,
one letter to each square, to form
six ordinary words.

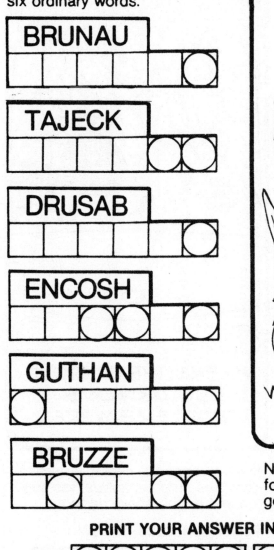

BRUNAU

TAJECK

DRUSAB

ENCOSH

GUTHAN

BRUZZE

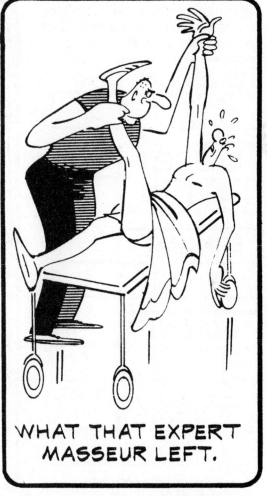

WHAT THAT EXPERT
MASSEUR LEFT.

Now arrange the circled letters to
form the surprise answer, as suggested by the above cartoon.

PRINT YOUR ANSWER IN THE CIRCLES BELOW

NO

JUMBLE®

Unscramble these six Jumbles,
one letter to each square, to form
six ordinary words.

RUBECH

LABBED

MINUME

IMDOYF

BLUHME

LUPPIT

WHERE THE SCHOOL
BUS DRIVER'S
PROBLEMS WERE.

Now arrange the circled letters to
form the surprise answer, as suggested by the above cartoon.

PRINT YOUR ANSWER IN THE CIRCLES BELOW

JUMBLE®

Unscramble these six Jumbles,
one letter to each square, to form
six ordinary words.

PORTHY

GEDUBB

CUMPIE

ANZATS

WYLLOH

DRAFTI

Oops! Sorry,
dear

Cash or
credit?

WHAT THE CLUMSY
PROSECUTOR DID ON
THE SHOPPING TRIP.

Now arrange the circled letters to
form the surprise answer, as suggested by the above cartoon.

PRINT YOUR ANSWER IN THE CIRCLES BELOW

◯◯◯◯◯◯◯ THE ◯◯◯◯◯◯◯

JUMBLE ®

Unscramble these six Jumbles,
one letter to each square, to form
six ordinary words.

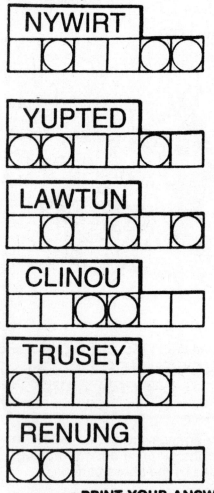

NYWIRT

YUPTED

LAWTUN

CLINOU

TRUSEY

RENUNG

BUILDERS OF
SUMMER HOMES ARE
PART OF THIS.

Now arrange the circled letters to
form the surprise answer, as suggested by the above cartoon.

PRINT YOUR ANSWER IN THE CIRCLES BELOW

A

JUMBLE®

Unscramble these six Jumbles, one letter to each square, to form six ordinary words.

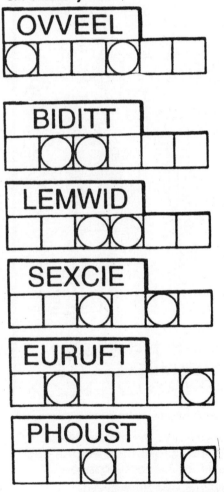

OVVEEL

BIDITT

LEMWID

SEXCIE

EURUFT

PHOUST

HOW THE SCIENTIST SPENT HIS TIME IN PRISON.

Now arrange the circled letters to form the surprise answer, as suggested by the above cartoon.

PRINT YOUR ANSWER IN THE CIRCLES BELOW

HE

JUMBLE®

Unscramble these six Jumbles, one letter to each square, to form six ordinary words.

TEECIX

DEAMOP

OSANTA

COLUNK

LIMSAD

YERMOM

I'll need a new loan

You don't have a very big farm

SPUDS FOR SALE

WHAT THE BANKER CONSIDERED THE FARMER'S LIVELIHOOD.

Now arrange the circled letters to form the surprise answer, as suggested by the above cartoon.

PRINT YOUR ANSWER IN THE CIRCLES BELOW

answers

1. **Jumbles:** ACUTE DAISY PEWTER MUSCLE
   Answer: What happened to the baked goods?—
   THEY WERE "PIE-RATED"

2. **Jumbles:** AWFUL FORTY PROFIT HERMIT
   Answer: What cold cash often makes people do—WARM UP

3. **Jumbles:** ARDOR KNIFE SATIRE RECTOR
   Answer: Where some guys get bright ideas—IN DARK CORNERS

4. **Jumbles:** BASIN MIRTH FUSION PUDDLE
   Answer: Old clothing made from letters—A SUIT OF MAIL

5. **Jumbles:** TIGER AUDIT REBUKE MOHAIR
   Answer: What the medicine man had trouble selling—
   A DRUG ON THE MARKET

6. **Jumbles:** PECAN MERCY OBTUSE INVOKE
   Answer: There is little to see through it—A MICROSCOPE

7. **Jumbles:** OUTDO CLOTH MARAUD GLANCE
   Answer: A note of harmony in most households—"DOUGH"

8. **Jumbles:** HOIST ENSUE CEMENT MUSLIN
   Answer: This tells you what the fare is—THE MENU

9. **Jumbles:** ABBEY CRANK NATURE TIMELY
   Answer: Bigmouthed at the summit!—A CRATER

10. **Jumbles:** DELVE FIFTY TRIPLE INLAID
    Answer: Why the results of his physical were music to his ears—
    HE WAS FIT AS A FIDDLE

11. **Jumbles:** PEONY GRAIN BIKINI SAVORY
    Answer: Once is OK, but a repeat means prison—SING

12. **Jumbles:** MOUSY APPLY WEAKEN TUMULT
    Answer: What the stupid shoplifter was—SLOW ON THE UPTAKE

13. **Jumbles:** RIVET BRAIN CENSUS FACILE
    Answer: The cartoonist drew this in order to hide what he was
    doing—A CURTAIN

14. **Jumbles:** OCTET STEED POPLIN CAVORT
    Answer: What the scared tree was—ROOTED TO THE SPOT

15. **Jumbles:** BASIS YEARN CLOVER POUNCE
    Answer: Openings provided for stereo sound—YOUR EARS

16. **Jumbles:** GRIEF TWEET DAMASK NIPPLE
    Answer: How women are after shopping sprees—
    TIRED—AND SPENT

17. **Jumbles:** WHOOP SNORT DABBLE CURFEW
    Answer: What the traffic cop turned doctor warned his patient to
    do—SLOW DOWN

18. **Jumbles:** AFOOT GRIMY DARING HECKLE
    Answer: What you have to get to wallpaper a room—
    THE HANG OF IT

19. **Jumbles:** SOAPY TULIP BLEACH EMBODY
    Answer: What one woman's past often is—ANOTHER'S PASTIME

20. **Jumbles:** BROOK AGLOW NINETY IMPEND
    Answer: Why you shouldn't criticize nudists—
    THEY WERE BORN THAT WAY

21. **Jumbles:** TOXIC SPURN DECODE YEOMAN
    Answer: What to avoid if you married your wife for her looks—
    DIRTY ONES

22. **Jumbles:** CHAMP JUDGE BUMPER PAGODA
    Answer: What the hip grocer said his "bag" was—PAPER

23. **Jumbles:** GOING VALVE POORLY FATHOM
    Answer: Your wife might do this when you give—FORGIVE

24. **Jumbles:** BRINY CRAWL GRIMLY CRAFTY
    Answer: What some women do if at first they don't succeed—
    CRY, CRY AGAIN

25. **Jumbles:** MOUND AROMA TIPTOE BAFFLE
    Answer: What Adam wasn't—ADAMANT

26. **Jumbles:** AIDED VERVE PSYCHE CALIPH
    Answer: What some of today's youth seem to prefer—
    VICE TO ADVICE

27. **Jumbles:** VIGIL SCARY DITHER TARTAR
    Answer: A dress should be this when it's attractive—
    DISTRACTIVE

28. **Jumbles:** BIPED YODEL VIRTUE CONVOY
    Answer: This leaves no one out!—EVERYBODY

29. **Jumbles:** WRATH VOUCH SIMILE MISHAP
    Answer: The only thing some women ever do on time—
    PURCHASE

30. **Jumbles:** TOXIN QUEER UPWARD JINGLE
    Answer: A more lasting finish for a car than lacquer—LIQUOR

31. **Jumbles:** NEWSY GUARD EXHORT PATTER
    Answer: What a lot of marriage ties are severed by—
    A SHARP TONGUE

32. **Jumbles:** TAWNY VIXEN MARLIN EIGHTY
    Answer: Growing old isn't so bad if you consider this—
    THE ALTERNATIVE

33. **Jumbles:** AMITY CRESS PRIMED SUNDAE
    Answer: What both landlords and tenants often try to do—
    RAISE THE RENT

34. **Jumbles:** ZOMBI JERKY BYGONE DINGHY
    Answer: What those who drink to forget always seem to
    remember—TO DRINK

35. **Jumbles:** PUDGY SKULK UPROAR ELEVEN
    Answer: What a man whose hand is quicker than the eye might
    get—SLAPPED

36. **Jumbles:** KAPOK QUIRE ASTRAY SAILOR
    Answer: What you can expect a dozen rosebuds to come to—
    ROSES

37. **Jumbles:** FOLIO BEFOG INSIST POWDER
    Answer: The easiest way to make ends meet—
    GET OFF YOUR OWN!

38. **Jumbles:** KNOUT SUMAC HANSOM BAUBLE
    Answer: A light kind of book—A MATCHBOOK

39. **Jumbles:** GAILY BALMY AFFRAY ENGULF
    Answer: What getting up in the morning can be—ALARMING!

40. **Jumbles:** DITTY COWER GRAVEN APIECE
    Answer: Ready to eat!—RIPE

41. **Jumbles:** DUNCE WAGER SCRIBE VERMIN
    Answer: This can produce a tight kind of feeling—
    A SCREWDRIVER

42. **Jumbles:** CROUP JOUST OFFSET PENURY
    Answer: What ladles do—SCOOP SOUP

43. **Jumbles:** BARGE LADLE TIMING BODILY
    Answer: It's all it's cracked up to be!—THE LIBERTY BELL

44. **Jumbles:** CABIN GUIDE JUMBLE HELIUM
    Answer: How the magistrate who was playing truant in the park
    acted—LIKE A JUDGE ON THE BENCH

45. **Jumbles:** AISLE EXERT IMPUGN VACANT
    Answer: One thing you can say for being poor—
    IT'S INEXPENSIVE

46. **Jumbles:** LEAVE MONEY WHALER AWHILE
    Answer: What the rake was turned into after he got married—
    A LAWN MOWER

47. **Jumbles:** WIPED AFTER MODISH NEARLY
    Answer: What he thought his wife's mother was—
    A MOTHER-IN-AWE

48. **Jumbles:** FETID LOGIC VANISH BRUTAL
    Answer: How modern housewives sometimes get rid of unsatis-
    factory dishwashers—THEY DIVORCE 'EM

49. **Jumbles:** ALTAR ENACT BUTANE TWINGE
    Answer: You don't know if you're this!—UNAWARE

50. **Jumbles:** HENCE SWOOP ABUSED CACTUS
    Answer: The best thing to use for feathering your nest—
    CASH DOWN

51. **Jumbles:** CLOVE ERASE LEGACY BEAVER
    Answer: How the reducing business is carried on—
    ON A LARGE SCALE

52. **Jumbles:** ABOUT CEASE WHOLLY LANCER
    Answer: What there was at the end of the burlesque act—
    A CLOTHES CALL

53. **Jumbles:** LEAKY EATEN TAMPER PEPTIC
    Answer: Up to the neck in hot water but continues to sing—
    A TEA KETTLE

54. **Jumbles:** FEINT ENEMY RATION VACUUM
    Answer: When you want to sleep this way, better put your watch
    under your pillow—"OVER TIME"

55. **Jumbles:** HEDGE SCOUR MALTED UNLESS
    Answer: What politicians who promise pie in the sky often do—
    USE *YOUR* DOUGH

515

56. **Jumbles:** SANDY AWARD BLOUSE GOLFER
Answer: How she sounded when she tried to sing high C—
"LOW-SY"

57. **Jumbles:** RABBI ELEGY BAKING FORBID
Answer: This is the best thing out!—A FIRE

58. **Jumbles:** CAKED SORRY FORCED MENACE
Answer: Because of this some movie stars are "cool"—FANS

59. **Jumbles:** WEIGH TASTY BEHIND UNLOCK
Answer: Why most things don't have to be thought out in modern kitchens—THEY'RE THAWED OUT

60. **Jumbles:** BLAZE HUMAN WHEEZE POSTAL
Answer: What the inattentive student said when teacher asked him to name two pronouns—"WHO, ME?"

61. **Jumbles:** NIECE POWER CANNED MISLAY
Answer: You can make this but you'll never live to see it!—NOISE

62. **Jumbles:** ADAGE BRIBE PELVIS MYOPIC
Answer: Men look harder at girls who look this way—"EASIER"

63. **Jumbles:** FOYER KNAVE GALAXY BEMOAN
Answer: What a taxpayer hopes for—A BREAK IN THE LEVY

64. **Jumbles:** LIBEL MADAM PYTHON FEUDAL
Answer: Serves to hold important things up—A DELAY

65. **Jumbles:** FORCE LYRIC PRYING INHALE
Answer: What the prude said miniskirts couldn't be worn for—
LONG

66. **Jumbles:** TRILL HEAVY MOTIVE BROGUE
Answer: How the miser held on to his dough—TIGHTLY

67. **Jumbles:** LOFTY USURY BECKON GOODLY
Answer: How he slept when he snored—"SOUND-LY"

68. **Jumbles:** AGENT OCCUR POLITE BECAME
Answer: An author to read at the breakfast table—BACON

69. **Jumbles:** APRON FAINT BESIDE DEMISE
Answer: Sometimes connected with a state of unrest—INSOMNIA

70. **Jumbles:** BEGUN LIGHT LAVISH THRUSH
Answer: Where the aging ballerina was—ON HER LAST LEGS

71. **Jumbles:** DIVOT GUEST BAKERY NORMAL
Answer: The Boy Scout felt dizzy because he did so many of these—GOOD TURNS

72. **Jumbles:** NEEDY LAUGH GROUCH FEALTY
Answer: What the doctor said to the patient who was always complaining of sinus—IT'S ALL IN YOUR HEAD

73. **Jumbles:** ANKLE JUICY CANINE HEAVEN
Answer: How the health official greeted his wife—"HI, JEAN!"

74. **Jumbles:** TUNED CHIEF LATEST MARVEL
Answer: What they said when they were locked out of the market—"LETTUCE IN"

75. **Jumbles:** COMET FAMED PICKET GOVERN
Answer: This might separate two quarreling thieves—A FENCE

76. **Jumbles:** AXIOM DOWNY HAZARD PIGEON
Answer: What eventually happened to the guy who stayed up all night wondering where the sun went to when it set—
IT DAWNED ON HIM

77. **Jumbles:** ABHOR NUTTY PILLAR LIQUOR
Answer: How the dentist and his manicurist wife fought—
TOOTH & NAIL

78. **Jumbles:** ICING OBESE MILDEW DILUTE
Answer: What the grease monkey got after working hours—
"OILED"

79. **Jumbles:** ANNUL FAULT BAMBOO HOMING
Answer: What the boss said when asked how many people worked in his office—ABOUT HALF

80. **Jumbles:** ICILY KNACK SHOULD MANAGE
Answer: What the manicurist wanted to do—NAIL HIM

81. **Jumbles:** POKED VISTA UNLIKE SCENIC
Answer: What he thought the restaurant was—CLOSED

82. **Jumbles:** UNWED BRAVO SIPHON INVADE
Answer: What the nudist demonstrators did—
AIRED THEIR VIEWS

83. **Jumbles:** PATIO ARRAY SCHOOL NETHER
Answer: Why he took a hammer to bed with him—
TO HIT THE HAY

84. **Jumbles:** COUPE PIKER NOTIFY HELPER
Answer: How to stop that ringing in your ears—
PICK UP THE PHONE

85. **Jumbles:** QUOTA DEITY LAXITY SHERRY
Answer: What she knew how to do—"DISH IT OUT"

86. **Jumbles:** FAVOR GUILE CUDDLE EXODUS
Answer: How he carried his business problems home—
IN HIS GRIEF CASE

87. **Jumbles:** MANGE PLAID AMPERE JACKAL
Answer: Where the usher put an overattentive theatergoer—
IN HIS PLACE

88. **Jumbles:** BUMPY FACET NAUSEA ALPACA
Answer: The caveman's favorite sandwich—CLUB

89. **Jumbles:** RAINY PIPER BEHAVE UNHOOK
Answer: What the rich wigmaker's son was—THE HAIR HEIR

90. **Jumbles:** DIZZY ABASH GUIDED BANANA
Answer: What the lunch wagon owner named his daughter—
DINAH

91. **Jumbles:** UNCLE PUTTY FLORID JABBER
Answer: What she was when he complained about her over-cooked biscuits—"BURNED UP"

92. **Jumbles:** ERUPT SKIMP VERSUS DIVIDE
Answer: There's a female in the middle of this type of society—
"PER-MISS-IVE"

93. **Jumbles:** RODEO SNARL CAMPUS PAYOFF
Answer: The wool salesman's stock-in-trade—
COARSE YARNS

94. **Jumbles:** CHAIR WHEAT FACTOR DEAFEN
Answer: A shotgun wedding—WIFE OR DEATH

95. **Jumbles:** RAJAH SUEDE ADJUST FAULTY
Answer: What low-calorie shampoos are good for—FATHEADS

96. **Jumbles:** MAGIC THICK ANYHOW PLEDGE
Answer: How Santa arrived—IN THE "NICK" OF TIME

97. **Jumbles:** LINGO DRAMA PARODY ALWAYS
Answer: What a gal who took up law did after she got married—
LAID IT DOWN

98. **Jumbles:** GOOSE PHONY FROSTY BOTANY
Answer: Odd if they're both right!—SHOES

99. **Jumbles:** POUND CROUP ASYLUM SIPHON
Answer: This is neither very good nor very bad—so, repeat it!—
SO-SO

100. **Jumbles:** PHOTO DAILY BOTTLE FLORID
Answer: Why the gunman and his gun were dangerous—
BOTH WERE LOADED

101. **Jumbles:** DEPOT ANKLE MORBID PLAGUE
Answer: Late in bed and delayed—"BE-LATE-D"

102. **Jumbles:** CHAIR PATIO FAMOUS MANAGE
Answer: Twice a mother—MAMA

103. **Jumbles:** VAGUE TRILL FAULTY BODICE
Answer: This would indicate that someone has just stopped smoking—A LIVE BUTT

104. **Jumbles:** IRONY SAUTE PEPSIN FARINA
Answer: Goes off to report trouble—A SIREN

105. **Jumbles:** ANNUL SCOUT GRATIS MIDWAY
Answer: It's more usual to have only half of this—TWINS

106. **Jumbles:** LURID SWAMP MARVEL CALIPH
Answer: Completely tied up in postal regulations!—PARCELS

107. **Jumbles:** FORCE ARBOR MARROW PLEDGE
Answer: Might be mad about the engine—"LOCO"

108. **Jumbles:** OUNCE FUROR PAYOFF DEFACE
Answer: This street meeting might give you a turn!—A CORNER

109. **Jumbles:** LINEN VISTA POETRY CONVEX
Answer: Your financial problems melt away when you're this—
SOLVENT

110. **Jumbles:** AHEAD SWOON TRICKY GIGGLE
Answer: How good models are built—TO SCALE

111. **Jumbles:** UNITY HIKER OSSIFY ARTFUL
Answer: Provides marriage guidance—AN USHER

112. **Jumbles:** NAVAL GIVEN DEPUTY GLOBAL
Answer: Sometimes goes around to provide comfort—
A BANDAGE

113. **Jumbles:** DERBY PLAID SLEIGH FACADE
Answer: What the tattoo artist turned gunman drew on his victims—BEADS

114. **Jumbles:** LAUGH PYLON RELISH FLAUNT
Answer: How a miser practices philanthropy—SPARINGLY

115. **Jumbles:** ADAPT SLANT COUPLE ROSARY
Answer: How to get good looks—STARE

116. **Jumbles:** AGATE FEIGN NOBODY COMMON
Answer: He won't stand for anything!—AN INFANT

117. **Jumbles:** LANKY AFIRE CRAVAT FICKLE
Answer: You have to be it with the first letter before you can be it without the first—L-EARNER

118. **Jumbles:** ELITE SNARL OPIATE MORTAR
Answer: Theater performances not open to the public—OPERATIONS

119. **Jumbles:** PUPIL HOVEL DISCUS QUARTZ
Answer: This would describe a high-spirited chiseler—"CHIPPER"

120. **Jumbles:** FAMED ENVOY OCCULT PULPIT
Answer: Sometimes carries poison and sounds awful—"VIAL"

121. **Jumbles:** IRATE VALUE SKEWER BLEACH
Answer: Might be straining to do a job—A SIEVE

122. **Jumbles:** AWOKE MINOR CLIENT BONNET
Answer: You just can't shut your eyes to this!—LOOK

123. **Jumbles:** VIGIL WAKEN THRESH LAWYER
Answer: This view may help you get a job—AN INTERVIEW

124. **Jumbles:** BUXOM INKED CAUCUS FALTER
Answer: This might be composed of mud and air—RADIUM

125. **Jumbles:** DAISY CREEL AROUSE STURDY
Answer: They insure the correct delivery of speeches—ADDRESSES

126. **Jumbles:** BEGUN SAVOR GARISH PROFIT
Answer: Today's answer will dawn on you tomorrow—SUNRISE

127. **Jumbles:** LUSTY FENCE POROUS GRISLY
Answer: From a ruse, you can make certain of this—SURE

128. **Jumbles:** PROBE TARDY BALLAD GIBBON
Answer: What he was was apparent—A PARENT

129. **Jumbles:** OPIUM ENJOY REALTY LIZARD
Answer: Once aroused you may lose it!—YOUR TEMPER

130. **Jumbles:** EPOCH APART BETAKE FLORAL
Answer: Might mean some drip let the secrets out—A "LEAK"

131. **Jumbles:** MUSIC TRIPE DAWNED ANEMIA
Answer: What you'd expect from a little devil—"IMP-UDENCE"

132. **Jumbles:** VERVE TOOTH DEVICE BANNER
Answer: Try and give this to a prisoner—THE VERDICT

133. **Jumbles:** DROOP EXULT BEWARE VOLUME
Answer: This is owing to being late—OVERDUE

134. **Jumbles:** NEWLY BARON POLLEN AUTUMN
Answer: Make nothing of it!—ANNUL

135. **Jumbles:** ONION PLAIT HOTBED TOUCHY
Answer: What you think is yours—OPINION

136. **Jumbles:** DANDY TWEET BOTHER RITUAL
Answer: How to offer them better meat—"TENDER" IT

137. **Jumbles:** YOUNG FANCY HAPPEN LEVITY
Answer: Makes many a slip!—NYLON

138. **Jumbles:** ABATE RANCH BIKINI TURNIP
Answer: You wouldn't want to go to the doctor if you suffered from this—INERTIA

139. **Jumbles:** OWING CHOKE SLOGAN IRONIC
Answer: It's definitely a racket!—NOISE

140. **Jumbles:** MERCY FAITH NICELY GOITER
Answer: Tell this guy to go to blazes—and you'll get a response out of him!—A FIREMAN

141. **Jumbles:** BIRCH GLAND OUTCRY RAGLAN
Answer: This is the least you can do!—NOTHING

142. **Jumbles:** DRAWL LOONY JURIST PODIUM
Answer: Made to come clean before the hanging!—LAUNDRY

143. **Jumbles:** BURLY GORGE ACTING CLOTHE
Answer: You can feel this but not get it!—YOUNGER

144. **Jumbles:** FLAME KHAKI EYELID BEFALL
Answer: This simply isn't done!—HALF-BAKED

145. **Jumbles:** CRAZE BUSHY IMPORT MISHAP
Answer: You might find "spice" in these poems—EPICS

146. **Jumbles:** SILKY BURST DEFAME FEMALE
Answer: What he suffered from on a boring date—"LASS-ITUDE"

147. **Jumbles:** ARRAY MOOSE DETAIN BARREN
Answer: What you could find if you just opened the dictionary at random—"RANDOM"

148. **Jumbles:** GLEAM HONOR BODILY INWARD
Answer: Might be a sound investment for those who don't get everything—A HEARING AID

149. **Jumbles:** VILLA SNORT EITHER BOUNCE
Answer: Something new in neckwear—"NOVEL-TIES"

150. **Jumbles:** BRAND FROZE SOLACE AIRWAY
Answer: One USED to be this in or at when he enlisted—SWORN

151. **Jumbles:** GROOM HITCH FRIGID RATIFY
Answer: She doesn't like to receive one or look one—A FRIGHT

152. **Jumbles:** COCOA HASTY PONDER TACKLE
Answer: This drink might put an end to rumors—SCOTCH

153. **Jumbles:** LEECH BLOOM GENTLE EMBALM
Answer: Sounds like a bit of a nut in the army—COLONEL ('kernel')

154. **Jumbles:** FINNY AMUSE LOCATE JUNKET
Answer: Hard on the hands!—NAILS

155. **Jumbles:** FETID GUMBO SUPERB GADFLY
Answer: What shoes often are, after being bought—"SOLED"

156. **Jumbles:** FATAL EATEN INNING MISERY
Answer: When does a woman do all her talking—IN HER LIFETIME

157. **Jumbles:** LOATH AWARD FERRET SCHOOL
Answer: Why a wig can help you to lie about your appearance—IT'S A "FALSE HOOD"

158. **Jumbles:** TEMPO ROBOT HINDER TORRID
Answer: Spreads out under a tree—THE ROOT

159. **Jumbles:** DUCAT PANSY LOUNGE BISHOP
Answer: This material must be checked!—PLAID

160. **Jumbles:** NOOSE LIBEL HEALTH ANGINA
Answer: They show signs of brilliance—NEON LIGHTS

161. **Jumbles:** VIPER MADLY OCELOT DINGHY
Answer: What an unemployed film star is—A MOVIE IDLE

162. **Jumbles:** KNAVE CEASE INVEST KISMET
Answer: They contain more feet in winter than in summer—ICE SKATES

163. **Jumbles:** WELSH TACKY AFLOAT SUBDUE
Answer: Sounds like it could be worn in the window—A SASH

164. **Jumbles:** EXUDE FAUNA REDUCE GALAXY
Answer: This could make you feel you ought to do something—AN URGE

165. **Jumbles:** HOBBY TWILL FLAGON ADDUCE
Answer: A kind of butter that's spelled with four letters—G-O-A-T

166. **Jumbles:** SPITE KETCH EASILY ABACUS
Answer: Might make you cross at the end of a letter—KISSES

167. **Jumbles:** TAKEN BANDY STOLID DULCET
Answer: You wouldn't take this sitting down!—A STAND

168. **Jumbles:** GAWKY TARRY NUTRIA DEFINE
Answer: The first part is rather heavy, but the whole can be lifted easily—and willingly!—A "TANK-ARD"

169. **Jumbles:** JADED BYLAW BUCKLE HIATUS
Answer: A mopping-up operation by the Navy—SWAB

170. **Jumbles:** GOUTY TYING MINGLE COMEDY
Answer: Often grows sharper with use—A TONGUE

171. **Jumbles:** SUMAC PRONE VANITY ATTAIN
Answer: This Russian has four to start with!—IV-AN

172. **Jumbles:** LEAVE BATON UNLESS ABDUCT
Answer: How to complain about a dull knife—BE BLUNT

173. **Jumbles:** SURLY GROUP PLOVER ENOUGH
Answer: What the barker's offspring were called—PUPS

174. **Jumbles:** ABOUT WAGER PERMIT KINGLY
Answer: He had some redeeming features—THE PAWNBROKER

175. **Jumbles:** ARMOR POACH MARKUP SOIREE
Answer: Could be a useless thing—to fight over!—A SCRAP

176. **Jumbles:** SAHIB GUISE DECENT PLURAL
Answer: This warm liquid can have a melting effect—TEARS

177. **Jumbles:** BASSO VOUCH DIVIDE MELODY
Answer: "Dropped" by a nosy person—"EAVES" (eavesdropped)

178. **Jumbles:** FRAME BARGE NORMAL MURMUR
Answer: You might break into this when in a hurry—A RUN

179. **Jumbles:** THINK SOAPY BEADLE FIDDLE
Answer: "Must be nails in your shoe!—"TOENAILS"

180. **Jumbles:** HUMAN TESTY RATION PENCIL
Answer: "Could connect us with that woman!"—"US-HER"

181. **Jumbles:** ESSAY SCARY SHOULD LIMPID
Answer: Divides by uniting and unites by dividing—SCISSORS

182. **Jumbles:** FORTY BRAIN MULISH POORLY
Answer: What people who boo at performers sometimes are—"BOO-RS"

183. **Jumbles:** DUCAL FIFTY MENACE IODINE
Answer: Not to be played with when loaded—DICE

184. **Jumbles:** LEAKY POISE CHALET PHYSIC
Answer: Far from alert but outwardly sly—"SL-EEP-Y"

185. **Jumbles:** POKER BASIC UNCURL CORPSE
Answer: A kind of European curtain material—IRON

186. **Jumbles:** NEEDY USURP EMERGE INVOKE
Answer: Where an astronomer might find poetry—IN THE "UNI-VERSE"

187. **Jumbles:** WEDGE TOXIC COMPEL WEAPON
Answer: Dragged away—to get married—"TO-WED"

188. **Jumbles:** GLADE ELEGY MYRIAD ABRUPT
Answer: What you'll find in the room of your dreams—A BED

189. **Jumbles:** GLOVE PUTTY MILDEW BROGUE
Answer: How to sell an electrical gadget—PLUG IT

190. **Jumbles:** BOUGH FLUTE WEAKEN DARING
Answer: You might be powerless to accept this—A TOW

191. **Jumbles:** RAINY LATHE CLEAVE FEUDAL
Answer: Working he gets all THE DIRTIER—THE CLEANER

192. **Jumbles:** PIETY AUDIT HAMMER MALTED
Answer: It's always done in the evening!—THE DAY

193. **Jumbles:** EAGLE THYME HOOKED SHANTY
Answer: What "a man of leisure" might look down at—THE HEELS

194. **Jumbles:** TONIC BISON DONKEY YELLOW
Answer: Loot taken from a shoe store—"BOOT-Y"

195. **Jumbles:** HAZEL GLORY COUSIN AFRAID
Answer: What the general said when they ran out of money to fight the war—CHARGE!

196. **Jumbles:** RURAL ADMIT ENSIGN BOUGHT
Answer: What he said all that astrology bull was—"TAURUS"

197. **Jumbles:** FABLE LOWLY MASCOT INDIGO
Answer: Thin upright figures—"ONES"

198. **Jumbles:** BUILT GLOAT DENOTE PANTRY
Answer: What the ceramics worker was developing—A POT

199. **Jumbles:** ELDER PRIME GIBLET OBLIGE
Answer: You wouldn't eat it when in this!—"(IN)EDIBLE"

200. **Jumbles:** MAIZE WRATH DROWSY SPONGE
Answer: Why she always had something on whenever he asked for a date—SHE WAS MODEST

201. **Jumbles:** LOGIC KNEEL INVENT MYSTIC
Answer: This light touch could produce laughter in the theater—A TICKLE

202. **Jumbles:** TRACT SOUSE ADJOIN LAVISH
Answer: Not the sort of case he expected to find in the bungalow—A STAIRCASE

203. **Jumbles:** PAPER CABLE FRENZY HAIRDO
Answer: Followed in the kitchen—A RECIPE

204. **Jumbles:** WALTZ STOKE THIRTY PILLAR
Answer: A figure in the middle of a figure—THE WAIST

205. **Jumbles:** LOUSE CHESS TYPHUS MOHAIR
Answer: A piece of Chopin suitable at dinnertime—"CHOP"

206. **Jumbles:** CRUSH DITTO BELONG TINKLE
Answer: What you might feel like doing after dinner—BURSTING

207. **Jumbles:** TASTY FLUTE WHINNY ORIGIN
Answer: The train carrying the laundrymen to work was delayed because of this—"WASH OUT" ON THE LINE

208. **Jumbles:** ADULT LINEN PONCHO INFANT
Answer: What you have to take into consideration these days when you have your tires pumped up—INFLATION

209. **Jumbles:** CHESS CRAFT MORBID GRAVEN
Answer: Threatened to rain on the actors at the outdoor theater—"OVER CAST"

210. **Jumbles:** OAKEN WHISK ARTFUL MASCOT
Answer: Agitated where cocktails are concerned—THE SHAKER

211. **Jumbles:** PANIC MAKER SQUALL ASSAIL
Answer: A "chasm" that might create a deep gap between husbands and wives—"SARCASM"

212. **Jumbles:** LURID IVORY JUMBLE SEAMAN
Answer: What he called his pretty female assistant—A VISUAL AID

213. **Jumbles:** TOPAZ LEECH OUTWIT CARPET
Answer: What the guy who swore he was going to lose weight ended up eating—"CROW"

214. **Jumbles:** LUCID CHASM BABOON EQUITY
Answer: Should you cut them and throw them away—or just file them?—NAILS

215. **Jumbles:** POUND QUASH LOUNGE FARINA
Answer: What they called the beautician—THE "PAN-HANDLER"

216. **Jumbles:** CURRY BOUGH AFRAID MUFFLE
Answer: What you might see if you refuse her request for a mink coat—THE FUR FLY

217. **Jumbles:** QUAIL HAREM RATHER ASSURE
Answer: What the broken phonograph record must have been—A SMASH HIT

218. **Jumbles:** FACET CHAFE MUSTER EXHALE
Answer: Many a "true" word is spoken between them—FALSE TEETH

219. **Jumbles:** CROWN BERET EASILY ZENITH
Answer: What the mad chef was—STIR CRAZY

220. **Jumbles:** PIOUS HARPY CANINE DROWSY
Answer: What turtle soup is—A SNAPPY DISH

221. **Jumbles:** INEPT BAKED ANEMIA TRUSTY
Answer: Sales resistance is the triumph of this—MIND OVER PATTER

222. **Jumbles:** FUROR CHUTE DISCUS PAROLE
Answer: His wife bought all those clothes for a ridiculous figure—HERS

223. **Jumbles:** FEWER QUAKE BUNION WHOLLY
Answer: This is terrible—but a letter would make it legal—AWFUL ("L-AWFUL")

224. **Jumbles:** MOUSY EMERY QUENCH MAMMAL
Answer: What the Pharaoh who ate crackers in bed was—A CRUMMY MUMMY

225. **Jumbles:** AGLOW DAISY MEMOIR VANISH
Answer: What you get if you eat too much—A "HANG OVER"

226. **Jumbles:** CABIN TWEET JUSTLY CROTCH
Answer: What you often have to do to stay within your budget—WITHOUT

227. **Jumbles:** GUEST THICK METRIC ABUSED
Answer: How the eye doctor might make your life—A "SIGHT" BETTER

228. **Jumbles:** AZURE TAFFY NEEDLE FAMOUS
Answer: What the lazy butcher was—A MEAT LOAFER

229. **Jumbles:** GULLY ELDER DENOTE WOBBLE
Answer: That oil tycoon sure was this!—"WELL"-TO-DO

230. **Jumbles:** GAWKY ELATE CALICO GAMBIT
Answer: What you might find plenty of in a burned-out post office—BLACK MAIL

231. **Jumbles:** AMITY BRASS NEWEST PLOWED
Answer: What a procrastinator has—A WAIT PROBLEM

232. **Jumbles:** TANGY DOGMA DEBATE BLAZER
Answer: What the doctor charged to fix up the guy who injured his elbow and knee—AN ARM & A LEG

233. **Jumbles:** WELSH CROAK POTTER CANKER
Answer: What a guy who doesn't like having time on his hands should get—A POCKET WATCH

234. **Jumbles:** PIVOT HONOR MISUSE BIKINI
Answer: What the gambling addict had trouble balancing—HIS BOOKIES

235. **Jumbles:** NERVY CHAFF ZIGZAG ENCORE
Answer: What you might do if you try to paint a girl in the nude—FREEZE

236. **Jumbles:** GAMUT PROXY FUSION DEBTOR
Answer: They decided to appoint him chief cook because he had this—THE "POT" FOR IT

237. **Jumbles:** CROUP LARVA HARROW BELONG
Answer: "How many pounds of Limburger cheese do you want?"—A "PHEW"

238. **Jumbles:** RURAL BANAL UNWISE IMPORT
Answer: A feeling you get when you open your mail on the first of the month—"BILL-IOUS"

239. **Jumbles:** DOUBT FOAMY EVOLVE NUDISM
Answer: When she asked for a diamond, he turned this—"STONE" DEAF

240. **Jumbles:** CREEK MAXIM ASYLUM FLAXEN
Answer: What the robber said as he made his getaway—"SAFE" BY A MILE

241. **Jumbles:** SOGGY ABASH PUZZLE RAVAGE
Answer: What he said that so-called barley soup was—
BARELY SOUP

242. **Jumbles:** JOKER MONEY PRAYER VALUED
Answer: What the down-and-out poet did—"ODE" EVERYONE

243. **Jumbles:** GIVEN TWILL BAMBOO INFIRM
Answer: What the solitary pawnbroker undoubtedly was—
A "LOANER"

244. **Jumbles:** JOLLY LYING LAYMAN FLIMSY
Answer: Another name for horse meat—FILLY MIGNON

245. **Jumbles:** SHYLY DADDY TRUDGE RELISH
Answer: Why she decided to watch her figure—
ALL THE GUYS DID

246. **Jumbles:** EXUDE MUSTY KILLER TWINGE
Answer: The only thing he did fast was this—GET TIRED

247. **Jumbles:** YODEL HABIT BROGUE EGOISM
Answer: What that nut who caught a cold must have been—
HOARSE & BUGGY

248. **Jumbles:** BIPED STEED INVOKE PLAQUE
Answer: What it was when the prisoner escaped—
A SLIP OF THE "PEN"

249. **Jumbles:** THINK MERGE INNATE GOITER
Answer: The doctor decided to "practice" medicine until he got—
IT RIGHT

250. **Jumbles:** ABBOT LUNGE CANYON GUZZLE
Answer: The hard part of being broke is watching the rest of the
world do this—GO "BUY"

251. **Jumbles:** BRINY OXIDE GOPHER EFFIGY
Answer: What the boss's son was, naturally—"FIRE PROOF"

252. **Jumbles:** HAVOC GRAIN INJECT SURELY
Answer: What a talkative barber might do—GET IN YOUR HAIR

253. **Jumbles:** GRIPE DERBY UNEASY OCCULT
Answer: What people often do at the beauty parlor—
CURL UP & DYE

254. **Jumbles:** HOUSE AFIRE GENTRY KIDNAP
Answer: What the chairman of the mathematics department was
called—THE FIGUREHEAD

255. **Jumbles:** AUGUR TOOTH WINTRY RACIAL
Answer: What the patient said when his doctor told him to diet—
WHAT COLOR?

256. **Jumbles:** KNACK TULIP NOZZLE CASHEW
Answer: What some people do at sneak previews—SNEAK OUT

257. **Jumbles:** CREEL MACAW SULTRY FEWEST
Answer: Alcohol will preserve almost everything except this—
SECRETS

258. **Jumbles:** BOOTY ODIUM TOTTER GYPSUM
Answer: If it's Dracula whom you meet on the street, he'll sure
know how to do this—PUT THE BITE ON YOU

259. **Jumbles:** TESTY ABIDE ELIXIR LACING
Answer: In order to select the finest wine, examine this—
THE BEST-CELLAR LIST

260. **Jumbles:** JOINT CUBIC COERCE DISMAY
Answer: There's plenty of this when a man doesn't pay alimony—
ACRIMONY

261. **Jumbles:** BARON TWICE WEDGED LAWFUL
Answer: What that incompetent politician seemed to live by—
THE LAW OF THE "BUNGLE"

262. **Jumbles:** NUDGE CRANK VARIED CAVORT
Answer: When you're in it, you never know—IGNORANCE

263. **Jumbles:** BRAVE LOONY VASSAL PUMICE
Answer: What the polite crook used when he held up the public
library—A SILENCER

264. **Jumbles:** GUIDE WOVEN ENTITY CLOVEN
Answer: "My husband found a new position—"
"LYING DOWN"

265. **Jumbles:** BLANK TRACT MARAUD LEGUME
Answer: What happened to the plastic surgeon who was working
in an overheated operating room?—HE MELTED

266. **Jumbles:** JUROR SIXTY KINGLY COOPER
Answer: What you're likely to take when you're invited to dinner by
witches—POTLUCK

267. **Jumbles:** AISLE NAIVE SUBDUE PUTRID
Answer: Why is venison so expensive?—IT'S "DEER"

268. **Jumbles:** DINER JUICY AMPERE FINITE
Answer: What the frightened rock was—"PETRIFIED"

269. **Jumbles:** WHOSE CHEEK LIZARD SIZZLE
Answer: What his rich uncle who was a famous artist knew how to
draw best—HIS WILL

270. **Jumbles:** DUCAT SOUSE CRAFTY KNOTTY
Answer: What to do when a plug doesn't fit—"SOCKET" (sock it)

271. **Jumbles:** BUMPY ACRID COBALT IODINE
Answer: How does Jack Frost get to work?—BY "ICICLE"

272. **Jumbles:** OLDER FRANC YEARLY NAUSEA
Answer: What the umbrella merchant was saving his money for—
A SUNNY DAY

273. **Jumbles:** DRAWL COACH WHALER MUSKET
Answer: The ship docked near the barbershop because they all
needed this—"CREW" CUTS

274. **Jumbles:** OUTDO CLEFT DREDGE HARBOR
Answer: What the secret agent was complaining of—
A "CODE" IN THE HEAD

275. **Jumbles:** NOOSE DOWNY BAUBLE TYRANT
Answer: Why they had to put the vampire away—HE WENT BATS

276. **Jumbles:** BLOOM FENCE MUSLIN LIQUID
Answer: What the doctor said when the patient complained of
ringing in his ears—YOU'RE SOUND AS A BELL

277. **Jumbles:** DOILY BRAVO STICKY FOMENT
Answer: When a vandal made a hole in the fence at the nudist
camp, the cops said they'd do this—LOOK INTO IT

278. **Jumbles:** RAPID CRAWL ICEBOX LARYNX
Answer: What he got when he read the story about those body
snatchers—CARRIED AWAY

279. **Jumbles:** GLOVE DROOP JAUNTY HOMING
Answer: He decided to become an astronaut when his wife told
him he was this—NO EARTHLY GOOD

280. **Jumbles:** NIPPY BASIN INTONE ADRIFT
Answer: If you want to start losing weight, you can get initiated
from this—A "DIETITIAN"

281. **Jumbles:** EIGHT TRYST EYEFUL MORGUE
Answer: When is the cheapest time to phone your friends by long
distance?—WHEN THEY'RE OUT

282. **Jumbles:** MOUTH TACKY DRAGON MYSELF
Answer: The man who stole a pudding was taken into this—
"CUSTARDY" (custody)

283. **Jumbles:** FRAUD TAWNY HOURLY LAVISH
Answer: What he said when teacher gave him an "F" on the
vocabulary test—WORDS FAIL ME

284. **Jumbles:** RUSTY EJECT MAINLY OPPOSE
Answer: Where you might find the schoolmaster—
IN "THE CLASSROOM"

285. **Jumbles:** DRAMA BEFOG UNSAID MAGNUM
Answer: From the surgeon came these words—"GO, NURSE!"

286. **Jumbles:** DRYLY SYNOD ENTAIL BANGLE
Answer: What her ideal became after she married him—
AN ORDEAL

287. **Jumbles:** LAPEL OPERA COUSIN PACKET
Answer: What that old-time garage mechanic was bothered with—
"CRANK" CALLS

288. **Jumbles:** GRAVE FETID BOILED MANIAC
Answer: He thought his new computer was going to give him this
kind of an illness—A "TERMINAL" ONE

289. **Jumbles:** GLOAT SUMAC INDUCE RADISH
Answer: What that crazy artist made of his model—A MUDDLE

290. **Jumbles:** FUSSY TASTY EXPOSE HAMMER
Answer: What a good history teacher should be—
A "PAST" MASTER

291. **Jumbles:** MERCY LUSTY TARGET NAPKIN
Answer: What a cent tip would certainly make these days—
A "PITTANCE"

292. **Jumbles:** DUNCE GUESS VOLUME QUAINT
A word of five letters the last four of which are unnecessary—
"Q-UEUE"

293. **Jumbles:** BILGE TEPID HUNTER FABLED
Answer: What to do when you get the feeling that you want to
splurge—NIP IT IN THE "BUD-GET"

294. **Jumbles:** JUICE MAJOR EXPEND STYMIE
Answer: What the government expects to get from income taxes—
"EXACT MONIES"

295. **Jumbles:** INLET TWINE FRENZY MALICE
Answer: What the author's pseudonym was—HIS "WRITE" NAME

296. **Jumbles:** FLOUR WHEEL OPIATE BECALM
Answer: What she did every time she washed her hair—BLEW HER TOP

297. **Jumbles:** HAIRY SCOUR JUMPER ARMADA
Answer: What a sleepwalker's habit usually is—PAJAMAS

298. **Jumbles:** KINKY WALTZ BURIAL FACADE
Answer: What a quack doctor usually tries to do—DUCK THE LAW

299. **Jumbles:** TRIPE HOBBY STUCCO MEMORY
Answer: How you have to learn to take care of a baby—FROM THE BOTTOM UP

300. **Jumbles:** FAVOR PLUSH DEFAME BUSILY
Answer: Held up in bad weather—AN UMBRELLA

301. **Jumbles:** AGENT HYENA PURIFY RUBBER
Answer: What a fashion model might figure on—HER FIGURE

302. **Jumbles:** AGING FOYER BAFFLE GLOBAL
Answer: "Does it all come from an allergy?"—"LARGELY"

303. **Jumbles:** FLOOD SWOON WALLOP FINISH
Answer: What that Peeping Tom was—A WINDOW FAN

304. **Jumbles:** DITTO WHEAT TRICKY HALLOW
Answer: How children arrive at your door tonight—EVERY "WITCH" WAY

305. **Jumbles:** LEAKY ERASE INVITE FACILE
Answer: What too much of an open mind might be like—A SIEVE

306. **Jumbles:** FAIRY ELITE POWDER LAUNCH
Answer: What they called that crooked politician turned doctor—THE WARD "HEALER"

307. **Jumbles:** BASIC COCOA CALIPH FRIEZE
Answer: It's "said" to be a test—"ORAL"

308. **Jumbles:** PIPER EXILE MAKEUP TAMPER
Answer: Another name for a pawnbroker—A "TIME KEEPER"

309. **Jumbles:** BATON AGILE ENJOIN HITHER
Answer: What to do in order to have soft white hands—NOTHING

310. **Jumbles:** FORUM GAUZE EXTANT DULCET
Answer: The reason so many of us are discontented with our lot these days is that it's no longer this—A LOT

311. **Jumbles:** LOVER ANNOY SOOTHE REDUCE
Answer: How the pop singer turned politician ran—ON HIS RECORD

312. **Jumbles:** VIRUS EXCEL LOTION PIRATE
Answer: What an alibi usually is—A "SLIP" COVER

313. **Jumbles:** GRIEF ALIAS MANAGE PRIMER
Answer: The MARINES were "arranged" as a study group—"SEMINAR"

314. **Jumbles:** HOVEL BISON ECZEMA SUBURB
Answer: What a garbage truck is—A MESS "HAUL"

315. **Jumbles:** CYNIC AFTER ZODIAC MEMBER
Answer: What the prices of some of those frozen foods definitely weren't—"FROZEN"

316. **Jumbles:** OPIUM STOKE BUTTON ACTUAL
Answer: What pinup girls sometimes are—STUCK-UP

317. **Jumbles:** WHISK AWARD SPEEDY ENGINE
Answer: What the church sexton minds—HIS KEYS AND PEWS

318. **Jumbles:** FRUIT BRAIN AVENUE DISMAL
Answer: While she was getting a faceful of mud she was also getting this—AN EARFUL OF "DIRT"

319. **Jumbles:** LINER FAITH ORPHAN ANKLET
Answer: What a snowball might be—A "PANE" KILLER

320. **Jumbles:** AWFUL SQUAW MALADY JAILED
Answer: What there seemed to be in that noisy courtroom—MORE "JAW" THAN LAW

321. **Jumbles:** IGLOO CHAMP BALLET HYBRID
Answer: What New Year's Eve might be for some people—AN "ALCOHOLIDAY"

322. **Jumbles:** GUILT ABOVE WORTHY RITUAL
Answer: What does a small inlay cost these days?—A BIG OUT-LAY

323. **Jumbles:** PLUME ABHOR BUOYED DURESS
Answer: What that dude became after marriage—SUBDUED

324. **Jumbles:** FISHY GOUGE SUGARY BELFRY
Answer: Figures don't lie—but liars do this—FIGURE

325. **Jumbles:** STOOP CLOTH RADIAL HUNGRY
Answer: A fabulously successful baker might bring these words to mind—ROLLS IN DOUGH

326. **Jumbles:** THINK AWOKE FORCED HOMAGE
Answer: Some guys don't know when to stop until they're told this—WHERE TO GO

327. **Jumbles:** DOGMA POACH FELLOW BANTER
Answer: What a yawn often is—A HOLE MADE BY A BORE

328. **Jumbles:** WHILE ABIDE TACKLE OVERDO
Answer: What the blacksmith did to his incompetent apprentice—BELLOWED AT HIM

329. **Jumbles:** VIPER QUOTA MUSKET CUDGEL
Answer: Medicine men are seldom what they're this—"QUACKED" UP TO BE

330. **Jumbles:** ELUDE JERKY FALTER ELIXIR
Answer: What the Scotsman who returned home late one night almost got—"KILT"

331. **Jumbles:** AISLE BUSHY FLAUNT PICKET
Answer: Those cars never run as smoothly as this—HE TALKS

332. **Jumbles:** TWEAK JOKER TURTLE DAMPEN
Answer: What a bureaucrat is—A RED TAPE WORM

333. **Jumbles:** CRACK DADDY GIMLET BOYISH
Answer: What the tax collector did for the man who thought he was saving up for a rainy day—"SOAKED" HIM

334. **Jumbles:** DROOP OLDER MUSEUM LOCALE
Answer: How some so-called "music" that's being composed these days sounds to some people—"DE-COMPOSED"

335. **Jumbles:** TARRY FUDGE PIGPEN MORTAR
Answer: That bacteriologist made his famous discovery by starting out with this—THE GERM OF AN IDEA

336. **Jumbles:** VALET DITTY BUNION QUENCH
Answer: What he did after stealing a pair of scissors—"CUT OUT"

337. **Jumbles:** MANGY VILLA FONDLY COMPEL
Answer: A guy who's busy coping has no time for this—MOPING

338. **Jumbles:** HENCE YIELD PUTRID MYSELF
Answer: What the millionaire left—MUCH TO BE DESIRED

339. **Jumbles:** SCOUT TANGY NOZZLE GLOOMY
Answer: What a conversation between husband and wife sometimes is—A MONOLOGUE

340. **Jumbles:** MUSTY SIEGE DRIVEL POSTAL
Answer: What tears are—"GLUM" DROPS

341. **Jumbles:** MERGE RANCH EFFACE GAMBIT
Answer: How some prominent family trees were started—BY "GRAFTING"

342. **Jumbles:** PRIME BELLE PREFIX FORMAT
Answer: The only thing he had against the younger generation was that he was not this—A MEMBER OF IT

343. **Jumbles:** AORTA BANDY PESTLE NEEDLE
Answer: How the students felt about the examination—THEY "DE-TEST-ED" IT

344. **Jumbles:** ASSAY PARTY GUNNER INLAID
Answer: What he quit doing in trying times—TRYING

345. **Jumbles:** PUDGY BUMPY EGOISM FINERY
Answer: What it was when the doctor said, "This won't hurt"—A "M.D." PROMISE (empty promise)

346. **Jumbles:** MAXIM WAFER MAGPIE THRASH
Answer: The waiter finally comes to this—HIM WHO WAITS

347. **Jumbles:** BORAX AFIRE FOMENT BARROW
Answer: He was the type of man some women take to—and also this—FROM

348. **Jumbles:** GIANT AUGUR FORKED SNITCH
Answer: What they called the star of the monster show—A STAGE "FRIGHT"

349. **Jumbles:** YOUNG IDIOT DREDGE VANDAL
Answer: A beauty salon is a place where this might happen—THE LIVING GO TO "DYE"

350. **Jumbles:** CROUP BARGE ADJUST EULOGY
Answer: How he felt about feeling bad—GOOD

351. **Jumbles:** DRAWL EIGHT DEPICT NAUSEA
Answer: If you're going to act like a skunk just make sure that nobody does this—GETS WIND OF IT

352. **Jumbles:** YOKEL PIVOT NIBBLE GAMBLE
Answer: What some college students major in—"ALIBI-OLOGY"

353. **Jumbles:** VENOM TOOTH BYGONE MOTION
Answer: How those folks who enjoyed eating grits sang—IN "HOMINY" (harmony)

354. **Jumbles:** PRONE HUSKY SMOKER ELEVEN
Answer: "What do you think of that poet?"—I'VE SEEN "VERSE"

355. **Jumbles:** VAPOR FRAME NUMBER STYLUS
Answer: Why they called for the chimney sweep—
IT WAS THE "FLUE" SEASON

356. **Jumbles:** MOTIF WOVEN PARLOR FLORAL
Answer: How he felt after eating too many pancakes—
"WAFFLE" (awful)

357. **Jumbles:** LIGHT PRIOR CORNEA GUIDED
Answer: What the card game at the oil field must have been—
"RIGGED"

358. **Jumbles:** TRAIT FENCE EXPOSE GARLIC
Answer: What firewood used to be—FREE FOR THE "AXING"

359. **Jumbles:** PIKER FRAUD SOLACE NOTIFY
Answer: The best way to watch calories, if you want to lose
weight—FROM A DISTANCE

360. **Jumbles:** EVOKE SMACK POWDER NEPHEW
Answer: What the helicopter tycoon decided to get for himself—
NEW CHOPPERS

361. **Jumbles:** QUEER DOUSE TYRANT HERESY
Answer: What they said about the angry governor—
WHAT A "STATE" HE'S IN!

362. **Jumbles:** HOUSE NAIVE VIRTUE QUAVER
Answer: What Junior was when Mom accused him of breaking her
favorite urn—"E-VASE-IVE"

363. **Jumbles:** DINER NIECE UPROAR COUPON
Answer: How the hotel room clerk appeared—"PREOCCUPIED"

364. **Jumbles:** QUIRE GUMBO LAYOFF CROUCH
Answer: Did the X-rated movie make any money?—"BARE-LY"

365. **Jumbles:** WAGON PORGY BOUNCE WIZARD
Answer: What boys do when they grow up—GROW "DOWN"

366. **Jumbles:** LANKY AWASH HUNGRY DETACH
Answer: What sort of existence did that crapshooter lead?—
A "SHAKY" ONE

367. **Jumbles:** SINGE BROOD LAGOON MUSCLE
Answer: What a good book usually is—"BOUND" TO SELL

368. **Jumbles:** NUDGE SOUSE HEARTH BOUGHT
Answer: How you have to pay for some kinds of plastic surgery—
THROUGH THE NOSE

369. **Jumbles:** SIXTY ENVOY MANIAC ALKALI
Answer: A man who takes you into his "confidence" often does this
afterwards—JUST TAKES YOU IN

370. **Jumbles:** SNARL SCARF COERCE FUNGUS
Answer: Political candidates often stay on the fence in order to
avoid giving this—"OF-FENSE"

371. **Jumbles:** VERVE PATIO SICKEN CASHEW
Answer: Some college kids who spend too much time with a
pigskin sometimes fail to get this—A SHEEPSKIN

372. **Jumbles:** CRANK SHYLY HOOKED ACCESS
Answer: Before they'll cash your check, they'll probably do this—
CHECK YOUR CASH

373. **Jumbles:** ABBOT PROXY INFLUX DAMASK
Answer: What a chip on the shoulder usually is—
JUST PLAIN "BARK"

374. **Jumbles:** KNACK CUBIC CABANA PURITY
Answer: What most of the chiropractor's income came from—
"BACK" PAY

375. **Jumbles:** NERVY RURAL PODIUM BRANDY
Answer: What the counterfeiter wanted—MONEY "BAD"

376. **Jumbles:** VOCAL PUTTY NESTLE MODERN
Answer: A small boy might wear out everything, including this—
HIS PARENTS

377. **Jumbles:** NIPPY COWER NATURE POORLY
Answer: A calculator is a device used by these—
PEOPLE WHO COUNT

378. **Jumbles:** CRAWL HANDY JUNGLE RATION
Answer: Where you might go in order to make yourself more
attractive—OUT OF YOUR "WEIGH"

379. **Jumbles:** APART WHOSE IMPUGN TAMPER
Answer: Some people with the gift of gab never know when to do
this—WRAP IT UP

380. **Jumbles:** LILAC JADED PIRATE INVERT
Answer: He felt the only way to multiply happiness was this—
TO DIVIDE IT

381. **Jumbles:** RAPID SKIMP RAMROD KENNEL
Answer: What he suffered from when the relatives arrived—
"KIN-DREAD"

382. **Jumbles:** HASTY ABASH MARTYR CAMPUS
Answer: What any good junkman knows how to convert—
TRASH INTO CASH

383. **Jumbles:** POWER KAPOK GUILTY LIQUOR
Answer: Some girls close their eyes while kissing, but others do
this—LOOK BEFORE THEY "LIP"

384. **Jumbles:** BEGOT ORBIT FINISH PLOWED
Answer: That after-dinner speaker always knew when to rise to
the occasion—but seldom this—WHEN TO SIT DOWN

385. **Jumbles:** JETTY NOOSE TURKEY RECTOR
Answer: What he got when he bought that stock—STUCK

386. **Jumbles:** OBESE NOVEL JAUNTY DISMAL
Answer: What his wife had a steady job trying to keep him at—
A STEADY JOB

387. **Jumbles:** RUSTY SWASH AVENUE LEDGER
Answer: A political platform is something a candidate needs when
he hasn't this—A LEG TO STAND ON

388. **Jumbles:** WELSH QUAIL YELLOW CAVORT
Answer: What sort of conversation was going on at the library?—
A VERY "LOW" ONE

389. **Jumbles:** HIKER VIXEN BUTTON QUARTZ
Answer: Another name for that much talked about baby boom—
THE "BIRTHQUAKE"

390. **Jumbles:** RIGOR HAVEN INJURY STURDY
Answer: A handy device for finding furniture in the dark—
YOUR SHIN

391. **Jumbles:** ESSAY BRINY EMBARK COUPLE
Answer: What a person who believes in fortune-tellers might be—
A "SEER" SUCKER

392. **Jumbles:** CHAIR MEALY RATIFY EXPEND
Answer: What a stuffed shirt often goes with—AN EMPTY HEAD

393. **Jumbles:** BATON PIANO STICKY CAUGHT
Answer: When dentists aren't, their patients are—PAINSTAKING

394. **Jumbles:** INLET HAIRY INFUSE PRYING
Answer: The pianist was a musician to this—HIS FINGERTIPS

395. **Jumbles:** VOUCH FAUNA CONVEX APPEAR
Answer: A prejudiced guy is down on anything he's not this—
UP ON

396. **Jumbles:** AMUSE OPERA JARGON PARDON
Answer: What the tuba player's kids called him—"OOM-PA-PA"

397. **Jumbles:** SWOON ABOUT ECZEMA JETSAM
Answer: What that practical joker had—A ZEST FOR JEST

398. **Jumbles:** SHINY EPOCH GIGOLO NOUGAT
Answer: With that deadbeat, it's often a matter of this—
TOUCH & GO

399. **Jumbles:** DITTO LOONY EXHALE GAINED
Answer: What they were doing at the sewing circle—NEEDLING

400. **Jumbles:** AGILE GNARL MARTIN BRONCO
Answer: How the so-called "coming" generation spends much of
its time—"GOING"

401. **Jumbles:** OPIUM DAUNT CLEAVE RARITY
Answer: What kind of milk does an invisible baby get, naturally?—
EVAPORATED

402. **Jumbles:** ANKLE YODEL DEADLY EITHER
Answer: What a criminal who falls into cement has to be—
A HARDENED ONE

403. **Jumbles:** FIFTY SQUAW TROUGH DEMISE
Answer: What tantrums in childhood appear to be—
QUITE THE "RAGE"

404. **Jumbles:** JUICY MOUNT SUBURB CARPET
Answer: What did they give Dracula when he first went to Hollywood?—"BIT" PARTS

405. **Jumbles:** LINER ALIAS LAWFUL SOOTHE
Answer: What jokes told by mountain folk often are—
"HILL-ARIOUS"

406. **Jumbles:** TRIPE BAGGY LAWYER BISHOP
Answer: What today's hangover might be connected with—
THE WRATH OF GRAPES

407. **Jumbles:** EXILE AGENT STOLID PERSON
Answer: What she was, after a hard day's shopping—
TIRED & "SPENT"

408. **Jumbles:** LIMIT FLUID GENTRY TOWARD
Answer: What a person who calls a spade a spade is probably
about to give someone—A DIRTY "DIG"

409. **Jumbles:** ELITE POKER SUBWAY KERNEL
Answer: Another name for a plagiarist—A "STEAL" WORKER

410. **Jumbles:** TAWNY WOVEN PARITY MORGUE
Answer: What an untalented writer might earn by his pen—
"PEN-URY"

411. **Jumbles:** MAXIM PUTTY BELLOW GARLIC
Answer: How the scandalmonger let the cat out of the bag—
ONE CLAW AT A TIME

412. **Jumbles:** BAGGY AFTER FAMISH POUNCE
Answer: Wallpapering is easy once you get this—
THE HANG OF IT

413. **Jumbles:** AHEAD VOCAL DECEIT GASKET
Answer: What the politician did when his opponent "laid an egg"—
CACKLED

414. **Jumbles:** TONIC CHASM PARLOR RADIUS
Answer: The egotist found fault with everything except this—
HIS MIRROR

415. **Jumbles:** NEWSY VITAL MARTYR CLEAVE
Answer: Some people are richer than others—which proves that
wealth may be only this—"RELATIVE"

416. **Jumbles:** EXILE RUSTY GYRATE CHARGE
Answer: What the spendthrift ended up making—
HIS "HEIRS" TURN GRAY

417. **Jumbles:** APPLY CURRY DEPUTY NAPKIN
Answer: What kind of attention did the chairman get when he
rapped with his gavel?—RAPT

418. **Jumbles:** DALLY ENVOY PALATE HECTIC
Answer: What an impeccable con man is—A NEAT CHEAT

419. **Jumbles:** BOGUS DEITY GRUBBY IMPACT
Answer: What a wife without curiosity could be—A CURIOSITY

420. **Jumbles:** LINER OPIUM RECTOR FATHOM
Answer: Some people scratch for money; others do this—
ITCH FOR IT

421. **Jumbles:** FRUIT HUMID MUFFLE CALICO
Answer: Why no one laughed at that joke about the broken
heating system—IT LEFT THEM COLD

422. **Jumbles:** MANLY ERASE BOYISH NEWEST
Answer: He owes his success not to what he "knows," but to
this—WHOM HE "YESSES"

423. **Jumbles:** VAPOR ROUSE MOHAIR HAWKER
Answer: The loafer put more hours in his work than this—
WORK IN HIS HOURS

424. **Jumbles:** SINGE DOWNY WORTHY KINGLY
Answer: Another name for a suit of armor—A "KNIGHT GOWN"

425. **Jumbles:** VERVE DAUNT LEVITY SUPERB
Answer: What the robot surgeon operated on—BATTERIES

426. **Jumbles:** ADAPT DRAFT BARROW TOUCHY
Answer: Why was he such a great cook?—
HE HAD THE POT FOR IT

427. **Jumbles:** FIFTY RIGOR MYRIAD INLAID
Answer: Somebody who calls a spade a spade might want to give
you this—A DIRTY "DIG"

428. **Jumbles:** CLUCK QUAIL MARAUD WEAKEN
Answer: What the artist turned cowboy was—
QUICK ON THE DRAW

429. **Jumbles:** BRINY ACCUTE STUCCO FETISH
Answer: When his wife gave birth to quintuplets, he could hardly
believe this—HIS "CENSUS" (senses)

430. **Jumbles:** GLADE NEEDY ENTIRE CANDID
Answer: Where do zombies like to sit when they go to the
movies?—DEAD CENTER

431. **Jumbles:** TULIP SAUTE CARPET LAGOON
Answer: What teacher said when he sat on a tack—
I GET THE POINT

432. **Jumbles:** COUGH ALTAR SAILOR WISELY
Answer: What you might see at a planetarium—
AN ALL-STAR SHOW

433. **Jumbles:** FLOOR SHOWY MARTIN PARDON
Answer: What he did every time he bought a suit—HAD A FIT

434. **Jumbles:** LINGO JUICY CEMENT HOMING
Answer: What a lawyer sometimes helps you get—
WHAT'S COMING TO *HIM*

435. **Jumbles:** VOUCH CABIN BLAZER SOOTHE
Answer: What was all that talk down at the garbage dump?
A LOT OF RUBBISH

436. **Jumbles:** PIANO FIORD NOUGAT SCARCE
Answer: When looking for bargains, you might go there—
WHERE THE "AUCTION" IS

437. **Jumbles:** IGLOO PILOT VERSUS UNPACK
Answer: What the broken soft drink machine was—
"COIN-IVOROUS"

438. **Jumbles:** RIVET AWFUL SUGARY CHISEL
Answer: What good camouflage is—WISE GUISE

439. **Jumbles:** QUIRE NOISE FLEECE RATHER
Answer: What that great horror film was—"TERROR-IFIC"

440. **Jumbles:** BLAZE FORTY TINKLE SPRUCE
Answer: What to do about squeaky furniture wheels—
USE "CASTER" OIL

441. **Jumbles:** GROUP ADMIT YEOMAN SUCKLE
Answer: A tiresome person always takes his time doing this—
TAKING YOURS

442. **Jumbles:** EPOCH AGATE MADMAN GALAXY
Answer: What the victim thought when the robber stuffed his
mouth with a dirty cloth—"THAT'S AN OLD GAG"

443. **Jumbles:** EXACT FLAME MOSAIC HARROW
Answer: What do ghosts eat for breakfast?—
SCREAM OF WHEAT

444. **Jumbles:** ROBIN ELOPE CYMBAL POROUS
Answer: Seems to grow abundantly in this yard—
A BUMPER CROP

445. **Jumbles:** QUEUE BERET GOPHER DEMISE
Answer: What the rope tycoon built—A HUGE "HEMP-IRE"

446. **Jumbles:** DRAMA TEPID CIRCUS NOVICE
Answer: What you should get before investing in expensive audio
equipment—"SOUND" ADVICE

447. **Jumbles:** AZURE SWAMP FEUDAL CANOPY
Answer: What many a public speaker devotes his life to—
A "WORDY" CAUSE

448. **Jumbles:** CRUSH MADAM COERCE PICNIC
Answer: A miser lives poor so he can do this—DIE RICH

449. **Jumbles:** FOIST BIRCH SALOON ASSURE
Answer: These words sometimes describe a law suit—
A LOSS SUIT

450. **Jumbles:** LOONY BRAIN SMUDGE COSTLY
Answer: Where you might find those optometry students—
IN THE "GLASS" ROOM

451. **Jumbles:** FUTILE UPLIFT PRIMER DEVICE THWART DOMINO
Answer: Why Atlas was arrested—HE HELD UP THE WORLD

452. **Jumbles:** TRYING ALBINO SUBURB BELFRY MALLET DECEIT
Answer: A man who likes you to be at his service—
THE MINISTER

453. **Jumbles:** THRESH FENNEL RARITY BETAKE DAWNED
CYMBAL
Answer: What the feuding bricklayers finally did—
CEMENTED TIES

454. **Jumbles:** GEYSER QUENCH CALLOW STUCCO HALVED
BUTTON
Answer: What happened when Goliath tried some pot—
HE GOT STONED

455. **Jumbles:** LAWFUL AIRWAY BUBBLE PAYING HANGAR
DRAGON
Answer: What a husband who had recently been ill seemed to be
doing—HOLDING UP WELL

456. **Jumbles:** OUTCRY BEHEAD SADIST AGENDA HONEST
INDOOR
Answer: The farmer raised his boy to be a bootblack because he
wanted to do this—MAKE HAY WHILE THE SON SHINES

457. **Jumbles:** YEARLY DIGEST OMELET MAGNET WAITER APPEAR
Answer: What 1969 pennies are worth this year—
ALMOST TWENTY DOLLARS

458. **Jumbles:** NICELY TORRID MEMBER SHAKEN HOMAGE ASSAIL
Answer: How a Western doctor might give you an inoculation—
WITH HIS SICK SHOOTER

459. **Jumbles:** BEHALF FERVOR MAGPIE HERALD UNEASY
PURPLE
Answer: Why the run-down timepiece was rushed to the watch
hospital—ITS HOURS WERE NUMBERED

460. **Jumbles:** INFECT MOTION LAWYER ENOUGH PLURAL CHISEL
Answer: What to get when your diet fails—ALTERATIONS

461. **Jumbles:** PURIFY FIESTA CLERGY ENSIGN BESTOW GASKET
Answer: One of the most expensive things a husband has to
face—KEEPING UP HIS WIFE'S

462. **Jumbles:** ENTITY TINGLE HORROR BRIDGE CATCHY DISARM
Answer: What you generally get before you do the laundry—
THE CLOTHES DIRTY

463. **Jumbles:** MIDWAY EXPEND BANTER KNOTTY GROTTO STUPID
Answer: What a husband who won't stand for his wife's extravagance will probably have to do—TAKE IT SITTING DOWN

464. **Jumbles:** PUPIL BRAVE MARROW ADVICE
Answer: This might grow in a junkyard—A BUMPER CROP

465. **Jumbles:** BANISH MASCOT DEADLY ASSURE IGUANA GIBLET
Answer: What they said about the psychiatrist—MIND'S HIS BUSINESS

466. **Jumbles:** FIDDLE INDUCT DAHLIA YELLOW EITHER VERIFY
Answer: How to stop that noise in your car—LET YOUR WIFE DRIVE

467. **Jumbles:** OBLIGE BUSILY NAPKIN PHYSIC EMBARK ACTION
Answer: What the absentminded boy thought he'd do—PLAY HOOKY

468. **Jumbles:** GOOSE PHONY FROSTY BOTANY
Answer: Odd if they're both right!—SHOES

469. **Jumbles:** SECOND REFUGE DROWSY ADMIRE UNHOLY BASKET
Answer: What color did he paint the sun and the wind?—THE SUN ROSE, THE WIND BLUE

470. **Jumbles:** PENCIL LOCATE BEHOLD CUDGEL ABDUCT IMMUNE
Answer: What the sailor in the top bunk was—UP ALL NIGHT

471. **Jumbles:** QUARTZ SALUTE DURESS ACCENT ITALIC SQUALL
Answer: What tears are for many a wife—LIQUID ASSETS

472. **Jumbles:** TANGLE DEBTOR ALKALI LAUNCH POLISH FAUCET
Answer: What to wear when you're going to jump out of the window—A LIGHT FALL COAT

473. **Jumbles:** INJURE GATHER PACKET AMOEBA FINITE SAVAGE
Answer: What the Spanish fisherman turned dancer played—THE "CAST-A-NET"

474. **Jumbles:** HEARTH WIDEST CELERY AVENUE DOMINO TAUGHT
Answer: What the thief got—TWELVE MONTHS

475. **Jumbles:** OUTING BROOCH DEFACE MOTHER KIDNAP POLICE
Answer: What the pretzel king made—CROOKED DOUGH

476. **Jumbles:** SEXTON MODEST TANKER EYEFUL BONNET HAPPEN
Answer: What the mother ghost said to the baby ghost—FASTEN YOUR SHEET BELT

477. **Jumbles:** MARTYR POLICY INFORM BIGAMY UNCOIL ABOUND
Answer: What George Washington made—A DOLLAR GO FAR

478. **Jumbles:** UNWISE POTENT COMEDY AFFIRM SOCIAL FUTURE
Answer: What he said when the judge informed him that he'd been brought before the court for drinking—LET'S GET STARTED

479. **Jumbles:** BROKEN LIZARD FALTER CROTCH IMPAIR PALACE
Answer: They gave the crook a bath so he could do this—"COME CLEAN"

480. **Jumbles:** ASPECT GHETTO WISDOM BELFRY POLLEN CABANA
Answer: Why the vampire avoided her—WRONG BLOOD TYPE

481. **Jumbles:** STOOGE DUPLEX ARCTIC REALTY INDOOR GADFLY
Answer: What the ghoul said when asked whether he had stolen the body—"OF CORPSE!"

482. **Jumbles:** GOSPEL ORIOLE HOTBED TRUANT AIRWAY BETAKE
Answer: An alarm clock can scare this—THE DAYLIGHT INTO YOU

483. **Jumbles:** SPRUCE JAGGED ELICIT GUZZLE LUNACY EGOISM
Answer: Why some couples go to "court"—TO PLAY "SINGLES"

484. **Jumbles:** MAGNET JARGON VALUED OUTLET WAITER DABBLE
Answer: In olden times this was often turned out by a well-bred maid—WELL-MADE BREAD

485. **Jumbles:** PALLID ACTING EITHER CAJOLE FECUND COOKIE
Answer: Why he died laughing—HE WAS TICKLED TO DEATH

486. **Jumbles:** THIRTY FINISH ABACUS WEAKEN BEAVER PARADE
Answer: What you get when you're kidnapped by a ghost—SPIRITED AWAY

487. **Jumbles:** ELEVEN BRUTAL HIDING AMBUSH PUNDIT CANNED
Answer: He blushed right down to his fingertips because he was this—CAUGHT RED-HANDED

488. **Jumbles:** EMBARK SALOON TUXEDO HINDER LEGACY PHYSIC
Answer: What he was when he found a pearl in the oyster—"SHELL" SHOCKED

489. **Jumbles:** FIESTA TONGUE BEFORE STYMIE CATCHY POLITE
Answer: You might have a vested interest in this—A THREE-PIECE SUIT

490. **Jumbles:** WHENCE BELONG MODISH SUBDUE FOSSIL LOUNGE
Answer: What a good body snatcher wouldn't be without on a night like this—HIS "GHOUL-OSHES"

491. **Jumbles:** ENJOIN HOPPER DISARM BLOUSE ZIGZAG ENTITY
Answer: At a place like this expect them at closing time—PARTING SHOTS

492. **Jumbles:** WATERY BAFFLE CRAYON VOYAGE TANDEM ENSIGN
Answer: What you wouldn't expect to get from a man of few words—A LONG SENTENCE

493. **Jumbles:** YEOMAN GRASSY FEDORA DITHER CORRAL BURLAP
Answer: Where you might take steps to enjoy yourself during the holidays—AT A DANCE

494. **Jumbles:** HAIRDO PITIED GAMBIT ENGULF THWART WEASEL
Answer: People who are this have slightly lower standing—DOWN-AT-THE-HEEL

495. **Jumbles:** BYWORD MOTIVE FORBID COMPLY SEPTIC PUSHER
Answer: What you might find at a haunted college—SOME SCHOOL "SPIRIT"

496. **Jumbles:** FIZZLE PIRACY DARING GHETTO FACTOR JACKAL
Answer: When the bride and groom started quarreling, it must have been this—AN "ALTAR-CATION"

497. **Jumbles:** JABBER ALWAYS HINDER GUITAR DAHLIA ADVICE
Answer: What clothes make a woman—"DEAR" TO HER HUSBAND

498. **Jumbles:** DISMAY ANYONE FORAGE BUMPER SINFUL CRAFTY
Answer: What that clever miser was—A MAN OF RARE GIFTS

499. **Jumbles:** CEMENT GOPHER DISARM PUZZLE FICKLE BANISH
Answer: An instant on the lips—A LIFETIME ON THE HIPS

500. **Jumbles:** LEVITY MASCOT DRAGON MODEST HEARSE PACKET
Answer: What an ophthalmologist's office is—A SITE FOR SORE EYES

501. **Jumbles:** ESTATE GATHER TURNIP MYRIAD HUNTER SYSTEM
Answer: What getting up early in the morning is a matter of—MIND OVER MATTRESS

502. **Jumbles:** ACTING VOLUME KNOTTY POLISH OBJECT RADISH
Answer: What overeating might make you—"THICK" TO YOUR STOMACH

503. **Jumbles:** NEARBY ADMIRE MUFFLE PARODY INTACT HAMMER
Answer: What you might eat at a buffet dinner—A "BALANCED" DIET

504. **Jumbles:** EYEFUL BUCKET EXOTIC QUAINT MINGLE CENSUS
Answer: What a big noise at the office often is at home—A LITTLE SQUEAK

505. **Jumbles:** NEGATE TIMELY DAINTY LOTION INSIST WALLOP
Answer: What an attractive sweater sometimes pulls—MEN'S EYES OVER THE WOOL

506. **Jumbles:** AUBURN JACKET ABSURD CHOSEN NAUGHT BUZZER
Answer: What that expert masseur left—NO STERN UNTONED

507. **Jumbles:** CHERUB DABBLE IMMUNE MODIFY HUMBLE PULPIT
Answer: Where the school bus driver's problems were—ALL BEHIND HIM

508. **Jumbles:** TROPHY PUMICE WHOLLY BEDBUG STANZA ADRIFT
Answer: What the clumsy prosecutor did on the shopping trip—DROPPED THE CHARGES

509. **Jumbles:** WINTRY WALNUT SURETY DEPUTY UNCOIL GUNNER
Answer: Builders of summer homes are part of this—A COTTAGE INDUSTRY

510. **Jumbles:** EVOLVE MILDEW FUTURE TIDBIT EXCISE UPSHOT
Answer: How the scientist spent his time in prison—HE STUDIED CELLS

511. **Jumbles:** EXCITE SONATA DISMAL POMADE UNLOCK MEMORY
Answer: What the banker considered the farmer's livelihood—SMALL POTATOES

Need More Jumbles®?

Jumble® Books

More than 175 puzzles each!

Cowboy Jumble®
$10.95 • ISBN: 978-1-62937-355-3

Jammin' Jumble®
$9.95 • ISBN: 978-1-57243-844-6

Java Jumble®
$10.95 • ISBN: 978-1-60078-415-6

Jet Set Jumble®
$9.95 • ISBN: 978-1-60078-353-1

Jolly Jumble®
$10.95 • ISBN: 978-1-60078-214-5

Jumble® Anniversary
$10.95 • ISBN: 987-1-62937-734-6

Jumble® Ballet
$10.95 • ISBN: 978-1-62937-616-5

Jumble® Birthday
$10.95 • ISBN: 978-1-62937-652-3

Jumble® Celebration
$10.95 • ISBN: 978-1-60078-134-6

Jumble® Champion
$10.95 • ISBN: 978-1-62937-870-1

Jumble® Cuisine
$10.95 • ISBN: 978-1-62937-735-3

Jumble® Drag Race
$9.95 • ISBN: 978-1-62937-483-3

Jumble® Ever After
$10.95 • ISBN: 978-1-62937-785-8

Jumble® Explorer
$9.95 • ISBN: 978-1-60078-854-3

Jumble® Explosion
$10.95 • ISBN: 978-1-60078-078-3

Jumble® Fever
$9.95 • ISBN: 978-1-57243-593-3

Jumble® Galaxy
$10.95 • ISBN: 978-1-60078-583-2

Jumble® Garden
$10.95 • ISBN: 978-1-62937-653-0

Jumble® Genius
$10.95 • ISBN: 978-1-57243-896-5

Jumble® Geography
$10.95 • ISBN: 978-1-62937-615-8

Jumble® Getaway
$10.95 • ISBN: 978-1-60078-547-4

Jumble® Gold
$10.95 • ISBN: 978-1-62937-354-6

Jumble® Jackpot
$10.95 • ISBN: 978-1-57243-897-2

Jumble® Jailbreak
$9.95 • ISBN: 978-1-62937-002-6

Jumble® Jambalaya
$9.95 • ISBN: 978-1-60078-294-7

Jumble® Jitterbug
$10.95 • ISBN: 978-1-60078-584-9

Jumble® Journey
$10.95 • ISBN: 978-1-62937-549-6

Jumble® Jubilation
$10.95 • ISBN: 978-1-62937-784-1

Jumble® Jubilee
$10.95 • ISBN: 978-1-57243-231-4

Jumble® Juggernaut
$9.95 • ISBN: 978-1-60078-026-4

Jumble® Kingdom
$10.95 • ISBN: 978-1-62937-079-8

Jumble® Knockout
$9.95 • ISBN: 978-1-62937-078-1

Jumble® Madness
$10.95 • ISBN: 978-1-892049-24-7

Jumble® Magic
$9.95 • ISBN: 978-1-60078-795-9

Jumble® Mania
$10.95 • ISBN: 978-1-57243-697-8

Jumble® Marathon
$9.95 • ISBN: 978-1-60078-944-1

Jumble® Neighbor
$10.95 • ISBN: 978-1-62937-845-9

Jumble® Parachute
$10.95 • ISBN: 978-1-62937-548-9

Jumble® Safari
$9.95 • ISBN: 978-1-60078-675-4

Jumble® Sensation
$10.95 • ISBN: 978-1-60078-548-1

Jumble® Skyscraper
$10.95 • ISBN: 978-1-62937-869-5

Jumble® Symphony
$10.95 • ISBN: 978-1-62937-131-3

Jumble® Theater
$9.95 • ISBN: 978-1-62937-484-0

Jumble® University
$10.95 • ISBN: 978-1-62937-001-9

Jumble® Unleashed
$10.95 • ISBN: 978-1-62937-844-2

Jumble® Vacation
$10.95 • ISBN: 978-1-60078-796-6

Jumble® Wedding
$9.95 • ISBN: 978-1-62937-307-2

Jumble® Workout
$10.95 • ISBN: 978-1-60078-943-4

Jump, Jive and Jumble®
$9.95 • ISBN: 978-1-60078-215-2

Lunar Jumble®
$9.95 • ISBN: 978-1-60078-853-6

Monster Jumble®
$10.95 • ISBN: 978-1-62937-213-6

Mystic Jumble®
$9.95 • ISBN: 978-1-62937-130-6

Rainy Day Jumble®
$10.95 • ISBN: 978-1-60078-352-4

Royal Jumble®
$10.95 • ISBN: 978-1-60078-738-6

Sports Jumble®
$10.95 • ISBN: 978-1-57243-113-3

Summer Fun Jumble®
$10.95 • ISBN: 978-1-57243-114-0

Touchdown Jumble®
$9.95 • ISBN: 978-1-62937-212-9

Oversize Jumble® Books

More than 500 puzzles!

Colossal Jumble®
$19.95 • ISBN: 978-1-57243-490-5

Jumbo Jumble®
$19.95 • ISBN: 978-1-57243-314-4

Jumble® Crosswords™

More than 175 puzzles!

Jumble® Crosswords™
$10.95 • ISBN: 978-1-57243-347-2